D1478819

Fort Bascom

Fort Bascom

SOLDIERS, COMANCHEROS, AND INDIANS IN THE CANADIAN RIVER VALLEY

James Bailey Blackshear

UNIVERSITY OF OKLAHOMA PRESS : NORMAN

Portions of chapters 2, 6, and 8 were previously published in "Boots on the Ground: A History of Fort Bascom in the Canadian River Valley," *New Mexico Historical Review* 87, no. 3 (Summer 2012), and appear here, with permission, in altered form.

Library of Congress Cataloging-in-Publication Data

Blackshear, James Bailey, 1954– author.
  Fort Bascom : soldiers, comancheros, and Indians in the Canadian River Valley / James Bailey Blackshear.
    pages   cm
  Includes bibliographical references and index.
  ISBN 978-0-8061-5209-7 (hardcover : alk. paper)
1. Fort Bascom (N.M.) 2. New Mexico—History, Military—19th century.
3. Frontier and pioneer life—New Mexico. 4. Comanche Indians—Canadian River Valley—History—19th century. I. Title
  F801.B58 2016
  355.009789'55—dc23   2015028435

1 2 3 4 5 6 7 8 9 10

For Lily, Christian, Blake, Cole, and Chloe

Contents

Illustrations

Preface

The publication of any work is always a journey. This journey began when my wife and I built a cabin in the Sangre de Cristo Mountains of New Mexico in 2001. On one particular trip up from Texas we exited the interstate at Tucumcari while looking for a shortcut and drove north on Highway 104 toward Las Vegas, New Mexico. About eleven miles outside Tucumcari, I spied a forlorn wooden sign on the side of the road. It read "Fort Bascom." The landscape of New Mexico is varied in its beauty, painted with a timelessness that only nature in its untouched form can create. I felt that timelessness when I stopped to look at this sign. Fort Bascom. Surrounded by broken mesas, deep arroyos, and a rolling sea of prairie grasses, I looked for adobe ruins, a collapsed roof, or anything else that could have resembled an old fort. Unfortunately, other than the sign, a barbed-wire fence, and the two-lane road, there was no such evidence. So we continued on our journey. On subsequent trips, every time we neared the faded Fort Bascom sign, I began to look for ruins, but never found them. This eventually prompted my research. Why was the fort built? Who built it? Who served there? All these questions eventually led me down many other roads.

Any historian who is fortunate enough to have his work published owes a debt of gratitude to many individuals and institutions. That certainly applies to me. I want to begin by thanking Ricky F. Dobbs of Texas A&M–Commerce, who gave me early encouragement regarding my work on New Mexico history. When I decided to get serious about researching Fort Bascom, several professors and fellow graduate students at the University of North Texas gave me excellent advice and support. Rick McCaslin of UNT offered continual encouragement and firm guidance when I began to feel as if I had taken a wrong turn in the Llano Estacado. Gus Seligmann provided relevant recommendations and unique insight into nineteenth-century New Mexico that proved invaluable. F. Todd Smith's expertise on Southern Plains Indians provided me with knowledge and leads that, I hope, allowed this to be more than just another history of a frontier post. Alex Mendoza was a constant supporter of this project, and his maps have been instrumental in revealing the history of this region. Mendoza also included an early version of chapter 4 in *Military History of the West* 44 (forthcoming, 2015), which he edits. While we were at UNT, fellow graduate student Mick Miller provided me with a sounding board regarding the direction I wanted to go, as well as offering a relevant critique of an early version of a portion of this work. Durwood Ball was an early inspiration, assuring me that research into this post was of historical value. A portion of this research was eventually turned into a journal article for the *New Mexico Historical Review*, which he edits. Portions of chapters 2, 6, and 8 first appeared in "Boots on the Ground: A History of Fort Bascom in the Canadian River Valley," *New Mexico Historical Review* 87:3 (Summer 2012): 329–58.

When I look back at the various facilities I visited in my research, I fondly recall what a rewarding experience I had at each one, visiting historians, archivists, and librarians who share the same love of history that I do. It was a great pleasure working with so many professionals. This was certainly true of the staff at the Donnelly Library of New Mexico Highlands University. I spent countless days in this library pouring over the James W. Arrott Collection, which is housed in their Special Collections section. Special thanks goes to Donnelly librarian Cheryl Zebrowski for helping me acquire Lt. Charles C. Morrison's map of the region. I also have to thank the kind staff at the Carnegie Library in Las Vegas, New Mexico, where I also spent many days scouring their "Locked Room" for sources. Additionally, another great day was spent at the Tucumcari Historical Museum with Duane Moore. Mr. Moore gave me some great insights into the region and the post. The day I spent in the archives of the Panhandle Plains Museum in Canyon, Texas, was just as beneficial. Warren Stricker saved me much time locating pertinent primary source materials that made this a better work. On my many visits to the New Mexico State Research Center in

Santa Fe, the staff there was both professional and helpful. It is always a pleasure to visit this great facility. The same is true of the National Archives in Washington, D.C., and College Park, Maryland. Like the documents they so diligently protect, the professionals who work at these facilities are national treasures. I had a similar experience at the Fort Union National Monument Archives, where Bill Broughton guided me toward some excellent sources. Likewise, Ellis S. Hambrick, director of the Third Cavalry Museum, came in on his day off to help me search the files when I visited his outstanding facility at Fort Hood, Texas. I would be remiss if I did not thank Emily Brock and her staff at the Palace of the Governors, Caitlan Lampman of the Arizona Historical Society, and John Hillmer of the National Parks Service for helping me locate period photos that have improved this work immeasurably. Of course, without the University of Oklahoma Press's interest, this book would still be a work in progress. I would like to extend my thanks and sincere appreciation to Charles Rankin, editor-in-chief, and Tom Krause, assistant acquisitions editor, for showing interest in this history of Fort Bascom and guiding me through the early stages of the publication process. The detailed and on-point corrections and suggestions offered by Steven Baker, managing editor, and Leslie Tingle, copyeditor, have improved this work considerably, as did the early recommendations and suggestions made by the peer reviewers who participated in this project. I would be remiss if I did not also thank the OU Press production department for their craftsmanship and professionalism.

My last road trip on this journey was the best. Jake Blackshear, my son, traveled east with me to the National Archives, where his expertise in all things related to the digital age came in handy. Together we discovered some amazing maps and sketches from 1865, and then he helped ensure that they were scanned properly before we left College Park. He also made sure the bus didn't leave without me. Thanks, Jake.

My son Mike also deserves some credit. His positive attitude about life, family, and work inspire me every day. His laughter and support are the best medicine a father could ask for.

Finally, I owe Barbara, my wife and anchor, the most. During this process, while I was focused on deadlines, she took care of everything else. A scholar in her own right, in 2006 she convinced me that I should quit my job and do something that I loved. Shortly thereafter, we came upon a sign in the middle of nowhere that read "Fort Bascom." There is no adequate way that I can properly express how instrumental she has been in the completion of this book. So I'll just say to the love of my life: "Thanks, Barb. We did it."

Material quoted from nineteenth-century archives and records retains its original spellings, punctuation, and capitalization in most instances. When clarification is required, an additional letter or word is inserted in brackets.

Fort Bascom

CHAPTER 1

An Awful Country

In the summer of 1870, a variety of civilian contractors swarmed over
Fort Bascom in New Mexico Territory, replacing many of its roofs;
repairing its adobe walls, the officers' quarters, and the guardhouse;
and finalizing plans for a standalone granary. Such activities indicated
this frontier post was in for a very busy future. Yet by early September
1870, Forts Arbuckle, Gibson, Smith, and Bascom were all notified that
they would no longer function as full-time forts. Brig. Gen. John Pope,
the new commander of the Department of the Missouri, issued the
closures, believing that the soldiers stationed at these garrisons could
be re-allocated to larger bases for the winter and then sent back to
the abandoned posts each summer on an as-needed basis.[1]

Once northeastern New Mexicans got word of Pope's plan, they
began a campaign to force him to change his mind. Trinidad Romero,
the probate judge of San Miguel County, and J. Francisco Cháves, then
one of New Mexico's leading political figures, immediately called local
citizens to action, creating and then submitting a petition to Secretary of War W. W. Belknap that implored him to countermand the
order. Above the signatures of 301 concerned New Mexicans on the
petition, Romero wrote: "Fort Bascom at present is the only Military
Post in the eastern frontier of the Territory. . . . We respectfully claim
that under the Treaty of Guadalupe Hidalgo we are entitled to the
fullest protection at the hands of the Government, both for our lives
and for our property." Romero told Belknap that the United States
was obligated to uphold the "spirit and intention of the document,"
as well as reminding him that many of the people who were about to

Map 1. In 1875 Lt. Charles C. Morrison, Sixth U.S. Cavalry, led a geographi
survey team across New Mexico Territory, charting all trails, forts, and topog
phy. This map, created by Lieutenant Morrison, details the world Fort Basco
soldiers inhabited. *Records of the Office of the Chief of Engineers, map file, map 1
no. 1, RG 77, NA, Washington, D.C. This copy in Special Collections, Maps, Donn
Library, New Mexico Highlands University, Las Vegas.*

Lieut. C. C. Morrison. 6th Cav.
Acting Engineer Officer.

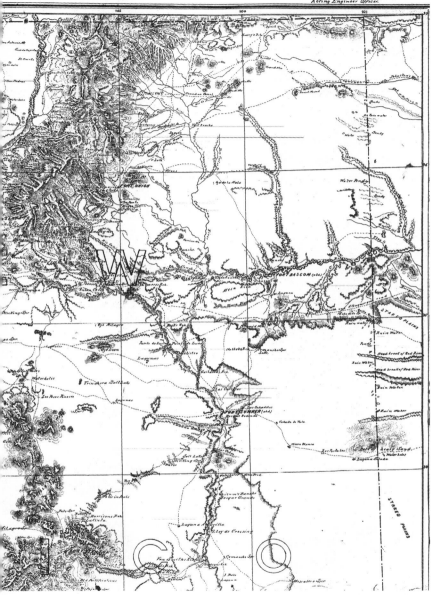

5

go unprotected "rendered their services to the government during
the late Rebellion." The Treaty of Guadalupe Hidalgo (1848) had stipulated that the U.S. Army must protect its new citizens from Indian
attacks. Twenty-two years later, many Hispano New Mexicans still took
such warranties seriously. Only a few months earlier, Teodosio Griego,
one of Romero's sheepherders, had been "killed and scalped," by a
band of Cheyenne and Kiowa Indians. Even before news of the closure
reached Romero, the concerned probate judge had written Territorial
Governor W. A. Pile about increased violence in San Miguel County:
"Our military commander [at Fort Bascom] with a very small and
inadequate force under his command is unable to protect us against
the outrage of the numerous tribes of barbarians who surround our
Territory." Certainly the army could make the case that it had expended
much blood and treasure doing just that over the last quarter century.
Yet New Mexican veterans, politicians, businessmen, and local ranchers
now reminded Belknap that the army's mission was not completed.
The government could expect more deaths and violent incidents once
this post closed. In addition, such raids would destroy a thriving sheep
and cattle industry. While leading political figures such as Eugenio
Romero (Judge Trinidad Romero's brother) and merchants Charles
Ilfeld and Adolph Letcher signed their names to the petition, the
majority of signatures were from local ranchers and farmers of Hispanic
origin whose main concern was their families' continued protection.[2]

John S. Watts, the man who leased the land for Fort Bascom to the
army, also got involved. A former territorial delegate to Congress and
recent chief justice of the New Mexico Supreme Court, Watts was back
in Santa Fe practicing law when he heard about Pope's order. First, he
contacted U.S. Army Quartermaster General Montgomery C. Meigs.
Watts wrote Meigs that, according to his lease agreement, if Fort Bascom was abandoned before its twenty-year lease expired, every building
on the military reservation reverted back to him. Meigs responded
by communicating this information to General-in-Chief William Tecum-
seh Sherman.[3]

Watts next wrote a more detailed letter to Secretary Belknap. He
began by repeating what he had told Meigs about the lease, then made
a claim that many of Fort Bascom's soldiers might have disagreed with:
"Fort Bascom is in a manner new—now built—in good repair, and suit-
able for the comfortable accommodations of two companies of United

States troops[—]and cost the United States fifty thousand dollars."
Once he had established its value, Watts admitted that while acquiring
the fort's buildings would benefit him personally, with the "evacuation of Fort Bascom [nearby citizens] will be left to the mercy and
foreberance [sic] of twenty thousand Kiowa, Arappahoes [sic], and
Comanche Indians, whose history for the last fifty years has been a
dark and bloody record of theft, plunder, and murder." For that reason,
he preferred the post remain fully operational so it could continue
to protect New Mexico's citizens. Watts was sure that once Secretary
Belknap reviewed all the issues, he would come to the same conclusion. Instead, Belknap replied that he had "received assurances that
ample provisions have been made by the proper authorities for the
continued protection of the people of New Mexico."[4]

Those assurances came from Brigadier General Pope. By then, Col.
George W. Getty, commander of the District of New Mexico, had sent
"all available transportation" from Fort Union to the Canadian River
Valley post to remove its supplies (with the exception of three months'
rations, some medical supplies, and arms for eight men). Meanwhile,
Pope had received a copy of the petition from San Miguel County
residents. Adjutant General of the United States E. D. Townsend also
sent him a copy of the letter that Quartermaster General Meigs had
sent to General Sherman regarding the quartermaster's own letter
from John Watts. Townsend also forwarded Pope a copy of the letter
Watts sent to Secretary Belknap. By 26 October 1870 government
wagons full of Fort Bascom supplies were on their way back to Fort
Union. In Pope's response to General Townsend, he made clear his
confidence that his decision to close Fort Bascom would not put
local citizens in more danger, emphasizing that it was an unnecessary
post; yet in the next sentence, which the general underlined, he noted,
"It was not and never had been my purpose to abandon Bascom or
any of the other posts named, in the sense of relinquishing possession of the buildings nor has Fort Bascom been thus vacated." He
explained that soldiers would return "early in the spring near Fort
Bascom to cover that section of the country during the summer and
autumn, when danger exists, if there be any now." He informed
Townsend that the post would continue to be used as a base of operations, which in his mind should keep the army's assets out of John
Watts's possession. He admitted that he was unsurprised by the protests

and was prepared to hear "misrepresentations of all kinds" regarding why the post should not be closed. Watts's attempt to circumvent Pope's plans by going over his head certainly angered the general, as was evident in his closing, somewhat caustic remarks to Townsend: "It is perhaps not presumptuous to say that my opinion about the location of the military posts is as valuable as that of Mr. Watts ["Mr. Watts" is underlined], and that my devotion to the public interests may possibly compare favorably with his."[5]

General Belknap also forwarded the San Miguel County petition and his own correspondence with Watts to General-in-Chief Sherman. Sherman responded: "I have never been to Fort Bascom, but I have been to the head of the Red and Pecos Rivers of New Mexico, not far from Bascom. It is an awful country from which to draw men before death. . . . Fort Bascom is on the Red River to the east, between New Mexico and the wild comanches [sic] of the Llano Estacado." Sherman's misidentification of the Canadian as the Red River was not unusual for the period. Many officers, soldiers, and merchants who lived in the region had made similar mistakes. Just as many people had also characterized this section of New Mexico Territory to be "an awful country," or something close to it. It is unknown how many soldiers associated this isolated post with death, but the correlation reveals what top military men in the nation's capital thought about the region. Army personnel considered the Eroded Plains, situated between the Sangre de Cristo Mountains and the Llano Estacado, to be a confusing no-man's-land of scant water and hard duty. Positioned along the Canadian River amidst Comanche and Comanchero trails, Fort Bascom was not far from Comanchería. Its importance to military operations continued long after Pope ordered it closed. This book seeks to explain why so many New Mexicans signed the petition to keep the post open.[6]

Fort Bascom was built in 1863, strategically positioned about sixty miles west of the Texas border. Its construction was prompted by Union fears of a second Confederate invasion from Texas and a desire to check incursions by Southern Plains Indians. Placed about eleven miles north of present-day Tucumcari, New Mexico, the fort was a day's ride from the western edge of the Llano Estacado. Fort Bascom operated as a permanent post from 1863 to 1870. From late 1870 through most of 1874, it functioned as an outpost of Fort Union, and it was used as a base of operations for patrols in New Mexico and expeditions into Texas. Soldiers stationed at this Canadian River garrison were positioned on the point of the spear, within the northern edges of the Comanches' homeland, during the height of the U.S. Army's war against the Southern Plains Indians.[7]

Comanchería encompassed the eastern face of the Sangre de Cristo Mountains, the Llano Estacado, and much of Central Texas, extending as far south as the southern rim of the Edwards Plateau. Within this region, an area larger than many European countries, various Comanche communities refused to defer to American expansion and violently resisted attempts to relocate them. Despite its location within what almost could be considered a foreign country at war with the United States, Fort Bascom has garnered little attention. Examples of this oversight are found within the works of two of the region's best historians. In 1964 Ernest Wallace detailed the efforts of Col. Ranald S. Mackenzie to defeat the Comanches in the Texas Panhandle. Regarding an expedition that occurred in the fall of 1871, Wallace wrote, "Mackenzie and his Fourth Cavalry had penetrated the very heart of the hostile Indian country, even venturing into the abysmal Llano Estacado in an area hitherto unexplored by the United States military." Ten years later, esteemed scholar Frederick J. Rathjen wrote of an 1872 Mackenzie expedition: "One wonders, in fact, whether the colonel realized the historic significance or personal distinction of having led the first United States military force across the Staked Plains!" (The exclamation is Rathjen's.) Yet seven years before Mackenzie's first journey into the Texas Panhandle, Fort Bascom patrols had already penetrated the region while participating in routine scouts and more extensive military expeditions. Such information does not detract from Mackenzie's accomplishments, nor from Wallace's or Rathjen's contributions to frontier military history. However, if the military's first forays into this "unexplored" territory are so historically significant, then this post's contributions are worth a second look.[8]

Only two long works on Fort Bascom have been written, both very dated. In 1961 Father Stanley Louis Crocchiola, a historian and Franciscan priest who practiced his faith in New Mexico for fifty years, used the pseudonym F. Stanley to publish *Fort Bascom: Comanche-Kiowa Barrier*. It was based on anecdotal, first-generation recollections as well as archival sources, yet he did not footnote his material. Earlier, in 1955,

scholar James M. Foster wrote his master's thesis on the fort. The work
was footnoted and more detailed but narrow in focus. Moreover, the
triumphalist themes both Stanley and Foster incorporated into their
histories have long needed updating in order to place the history of
this frontier outpost within the emerging historiographies that have
re-created Southwestern history in the last twenty years.[9]

In the past two decades many new histories of the Southwest have
revealed a world of cultural and economic vitality. Scholars now
argue that Southern Plains Indians were shapers of Southwestern
history, not mere participants. If this is true, then we must consider
the role played by Fort Bascom, situated fifteen miles from the Llano
Estacado, where many of the Indians lived. The fort's location within
this cultural shatter zone provides useful perspectives on existing and
evolving relationships during an important era in the expansion of the
United States. Spanish explorers, American merchants, and the U.S.
Army Corps of Topographical Engineers left historians the first written
descriptions of this region and its inhabitants. New Mexicans from
the Sangre de Cristo Mountains, Navajos from the Bosque Redondo,
Comanches from the Llano Estacado, African Americans from Kentucky, Anglo-Americans from Illinois, and European transplants all
crossed paths along roads that radiated from this post.[10]

After the Civil War, the cultural gulf between American soldiers and
the Southern Plains Indians widened. Many of the volunteers who
manned the frontier forts at the beginning of the war were locals, or
at least lived somewhere within the region, and were familiar with the
topography and people who inhabited it. They served in the First New
Mexico Volunteer Infantry and Cavalry. Volunteers from Colorado and
California also filled the Union ranks in New Mexico Territory. After
these westerners mustered out in 1866, army regulars raised east of
the Mississippi River or in Europe were left to gain control of the Southwest. Soldiers' familiarity with both the people and the landscape of
the region was paramount to success, yet the newcomers often had a
difficult time distinguishing Navajos from Puebloans, Comanches from
Utes, and honest Hispano ranchers from Comancheros. The Comancheros, composed of both Puebloans and local New Mexican mountain
people, traded with the Comanches, sometimes legally and sometimes
illegally. American soldiers posted to Fort Bascom and charged with
breaking up this trade were inserted into this "fluid borderland world."[11]

While these soldiers' subjugation of the Comanches may appear
in retrospect to have been inevitable, in the 1860s the future was not
so certain along the edge of the Llano Estacado. American dominance fed by claims of racial superiority, the acquisition of ancient
land grants, and the elimination of hunting ranges created a recipe
for dissent among a variety of people impacted by the army in general and Fort Bascom soldiers in particular. Although many Hispanos
fought for the Union during the Civil War, thus allying themselves
with the frontier army, others remained loyal to their lifelong trading
partners, the Comanches. This loyalty ensured that Fort Bascom's
areas of operation involved more than just chasing Indians. Troopers
were charged with interrupting a transnational, black market economy
that funneled manufactured goods and weapons south and east in
exchange for Texas cattle and horses, the illegal contraband of the
American Southwest during the 1860s. Wealthy New Mexicans and
Anglo ranchers from Kansas and elsewhere were interested in cheap
cattle and were hardly concerned with where the Comancheros had
acquired them, although they certainly knew. This book will illustrate
how this shadow economy worked and what Fort Bascom soldiers did
to help bring it to a halt.[12]

Texans were certainly just as concerned about Indian attacks as
citizens living in San Miguel County. The archival evidence supports
the argument that New Mexico Territory's Fort Bascom was Texas's
northernmost frontier fort. Its men were closer to the Comanche
homeland than any Texas post of the period. In the 1860s and 1870s,
its commanders repeatedly sent patrols into the Texas Panhandle to
break up the black market trade that plagued Texas ranchers and settlers. Three major expeditions sent large columns from Fort Bascom
on missions to eliminate the Comanches and Kiowas who prevailed
in the region. These columns, as well as regular scouts from the post,
were instrumental in finally gaining control of the region.[13]

Living in the Eroded Plains and patrolling the Llano Estacado,
soldiers were constantly battling the elements. In *The Great Plains,*
Walter Prescott Webb wrote that "the essential truth is that the West
cannot be understood as a mere extension of things Eastern." Lack of
water and arid climates restricted the use of landscapes in ways that
did not occur east of the Mississippi River. Such scarcity shaped culture
and influenced how people, including soldiers posted in the Canadian

River Valley, survived. In a land without maps, the Comanches and Kiowas were never lost, yet military patrols often were, often with disastrous results. As William deBuys notes, "In an unforgiving environment, small errors yield large consequences."[14] Part of Fort Bascom's story includes explaining how soldiers adapted to this borderland region.

To survive on the arid frontier, officers and troopers had to do more than adjust their frames of reference. East of the Mississippi River, crops and forage were readily available for harvest or purchase. West of the river, vegetation and hay were sparse, supply lines were often hundreds of miles long, and merchants were few and far between. Thus managing logistics would play as great a role in subduing the Southern Plains Indians as actual combat. This work will illustrate these difficulties from the perspective of those who manned Fort Bascom.

Such environmental challenges meant the federal government could not dictate where crops would be grown or who would grow them. Officials did use their powers to promote certain contractors over others. Ex-military men who served at Forts Bascom, Union, and Sumner often won those contracts. Hispano entrepreneurs, ranchers, and farmers also participated in this trade. Issues related to scarcity, climate, and dependence on local contractors play an integral role in Fort Bascom's history.[15]

While Fort Richardson, near Jacksboro, is recognized as Texas's northernmost fort, strong historical links tie the history of the Texas Panhandle to Fort Bascom, which was much closer to the Comanches' homeland. Such links are explored in detail in the latter chapters of this book. During and after the Civil War, many northwest Texas counties lost millions of dollars in livestock, and settlers were forced to abandon their ranches for their personal safety. While the published history of Fort Bascom's role in stopping the Plains Indian incursions is minimal, archival documents tell another story. Almost from its inception this fort's soldiers began patrolling in Texas, trying to halt Indian raids. Ranchers and farmers in Palo Pinto, Montague, Wise, and other northern and northwestern Texas counties were affected by its successes and failures. Thus Fort Bascom offers a case study on how frontier soldiers and their officers gained the experience needed to contain the Plains Indians and their borderland partners, the Comancheros.

The decision to build a new fort west of the Mississippi during the Civil War while many other western posts were being abandoned establishes Fort Bascom's significance in the history of the region. Manpower was shifted to the fort and integrated into the Department of New Mexico's defense of the Union frontier. The fort remained operational as either a full- or part-time post until the U.S. Army gained control of the Southern Plains Indians. Deployed within an "awful country," among people of many cultures who did not want them there, Fort Bascom soldiers evolved into what one trooper called "horse marines," an apt title for the borderland warriors who ultimately helped end the traditional way of life of the Comanches and Kiowas who roamed the Llano Estacado and beyond.[16]

CHAPTER 2

In the Shadow of Mesa Rica

Americans of all ethnicities have always followed the rivers. Whether it was the Kennebec or the Connecticut, the Mohawk or the Mississippi, similar survival and migration patterns played out along the rivers that vein the North American continent. Where there was water, there was life: fish, fowl, edible plants, a variety of mammals, and after a time, humans. Over the centuries, people used rivers as pathways and resource zones. The Canadian River Valley of northeastern New Mexico is such a place. From its source in the Sangre de Cristo Mountains to the plains of Texas and Oklahoma, various cultures have lived, hunted, and traded along this stream for at least one thousand years. Archaic cultures utilized the Canadian River Valley as a home long before the arrival of Puebloans, Plains Indians, Spaniards, or New Mexicans. Well-worn footpaths once shadowed this river from its headwaters near Raton Pass to its tributaries in the Oklahoma Panhandle.[1] In 1863, amid a variety of people who claimed this river valley as their homeland, the Union Army built Fort Bascom. The surrounding environment played no role in the decision to build this outpost, yet it played a feature role in military operations. Thus, a thorough examination of the geology, topography, flora, fauna, and cultures that existed along this river prior to Bascom's construction is essential to understanding the challenges that its soldiers faced in the 1860s and 1870s.[2]

Frederick Jackson Turner argued that the modern United States emerged from expansionist efforts to tame the frontier, yet the conversion of the American West into a fount of manageable resources did not apply to this portion of the Canadian River. Forests did not have to be leveled to make way for the plow. Despite being immune to this step in Turner's "process," the region seldom yielded bountiful crops. Additionally, prior civilizations had already claimed this corner of Turner's "wilderness" as their domestic and spiritual homes, and some of these prior settlers proved very resilient. This chapter, an investigation of the Canadian River Valley, will discuss both environmental and cultural aspects of the region's history. This includes a closer look at the Comancheros, the Hispano trading partners whom the Southern Plains Indians used to thwart the federal government's attempts to shuttle them off to reservations.[3]

It is true that any region's ecology impacts the people who live there, yet specific environments create particular concerns, such as a continual awareness of the locations of water sources and wood. In New Mexico, such resource-limited environments make up the greatest part of the landscape. Southern Plains Indians, who before the arrival of the Spaniards lived in a world without horses, and U.S. cavalrymen all faced the same environmental realities within this river basin.

When the Rocky Mountains pushed up out of the shallow sea millions of years ago, they shed an abundance of alluvial soils eastward for hundreds of miles. This relocation of old sea beds led to the creation of upland grassland prairies. For eons, water flowing out of the Rockies cut wide valleys and deep canyons through these high plateaus, creating a region known as the Eroded Plains. The new valleys separated the elevated plains into two distinct geographic formations: the Las Vegas Plateau and the Llano Estacado. The Canadian River Valley runs between these formations. The southern rim of the Las Vegas Plateau, called the Canadian Escarpment, rises from fifteen hundred to two thousand feet above the riverbed. Shortly after joining the Conchas River, the Canadian turns east, eventually cutting through the walls of the Caprock Escarpment, which rises to meet the plains of the Texas Panhandle. About a millennium ago, both plateaus were covered in blue and hairy grama grasses, as was the river basin that divided them. Centuries later, buffalo grass replaced large swaths of the gramas, its namesake spreading its seeds south each spring.[4]

Although the Canadian River Valley's latitude is about the same as Central Tennessee's, it is locked into an ecological zone more similar to that of northern Mexico.[5] Moving west from the Texas Panhandle toward the Sangre de Cristo Mountains, this Lower Sonoran life zone cuts through the Upper Sonoran grasslands of the upland plateaus before turning northwest and beginning an ascent into the pine-forested and snow-covered peaks of the Sangre de Cristos. These upper elevations are within what is called a transitional zone. The entirety of the Canadian drainage system includes 11,237 square miles, 34 percent of which contain mountains, 41 percent consisting of plateaus, and the remaining 24 percent left to lower-level mesalands and canyons that cut through the southern plains.[6]

The environmental focus of this chapter, for the most part, concerns about eighty miles of the river that lie within the Lower Sonoran zone, an area near present-day Tucumcari, New Mexico. Yet for proper context, the entirety of this stream must be understood. The Canadian exits the Sangre de Cristo Mountains at 7,834 feet above sea level and is a fast-running river at this point. For approximately 100 miles it flows south, paralleling the eastern slope of the Sangre de Cristos before reaching the edge of the Canadian Escarpment. Cutting deeply into the escarpment, the river quickly descends some 2,000 feet to the valley floor, where it meanders 40 miles or so before merging with the Conchas. From this juncture it continues south until it passes the old Fort Bascom site, where it bends east. By the time it reaches the Texas and Oklahoma Panhandles, this once full-bodied river has become a sluggish stream, ambling along about 2,505 feet above sea level. The journey from Raton to the Texas border encompasses about 240 miles of the river, which carries bits of the Sangre de Cristos into the Llano Estacado along the way.[7]

Although the Canadian has calmed considerably by the time it turns toward Texas, the land surrounding it, known as the Eroded Plains, retains a visible, geologic vitality. Oranges, reds, browns, and purples paint the numerous sandstone columns (remnants of old volcanic flows) and inner linings of the deep arroyos that lace this section of the valley. Little grass and few trees exist any distance from the stream. While many animals still follow the river, fossil imprints found high in the delaminating walls of the rocky outcrops and mesas that overlook it acknowledge creatures of another time once roamed here. Such geologic outliers stand throughout both the Canadian River Valley and the nearby Pecos River Valley. Two of the most prominent, the Tucumcari and Cuervo formations, lie to the south and southwest of the Canadian.[8]

Another important geologic formation in this region, Mesa Rica, looms between these two river valleys. This outlier's crumbling, stair-stepped façade, over four miles long and a quarter-mile wide, resembles the ruins of an enormous Aztec pyramid. Just below the buff-colored cap, which rises five hundred feet above the two valleys, lies a sheet of gray to greenish Purgatoire shale, followed by a layer of hard Dakota sandstone. The shale beneath such mesa's caps has been known to encase *capitosauroid labyrinthodonts* and *rauisuchid archosaurs,* both Washita fossils of the Middle Triassic epoch.[9] With each descending step, Mesa Rica reveals additional geologic layers of alternating colors. Farther below, maroon sandstone sections are interspersed with layers of brown and gray shale that are followed by a sixty-foot-deep layer of white Wingate sandstone. At the bottom of this formation rests two hundred feet of dark red earth. This base is a compilation of red and almost iridescent orange layers of shales and sandstones, called the Dockum group, which are also known as "red beds."[10]

The most striking geographic characteristic found in the Eroded Plains is these red beds.[11] The rippled and eroded layers of the Dockum group underlie the outliers and escarpments that rise and fall throughout the region where Fort Bascom was built. The Canadian River carved these stair-stepped mesas millions of years ago. The river's present course, anywhere from thirty to one hundred feet below the valley floor, is often hidden from the horizon, cutting below grade, exposing gray and greenish sandstone, limestone, and shales of the same Dockum group. Layers of medium-sized gravels and rocks, pushed down the valley during Sangre de Cristo spring thaws and rainstorms, rim the river's beds.[12]

Geologically speaking, the Canadian River Valley is still young. Mature soils take tens of thousands of years to develop, something that has not occurred among the sharp ridges and broken outliers that continue to crumble and find their way to the valley floor. In such areas, topsoils are generally light in color, low in organic material, and shot through with alkali compounds. Organic materials derived from the breakdown of plant particles and other organisms usually act as a soil's cohesive agent. One of the types of soil found in this region, aridisol, does not contain these cohesive materials. Frequently occurring between the Pecos and Canadian Rivers, aridisols are highly water

soluble, meaning their capacity to retain moisture and sustain plant
life is slim. Aside from specific issues regarding the valley's capacity
for plant growth, the arid nature of this environment also eliminates
ground moisture through evaporation. Acidic compounds wick up to
the surface as the water evaporates, leaving a white powdery material
exposed to the sun. As discussed later in this chapter, nineteenth-
century government officials realized too late that this white powdery
substance was destructive to local vegetation.[13]

When compared to the flora in subhumid or humid regions in
North America, Canadian River Valley plant life could be characterized
as sparse. Yet despite the region's alkaline topsoils, an accounting of the
vegetation found there reveals a wide variety of species. The greatest
diversity is found near the water's edge. Throughout the northern
portion of the valley, underground springs leach out of the arroyos
and run down to the main stream. Plains Indians and Comancheros
were cognizant of these springs and used them to great advantage.
Tall cottonwood trees dominate these junctures.[14] Chokecherries, hack-
berry, and poison ivy thrive near the river, clinging to the banks'
steep edges. Junipers and pinions grow in the basin. Since they do
not require as much water, these evergreens cling to the tops of the
mesas and vertical edges of the escarpment. Along with these brush-
like trees, spiny-fingered cholla cactus and white-flowered yucca dot
the slopes, plateaus, and canyon edges with various shades of green.[15]

At first glance, the dominant visual characteristic of this stretch of
the Canadian River appears to be emptiness, or lack of movement.
Yet like the shimmering blue blurs that occasionally dance off the
valley floor, such perceptions are merely mirages that evaporate upon
closer inspection. For generations, the black dots that hung in the
cottonwoods lining the river turned out to be wild turkeys. Beneath
the water's surface lurked native trout, and the western box tortoise
once moved along the water's shaded edges where the hackberries
grew. Red-sided garter snakes, eastern ribbon snakes, plains black-headed
rattlesnakes, and western diamondback rattlers still glide through the
reeds and hide in nearby rocks. Lizards skitter across the gravel beds
and through the prairie grasses. The collared, southern prairie, lesser
earless, six-lined racerunner, and Texas horned frog are just a sam-
pling of lizards still found along the Canadian. The hispid pocket
mouse, striped skunk, badger, black-tailed prairie dog, fox squirrel,

opossum, desert cottontail, black-tailed jackrabbit, and even porcupines
lived there, as well as larger, four-legged creatures such as mountain
lions, cougars, coyotes, gray foxes, gray wolfs, bobcats, and black bears.
Both merchant records and military documents often note the presence of antelope herds. Winged creatures included burrowing and
great horned owls, prairie and peregrine falcons, red-tailed hawks, and
golden and bald eagles. Bobwhites, yellow-billed cuckoos, mocking-
birds, cardinals, and golden-throated woodpeckers flit from the hackberries and junipers.[16]

Still, any description of the topography or listing of the creatures
that once lived and still live in the valley marginalizes and compacts
the expansive nature of the region. Thus, a study of the dual nature
of the relationships that existed between the inanimate and the animate creates the context needed to understand the challenges Fort
Bascom soldiers faced in the 1860s and 1870s. Josiah Gregg, an American merchant who in 1832 kept a diary of his travels through the
area, wrote that this part of the Canadian River Valley "constituted a
kind of chaotic space where nature seemed to have indulged in her
wildest caprices. Such was the confusion of ground-swells and eccen-
tric cavities, that it was altogether impossible to determine whereabouts the channel of the Canadian wound its way among them."
Newcomers like Gregg, unfamiliar with the valley's resources, were
amazed at the "sublimity of its desolation."[17] Such notions of desolation were foreign to natives who had been using its resources for
generations. Plains tribes and New Mexicans would not have characterized the Canadian River Valley as desolate.

Cultural history is buried deep in the broken topography of the
Canadian River Valley. It can be found along remnants of the footpaths and cart trails that once gouged the lip of the Caprock. It is
present along the riverbeds of the Eroded Plains, where smooth-bored
holes found in limestone benches indicate where Apaches long ago
mounted their lodge poles. Historians, anthropologists, and environ-
mentalists have written about distinct sections of this region, such as
the Sangre de Cristo Mountains and Palo Duro Canyon, yet little
work has been done on the Canadian River Valley of northeastern
New Mexico. Just like the stair-stepped mesas with their multicolored
layers that identify different ages of the earth, centuries of human
culture are pancaked on top of one another in this valley.[18]

These cultures were long ago separated by the same waters that cut through the upland prairies. The archaic Apishipa focus people of the northwestern Las Vegas Plateau used their elevated vantage to study the Canadian Valley for game and other humans. About the same time, another group of hunter-gatherers, the Antelope Creek focus, emerged on the western edge of the Caprock and lived along the lip of Llano Estacado. It is conceivable that the Antelope Creek people peered west across the Caprock at the same time the Apishipa looked east from the Canadian Escarpment, both searching for game or visitors.[19]

Environments are not constrained by imposed human borders, yet the Anglo-Europeans who laid claim to such environments often have perceptions of place defined by straight-lined, surveyor-plotted boundaries. Many Hispanos and Southern Plains Indians refused to accept Anglo ideas concerning laws and borders that inconceivably (to them), cut across rivers and mountain ranges and prevented them from carrying on a livelihood that began with their great-grandfathers.

By the time the Spanish entered New Mexico, generations of Jicarilla Apaches and Puebloans knew where the water bubbled out of the rocks in the Canadian Valley, which main path fur-bearing animals took to the stream, and where valuable herbs and edible plants could be located. During this period, the Faraones Apaches claimed much of the area between the Pecos and the Rio Grande Rivers and were there to greet an expeditionary force put together by Don Juan de Oñate in 1598. By that time, those Puebloans who had ventured east were forced back by the Apaches toward the Sangre de Cristos and the Rio Grande, where they lived in multilevel, fortified dwellings. Regardless of the raiding practices of some of the more nomadic tribes, all native groups found ways to avoid their enemies and make annual pilgrimages into the river basins and onto the High Plains in search of game. Apaches often hunted along the Canadian River and camped under its cottonwoods. Antelope, elk, and deer were plentiful, yet there was another animal most Plains Indians hunted when the grama grasses grew lush. In early summer, bison herds flowed into the valleys and onto the plains. Hunters who lived at the foot of the Sangre de Cristos followed them east.[20]

It was some of these Indians that Oñate's men encountered on their expedition. On 20 September 1598 Vicente de Zaldívar led sixty Spanish soldiers away from the Pecos Pueblo to get a firsthand look at the bison herds.[21] Zaldívar was on a larger mission to explore the area east of the Rio Grande pueblos. He had heard of the strange beasts that inhabited the plains and wanted to investigate. After spending a few nights at the Pecos Pueblo, Zaldívar and his men camped along the Gallinas River near its junction with the Pecos River. Later transcribing what his sargento mayor had reported, Oñate wrote that the Gallinas was "abounding of fish." He reported that many were caught with one hook. Moving southeast, Zaldívar saw his first bison north of present-day Tucumcari, about sixteen miles east of where Fort Bascom would be built. The first bison herd these Spaniards saw included about three hundred "cows." Soon after, they came upon a herd of four thousand moving through the Canadian River Valley. The conquistadores built a corral of cottonwood branches and tried to drive them into a make-shift trap, yet the animals refused to cooperate. After many attempts to capture them, Zaldívar gave up. He noted that bison were "brave beyond praise, and so cunning that if one runs after them, they run, and if one stops or moves slowly, they stop and roll, just like mules, and after this rest they renew their flight."[22]

On this same trip Zaldívar noted that the Canadian "flows from the direction of the Picuríes" (a Puebloan people who lived and still live in the mountains south of Taos, northwest of Zaldívar's location). While following the river, the expedition came upon a band of Fara-ones. Their teepees, draped with bright red-and-white bison skins, were "round like pavilions, with flags and openings, made as neatly as those in Italy." He described these Indians as vaqueros who had just come back from the plains. They packed meat, skins, fat, and tallow to trade with Puebloan peoples for pottery, maize, cotton products, and salt, evidence that barter between the different cultures was a long-standing tradition. Of the Llano Estacado, Oñate wrote, "We never came to the end of these plains; nor do they have sierras, trees or shrubs." When writing of the river basin, he said, "At the front of these mesas, in some places where they form valleys, there are numerous junipers, countless springs flowing out of the very mesas, and a half a league from them, there are large groves of cottonwoods." He con-cluded this description of the region by adding: "There are numerous Indians in those lands."[23]

Noted archeologist Alex D. Krieger believes Puebloans had been traveling from their Rio Grande villages to the Llano Estacado to trade with Plains peoples since at least the fifteenth century. Some of these Puebloans may have begun to farm along the Caprock.[24] It is certain that by the time Zaldívar made his way into the region, the flow of traffic up and down the Canadian and Pecos River Valleys had been ongoing for hundreds of years. During parts of the fifteenth and six-teenth centuries, the mountain agriculturalists and the Plains bison hunters were linked through trade. This barter economy thrived along the Canadian River, a main thoroughfare for both eastern- and western-bound caravans looking to convert corn into bison robes and meat into wool fabrics.

In 1680 the Pueblo Revolt forced the Spanish out of New Mexico, and they left behind many horses in their wake. When the Coman-ches pushed down from the Arkansas River in the first decades of the eighteenth century, they collected many of these animals and were soon breeding their own herds. As a result, the Comanches were at the forefront of the indigenous transportation revolution, and in the process created their own distinct vehicles of war. Utiliz-ing the horse, all Southern Plains Indians became capable of short-ening travel time and conquering distance, resulting in closer links between mountain and Plains cultures. The horse also transformed the Plains Indians into more dangerous adversaries.[25]

After the Pueblo Revolt, the Spanish did not return to New Mexico for twelve years. By then the Comanches had made an appearance in the Arkansas River Valley and would soon penetrate farther south. Various tribes of Apaches were still the dominant force in the region but that would begin to change in the first decade of the eighteenth century. Yet from 1706 to 1779, whether interacting with Navajos, Apaches, or, for most of the century, the Comanches, Spanish settlers participated in an economy fueled by revenge wars, livestock raids, kidnapped women and children, and slave labor. Such exchanges included every culture that populated the region. On the Spanish fron-tier, all living things could be converted into commodities.[26]

The Jicarilla Apaches resided near the headwaters of the Canadian just beyond Raton Pass, yet their homeland was not confined to the eastern face of this New Mexico mountain range. Jicarillas were taught from childhood that when their ancestors emerged from underground, the "Supreme God" asked them where they wanted to live. They chose the land between the Rio Grande and the Arkansas, Canadian, and

Pecos Rivers. Within this range, Jicarillas were both horticulturalists and hunters. Sargento mayor Juan de Ulibarrí noted their presence in 1706 when he passed by their community near the headwaters of the Canadian. He noted that they were growing pumpkins, corn, and frijoles, yet like other Sangre de Cristo Mountain people, they also followed the Canadian onto the plains each summer to hunt bison.[27] The Jicarillas' only boundaries on such excursions were those they set for themselves. What many Europeans considered desolate wilderness, a variety of American Indian tribes (as well as early Hispano settlers) found to be life-sustaining and holy.[28]

Nuevo Mexico remained a zone of strife until 1779, when Governor Juan Bautista de Anza's army killed Comanche war chief Cuerno Verde. From this Spanish victory, a peace was finally brokered on 21 April 1787. The treaty, a drawn-out affair that took several rounds of negotiations at Pecos Pueblo and Mexico City, officially formalized the already ongoing plains-mountain trade. This led to a relatively nonviolent period in Hispanic–Plains Indians relations that lasted into the Mexican period. The Spanish government issued licenses to Pueblo Indians and Hispanos that granted them the legal right to barter with the Comanches and other Southern Plains Indians. Spanish authorities encouraged these relationships, hoping they would halt outright theft. They also counted on eastward-trekking traders to bring back intelligence concerning any future raids. Such traders could also be used to alert officials of unwanted encroachment by Anglo explorers.[29]

In 1821, after Mexico gained its independence from Spain, the new government opened its borders to U.S. merchants.[30] Many of the first Anglo-Americans to travel to New Mexico along what became known as the Santa Fe Trail left journals of their exploits. Few, if any, of these journals were as descriptive as those of the previously mentioned diarist Josiah Gregg.[31] Although his characterizations of New Mexicans were unflattering, his descriptions of the countryside are some of the first Anglo-American observations of the Canadian River Valley. Gregg wanted to be a doctor, yet suffered from chronic dyspepsia and consumption and never completed his studies. In 1831, after trying his hand at teaching, he decided to head west for his health, keeping the accounts for a wagon train full of goods that was headed to Santa Fe. His health improved. Over the next nine years he ventured west from Missouri four times to sell merchandise to Mexicans, particularly New

Mexicans. In 1839–40 his round-trip journey led him along old Indian
and contemporary Comanchero trade routes that tied the Rio Grande
to the Llano Estacado. These same paths later evolved into the Fort
Smith route that led back to Arkansas and followed a portion of old
Route 66 and current Interstate 40 that runs from Amarillo to Albuquerque. On the westward trek, Gregg followed the Canadian River
as far as Tucumcari Peak. Yet here, not far from where Fort Bascom was
constructed, the river turned north. On this trip, Gregg abandoned
the stream and continued westward toward Albuquerque.[32]

This merchant's additional descriptions of the flora and fauna surrounding the eventual location of Fort Bascom are worth noting. Of
the grama grasses that drew the bison and other game into the valley
he wrote, "Our stock will eat but little corn; for the first appearance
of spring grass set the animals crazy—they will leave all other food to
seek after the few shooting sprouts."[33] He believed the exposed soils
lacked something in their composition, which led to the common
erosion of the *cejas,* or brows, along the Caprock: "The clayey foundation is exceedingly firm . . . [yet] while dry, it seems the most soluble
of earths, and melts almost as rapidly as snow under actions of water."
His animals were unable to drink from some of the streams he crossed
due to their brackishness. On a separate journey that took him eight
miles beyond the river's junction with the Conchas, he wrote of steep
walls along the Canadian Escarpment, noting that they rose two thousand feet above the river. He commented on the difficulty of travel
through this area, which he called "the narrows," yet at the same time
mentioned the presence of cart paths crisscrossing the valley.[34] He
found plums, grapes, chokeberries and "several kinds of onions" among
the river's creeks and marshes. He wrote of the presence of sunflowers,
dogtooth, and violets on the valley floor. He observed herds of deer
and found black bears foraging on various red, black, and white berries,
as well as on abundant acorns. He was particularly fascinated with
the pronghorn antelope that roamed the prairies and the "curious"
prairie dogs that stood atop their burrows and chattered at him when
he passed.[35]

Gregg encountered "large parties of New Mexicans," some on horses
and mules, others pushing the wooden-wheeled *carretas* east to where
they hunted game and searched out the Comanches to trade hard breads
and produce for robes and other bison products.[36] He also came into

contact with Southern Plains Indians. In the early part of his 1839 journey, near where the Little River joins the Canadian, a small group of Comanche and Kiowa men and their families joined Gregg's caravan to barter a few mules. About to embark westward into a land he had never traveled, Gregg asked Chief Tábba-quena if he might describe the area he was about to enter. After giving the chief "paper and pencil . . . he promptly executed . . . to our astonishment, quite a map-like appearance, with far more accurate delineation of all the principal rivers of the plains . . . than is to be found in many of the engraved maps of those regions."[37]

Gregg learned a fact in 1839 that would mystify Anglo-Americans for the next forty years. Comanches and Kiowas did not need marks on paper to tell them where they were. Like other American Indians, their homeland's topography was imprinted in their minds. Regardless of the seemingly monotonous nature of the landscape, each brook held special meaning. Cliffs and mesas were more than rocks and dirt, more than the remnants of another world. Whether Jicarilla, Comanche, or Puebloan, the land appeared to be saying something different to Indians such as Chief Tábba-quena than it did to Gregg and all the Americans who followed him.

By the 1840s Hispano and Puebloan farmers and ranchers loaded with goods left their villages in August and September of each year and journeyed east with their pack mules, carts, and wagons toward the Llano Estacado. At the same time, the Comanches moved north with bison hides and stolen horses and cattle. Kotsoteka and Yamparika bands met the Comancheros at predesignated locations to barter. In the decades to come, regional demographics shifted. The Kwahadis became the primary group of Comanches who met these traders on the Texas Panhandle, but Kiowas and Apaches also took part. The Hispano participants in this exchange lived in a string of villages that began near the New Mexico–Colorado border and ran down the eastern range of the Sangre de Cristos, a path also followed by the Canadian. Puebloans also participated, with the Santo Domingo traders being particularly active. The trade zone encompassed much of Comanchería, including the highland prairies of the Llano Estacado and the Edwards Plateau of Central Texas. Within the Wichita, Davis, and Sangre de Cristo mountain ranges, Comancheros carried on a substantial trade with their namesakes. For three-quarters of the nineteenth century, these New Mexican middlemen operated at the center of a trading nexus that at different times included Canadian fur trappers, Arapaho merchants, Anglo-American cattlemen, Hispano farmers, and Tiwa Indians from Taos.[38]

From the time of Juan de Oñate's 1598 expedition until the 1830s, this exchange was well established, as Gregg's journals verify. New Mexican and Puebloan travelers, early on called *viajeros,* drove their pack mules and carretas onto the Llano, finding the Comanches on the western edges of the Texas Panhandle. Even the governor of the Tesuque Pueblo participated in this trade and was called, like the others, a Comanchero.[39] These traders followed the Canadian and the Pecos Rivers out of the mountains, hauling their goods across the prairie sea to Las Tecovas, Quitaque, Cañón del Rescate, and Muchaque.[40]

In 1848 the U.S. annexation of half of the Mexican nation prompted many within the United States to commence with the business of connecting their new territories to the rest of the nation. Congress approved several surveys to be conducted by the U.S. Corps of Topographical Engineers. They were charged with determining and mapping the best route through the west for a transcontinental railroad. In 1853 Lt. Amiel W. Whipple led a team of surveyors, scientists, and engineers along the same Canadian River route Gregg had taken fourteen years earlier.[41]

With an engineer's eye for detail, Whipple recorded more than data pertinent to building a railroad. Just north of Amarillo, close to where the Antelope focus people once lived, the lieutenant met a group of Indians from the Santo Domingo Pueblo. Draped in Mexican blankets and wearing Indian headdresses and beads, they were on their way to trade with the Southern Plains tribes. These Puebloans rode mules and packed hard breads and flour to trade with the "k'ai-ó-wás." Whipple had stumbled onto one of the permanent rendezvous sites where the Comanchero trade took place.[42]

As he traveled from the Caprock to the Tucumcari outliers, Whipple wrote about a variety of subjects not related to railroad topography. He found wild grapes "as large as hazel nuts" growing by a brook and counted hundreds of antelopes grazing on the prairies. On both 18 and 21 September 1853, his party met several groups of Mexican traders heading east: "We had no idea of the extent of this Indian trade, or the impunity with which defenseless traders could mingle with these savages and treacherous tribes upon their own soil."[43]

As the expedition passed eleven miles south of the future site of Fort Bascom, botanist Dr. John Milton Bigelow climbed Tucumcari Peak. He deduced much of this outlier to be from the Jurassic period and expounded on the beauty of the valley that wound north toward the Sangre de Cristos. Along the way the expedition observed "lizards, horned frogs, and snakes in quite numerous and interesting new varieties daily." Whipple wrote that this valley "offers every faculty for a large settlement." He observed that the same Gallinas River where Zaldívar's Spaniards had caught so many fish had "pure running water, but with neither wood or grass upon its banks."[44]

While recent historiography regarding the Comanches' economic influence has compared them to other colonial powers, such a story seems a half-told tale. If the wealth that these Indians accumulated over a fifty-year period during the nineteenth century actually drove Southwestern economies and inculcated surrounding cultures, as Pekka Hämäläinen has argued, would not the barter Comancheros accumulated to trade for this wealth be just as valuable? And if this were so, what would that say about the men who provided this barter? Detailing these trade goods—where they came from, who participated in their exchange, and what impact that exchange had in New Mexico and Texas, which will be further investigated in subsequent chapters— sheds new light on the Comancheros' relevance to the history of the Southwest. Such a discussion should begin with a brief comparison to their more famous Anglo counterparts. Scholars have never doubted the historical significance of Rocky Mountain fur traders and trappers. If, upon inspection, we can deduce that the Comancheros were in many ways similar to their Anglo counterparts, perhaps it is time to reevaluate their significance.[45]

For most of the year, Comancheros were not Comancheros: they were farmers and ranchers living along the rivers and streams that ran out of the Sangre de Cristo Mountains. Many grew up in the small villages that were scattered along the Pecos River. Twice a year they traveled east and traded with the Comanches. Military records, maps, and government documents illustrate that much of this trade originated between San Miguel and Puerto de Luna, with its apex near the Gallinas River crossing (also known as Gallinas Spring).[46]

The Gallinas River runs into the Pecos River about seventeen miles east of Anton Chico. This junction was of the utmost interest to William Pelham in 1857. Pelham was the Surveyor General of New Mexico, charged with the herculean task of validating every land grant in the territory. Despite this almost inconceivable challenge, Pelham made time to query Hispano villagers who lived along the Pecos about their knowledge of any roads that led into Comanchería. After interviewing four Hispanos who lived on the Preston Beck and José Leandro Perea grants, he found that the Gallinas River crossing, just a few miles above this river's junction with the Pecos, sat between two major New Mexican trade routes.[47]

Pelham strayed from specifics on these land grants when questioning men who had lived along the Pecos for decades. Marcos Sandoval, Francisco Salazar, Luis Griego, and Antonio Saens testified that two main roads led away from the Gallinas's junction with the Pecos. The surveyor general's interview with Francisco Montoya was quite typical of the questions asked and the answers received.

Pelham: "Do you know the road to Conchas Springs?"

Montoya: "I do. There are two old roads [heading east]."

Pelhman: "Where do the two old roads cross the Gallinas River?"

Montoya: "One crosses a little above the house."[48]

The "house" was Juan Esteban Pino's hacienda. Pino ran a large sheep ranch at the confluence of the two rivers. Montoya and the others described two roads leading away from the Gallinas. One began about five miles to the north of Pino's hacienda, near the future village of Chaperito; the other started immediately in front of the hacienda and trailed south along the Gallinas until that river joined the Pecos. At this point, the road, which ran parallel to the river, followed the Pecos to the southeast. Both of these roads are significant in the history of the Comancheros and therefore figure in the fate of Fort Bascom.[49]

Conchas Springs was a well-known intersection of Southern Plains Indian and Hispano mountain trails that radiated outward to Texas, Indian Territory, Kansas Territory, and present-day Colorado. It was also an early Comanchero rendezvous site and trading station. This was why Pelham was interested in more than just validating land grants when he talked to people who lived nearby. One of these trails, the "upper road," which rancher Luis Griego called the "Rincón de las Conchas," originated not far from Pino's ranch and followed the Conchas

River east to its junction with the Canadian at Conchas Springs. This path furnished a good water route for traders who lived in San Miguel, La Cuesta, Anton Chico, and other Pecos Valley villages. Griego told Pelham that traders traveled this trail with small packs and mules brought by the Comanches. He explained that the lower path was more than a trail. He called it the "Comanchero road." It followed the Gallinas to the Pecos, then ran south with the larger river for a few miles before it split into two roads. In the 1830s this split was the epicenter of Bernalillo mercantilist Pedro José Perea's sheep ranch. Like Pino, Perea was one of the wealthiest men in the territory.[50]

Perea established himself just downstream from Gallinas Spring on Esteros Creek, a tributary of the Pecos. He ran thousands of sheep on this ranch, which is noted as Rancho de los Esteros in the surveyor general's records. Another herder Pelham interviewed, Miguel González, explained that Perea also grazed cattle, horses, and mules there. Mules were often used by Comancheros to pack their goods into Texas. According to later military maps, Esteros Creek, the center of Perea's grant, was also called Hurrah Creek. This tributary was very close to where the Comanchero road split into two roads. In 1857 local herders, or *pastores*, testified to Surveyor General Pelham that the Pereas had been grazing livestock at this location since 1815. Pedro's son, José Leandro Perea owned the land when Pelham began assessing the validity of New Mexico's land grants.[51]

After crossing Esteros Creek, one road headed east across the Eroded Plains, skirted south of Mesa Rica and Tucumcari Peak, then continued on toward Texas. Much of the later Fort Smith road followed this route. The second fork in the "good wagon road" followed the Pecos south to Alamogordo, where it also turned east, following the "Trail of Living Water" across the Portales Valley to Cañón del Rescate or Muchaque in northwest Texas near present-day Gail.[52]

It is unlikely that Mexican elites such as Juan Esteban Pino and Pedro José Perea were unaware of the traffic that passed through their property. We can speculate that Pino and Perea, and many others who later lived in the Pecos River Valley—including many Anglos—not only knew about the Comanchero trade but also participated in it. Some of the locals were certainly involved in both legal and illegal expeditions to Conchas Springs, Quitaque, and Muchaque. Who supplied them remains a sketchy proposition in most cases. Yet when reviewing

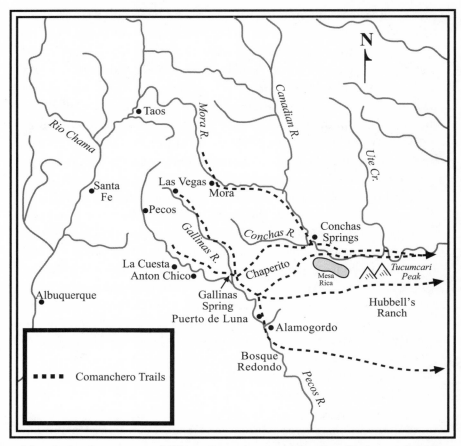

Map 2. A select group of Hispano ranchers and farmers filed out of their
mountain villages at least once each year, eventually turning east toward
Texas. Comancheros hauled hard breads, textiles, vermillion, guns, whiskey,
and much more down trails that followed the Canadian and Pecos Rivers
before turning east toward the Llano Estacado, where the traders linked up
with the Comanches and Kiowas for several days. Copyright © 2016 The University of Oklahoma Press, Publishing Division of the University. All rights reserved.

the history of those who lived along these trails, especially at critical
river junctures, a pattern emerges that allows the historian ample food
for thought.[53]

In the decade after annexation, Anglo-Americans began to move
into the area. Alexander Hatch, a former New Yorker, became a pros-
perous merchant in Santa Fe. Later he established a ranch and trading

post just north of Griego's upper road in the mid 1850s. After serving his country as an army captain at Fort Union, another Anglo, Preston Beck, also acquired land just south of Perea's ranch during this same period. Beck used the United States court system to gain legal title to land once owned by the Pinos. In 1856, not long after Hatch founded his ranch, two U.S. Army infantry companies were sent to build an outpost on his land. Hatch and Beck were soon selling hay and other provisions to the soldiers stationed there. Military officials called this new post Hatch's Ranch. Capt. Thomas Wilhelm, Eighth U.S. Infantry, stationed at Hatch's in 1860, noted in a history of the Eighth Infantry that they were sent there to protect the sutlers (civilian merchants who sell provisions to the army). Fort Union was seventy miles away. Men like Hatch offered the military a variety of supplies and forage it otherwise would not have been able to procure. Soldiers stationed at Hatch's Ranch patrolled the Pecos and Canadian River Valleys and the Eroded Plains in search of Kiowa and Comanche raiders. The army only used this location as a permanent post for a few years. Long after Hatch abandoned it, several ex-officers from Fort Bascom and Fort Sumner began to contract with local Comancheros to haul their goods east. They obviously believed there was money to be made if they could somehow corner the Comanche market. Men had been seeking such alliances for hundreds of years.[54]

Most Anglo descriptions of the Hispano traders who facilitated these transactions characterize them as a backward people who hauled their goods across the plains like so many itinerate gypsies. The first Anglo travelers to come into contact with New Mexican traders recorded their impressions in journals and reports that were often published on the East Coast. Historians still cite impressions of Comancheros conjured up by men like Josiah Gregg. His descriptions did not stir the kind of romantic notions that led to dime-store novels. Yet in the 1870s, Col. Ranald Mackenzie found José Piedad Tafoya, a noted Hispano trader, to be "reliable . . . brave, intelligent and sagacious."[55]

Many Anglo mountain men became popular American folk heroes, but much of what happened beyond the mountains did not make the newspapers back home. Media adulation came in part from the notion that such men had freely chosen such a dangerous and singular lifestyle. Yet, as in all frontier zones of interaction, various forms of violence were as much a part of the landscape as the snow-covered peaks

and green river valleys that cut from north to south across the continent. Anglo mountain men were traders as well as trappers. George
Ruxton, who traveled extensively in the Rockies in the 1840s, noted
that "mountaineers . . . [capture] women, whom they carry off, and
not unfrequently [*sic*] . . . sell to other tribes, or each other." Some
were known to practice ritual cannibalism, and many took their enemies'
scalps. Besides slaves and furs, traders were also interested in horses.
Several mountain men encouraged the Utes to raid into California
when it still belonged to Mexico. The herds these Indians confiscated,
numbering into the thousands, were led back to the Rocky Mountains,
where "expectant capitalists," as one historian called them, awaited
their arrival at rendezvous. Stolen horses were bartered for whiskey,
weapons, and gunpowder. Although Ruxton's fact-based, fictionalized
account of such experiences was distributed throughout the country,
it was East Coast "blood and thunder" paperbacks that gained traction
with the public. With little to no focus on slave trading or horse stealing, most historians' characterizations of mountain men likened them
to knights of the Round Table or Robin Hood and his Merry Men.
Although Wilbur R. Jacobs did describe them as "wasteful varmints,"
for the most part their reputations remained untarnished. William R.
Swagerty has noted that "other than politicians, [no one] has received
as much attention as this cadre of often overly romanticized . . . mytho-
logical and real personalities."[56]

In many respects, Comancheros carried on a similar livelihood,
but no George Ruxton cared to romanticize their actions in print.
Race is woven into why this is so, yet not always in traditionally understood ways. Factors such as distance from media outlets, language
barriers, foreign borders, and the inability to travel freely across Comanchería also help to explain why so little has been written about the
Comancheros, especially anything positive. On the surface, their world
embraced many of the same characteristics associated with Kit Carson,
Ceran St. Vrain, and other mountain men. Both groups of men lived
in the Indians' world. Both traded there, married native women, became
part of the local communities, warred with and against neighboring
tribes, and, in many cases, recoiled at returning to their previous lives.
Early historians and pulp writers never had a problem using their imagi-
nations to fill in the gaps left by men like Carson. If mentioned at all,

such traders' illegal activities accentuated their cunning and adventuresome spirit, while similar reports of Hispano actions seldom portrayed them as anything other than thieves.[57]

Defining the significance of the Comancheros within southwestern history involves acknowledging the multidimensional aspects of their story. They were the product of a social exchange system that originated out of New Spain's slave-trading heritage. As cultural intermediaries, they used this heritage to their advantage. Like Carson, they traveled easily between the Euro-American and Indian worlds. Their ability to converse with a variety of nationalities allowed them to become significant economic players in the region, as well as facilitators of a transnational black market phenomenon. The Comancheros would ultimately link Mexican nationals, Texas Comanches, New Mexican businessmen, and Kansas ranchers into one trade network.[58]

By the close of the Spanish period, racial and cultural interchanges between plains and mountain peoples were generations old. These exchanges created an ethnic borderland free of predetermined loyalties based on treaties or geographic boundaries. At least one thousand Southwestern Indians and several hundred Hispanic women and children had been "cross-cultured" through generations of trading, kidnapping, and slave raiding. These raids helped fuel the Comanche economy. New Mexicans' insatiable desire for servants encouraged similar behavior. While many of those captured by the Comanches were later bartered for horses, blankets, and weapons, kidnapped females of all ages and small boys were often incorporated into Southern Plains Indian society as equals within their communities. Similarly, nomadic Indians captured during conflicts with New Mexicans and sold or traded into slavery were enculturated into the Hispanic communities into which they were inserted. These *genízaros* (detribalized nomadic Indians) were some of the first Mexican citizens to venture away from the Rio Grande to start their own New Mexican communities.[59]

By the late 1850s, descriptions of Mexicans hauling bread and wool out of the mountains only partially described what the caravans were carrying to the plains. In the first decade after annexation, the demand for stolen horses and cattle increased exponentially, tied to a reduction in bison and an increase in cattle ranching that was related to Anglo-American westward expansion. Comancheros could not remain viable trading partners without providing barter equal to the value of live-stock flowing toward them from Mexico and Texas. Along with carts and pack mules, wagons were used to move merchandise toward the Llano Estacado. From a distance, such caravans could have been mistaken for the American merchant trains that rolled along the Santa Fe Trail, characterized in history and fiction as being piloted by intrepid, capitalistic pioneers.[60]

So many Hispanos were noted to be traveling east in the 1850s because the Comanches no longer visited the old trade fairs of Pecos or Taos. By mid-century, Comanches were powerful enough to demand their trading partners come to the plains. New Mexicans followed the Canadian and Pecos Rivers beyond the mesalands to the upland prairies that rose above the Caprock and the Edwards Plateau. Their trails pivoted off the rivers, breaking east and southeast along tributaries that ran into the Panhandle. La Pista de Vida Agua (Trail of Living Water) led to Cañón del Rescate and Muchaque in Texas. Las Escarbadas wound its way to Quitaque. New Mexican villagers from Mora, Las Vegas, Trujillo, and Colonias followed the Canadian to Texas, while residents of San Miguel, La Cuesta, Anton Chico, and Chaperito moved in a more southern direction down the Pecos River before turning east. Comanches also met these long-distance traders near Jayton, in northwest Texas, and also along the Canadian River north of present-day Amarillo. After annexation, some transactions continued to take place closer to the Sangre de Cristo mountain villages, yet with less frequency after the Civil War.[61]

The Canadian River Valley served as one of the main conduits of exchange. Hispano and Puebloan traders usually took between three to four weeks to reach their destinations. Mesa Rica, located between the Canadian and Pecos River Valleys, was one of the geographic markers such travelers and Plains tribes used to determine the distance and time needed to reach the Llano Estacado. Like the fur traders' rendezvous, Comanchero exchanges with the Southern Plains Indians often took on a festive air, with competitive events such as wrestling, horse races, and gambling. Each year hundreds of Hispano traders made their way into the canyons and river valleys that hosted these "fairs," indicating just how strong the demand for southwestern livestock had become, especially after annexation, as Anglo pioneers moved into Comanchería. On the hinge of this economic gateway, Comancheros exchanged their goods and returned to the Sangre de Cristos with thousands of head of stolen horses and cattle.[62]

American soldiers quickly learned that Comanche and Comanchero cultures were intertwined. This was certainly true in 1863 when the army constructed Fort Bascom. Thus it is important to assess the significance of Comanchero kinship ties with Southern Plains Indians. Assimilation had multiple intentions. Merging kidnap victims and former slaves into the families of both societies produced a cohort of bilingual subjects who could understand and communicate with business partners and become spies to circulate among a new common enemy, the Euro-American. Comanches assimilated Mexicans, Anglos, blacks, and a host of native people into their world. Similarly, for generations Hispanos had been enculturating captured American Indians into their communities. Such comingling created general confusion for U.S. soldiers charged with eliminating wayward Mescalero Apaches while observing orders to allow Pueblo traders to pass unharmed. Maj. Edward H. Bergmann, on patrol from Fort Bascom, was astonished by the number of Hispanics who rode with the Comanches on the Llano Estacado. He estimated that "one half of the Comanche warriors, which I have seen, were either Mexican Captives or such Mexicans who go among the Indians voluntarily, preferring this style of life." As early as 1845, on an expedition up the Canadian River, François des Montaignes saw a number of Hispanics riding with Kiowas and was told that "many American individuals [were] thus circumstanced among Camanches [sic]." In 1867 a "Mexican" trader caught trying to herd eight hundred head of stolen cattle past Fort Bascom told Capt. George W. Letterman that he had seen fifteen Anglo children and one negro with the Comanches. Many captives chose to remain with their captors when Anglo soldiers or Indian agents offered to purchase them. Capt. John V. D. Dubois reported to Acting Asst. Adj. Gen. Cyrus H. De Forrest that the Comanches had "many negroes among them." Such reports illustrate the fluidity of the borderland societies Fort Bascom troopers encountered along the Canadian. Soldiers often had a hard time distinguishing friend from foe.[63]

Fort Bascom was located just to the southeast of Mesa Rica, the geologic bridge that ties the Pecos and Canadian River Valleys together. Four miles long, the mesa's size made it the perfect screen to avoid military patrols. As a result, Fort Bascom cavalrymen were constantly scouting on Mesa Rica. Their reports often illustrated the frustration these soldiers experienced trying to chase down uncooperative Navajos or illegal traders. More escaped than were apprehended. Anglo soldiers from the east found it difficult to remain oriented in a land of few trees, where horizons occasionally disappeared into arroyos and canyons unknown to them.[64]

The environment that surrounds Mesa Rica was hard on soldiers and their animals. Evaporation rates strong enough to eliminate fifty inches of ground moisture prevail in a region that only averages twenty inches of rain per year.[65] American Indians and most New Mexicans did not know or care about such statistics. They depended on their senses, not precise instruments of measurement, to acquire the information they needed to survive and even to thrive. Comanches did not know what the land lacked, for it had always provided. Kiowas did not need paper maps to locate water or food. The Canadian River Valley, like much of the Southwest, provided New Mexicans, Puebloans, Comanches, and Jicarillas with a vibrant, multifaceted ecosystem. Its topography was entangled with their folklore and helped shape their cultures. For some, it was a holy land; for others, just home. For most Anglo-Americans, the land around Fort Bascom was never much more than a dry, rock-strewn, windy hellhole of sand and lizards where they never quite got their bearings. Yet within the history of Fort Bascom is the story of such soldiers ultimately adapting to what they considered a harsh environment. Gregg's "sublimity of desolation" was more desolate than sublime for troops stationed in the Canadian River Valley. Over the years, the New Mexico volunteers and army regulars posted to Fort Bascom took their cue from the Comancheros and the Comanches, memorizing where the water holes were.[66]

On the eve of the American Civil War, the U.S. Army knew the Comanchero traders were at the heart of many of its problems concerning Southern Plains Indians. One such trader, Thomas Padilla, known simply to the Kiowas and Comanches as "Thomas," was accused by Capt. William B. Lane of acting as a decoy or advance scout who reported the whereabouts of patrols to his trading partners. Captain Lane also charged Padilla with actively participating in recent attacks at Forts Dodge and Laramie, as well as fighting alongside the Comanches against Col. Kit Carson's troops at the Battle of Adobe Walls. Many officers believed Padilla had a wealth of company, insisting that the

Comanchero trade of the late 1860s was about more than exchanging cattle for rifles, or horses for hard bread and calico. Certainly there was an element of resistance embedded in these exchanges. Many Hispanics maintained stronger alliances with Comanches and Kiowas than with Anglo-Americans. When most regular army soldiers rode east to fight in Virginia and Pennsylvania during the Civil War, the Comanchero trade exploded. This left Hispano and Anglo-American cattle ranchers exposed to raids. The extraction of livestock, especially from Texas, provided the Comanches and Kiowas the barter they needed to acquire weapons and other manufactured goods from New Mexican entrepreneurs. In the decade following the Treaty of Guadalupe Hidalgo, this exchange helped the Southern Plains Indians reestablish, if only for a few years, much of their hold on old hunting grounds that they had grudgingly abandoned after 1848. Major military and trade routes, such as the Fort Smith road and the Santa Fe Trail, also saw an uptick in raids and skirmishes during this period. Thus, at a time when many U.S. Army posts in New Mexico were being abandoned, Fort Bascom, constructed in the shadow of Mesa Rica, became one of Union's most forward frontier bases.[67]

The soldiers posted to this fort and the officers they served soon learned military power would have little to do with gaining control of the region. Troopers had to acquire a better understanding of the Canadian River Valley environment and the people who already lived there before their mission could be accomplished. Strategy and tactics would change over the years to better challenge adversaries who did not need maps in a land of little water. First impressions concerning Hispanos who lived in the territory proved to be inaccurate. Mountain traders' ties to Plains cultures were much stronger than U.S. government officials first realized. Understanding these relationships, which originated as far back as the sixteenth century, was crucial to developing the tactics needed to efficiently police the area. With the establishment of Fort Bascom, on-the-job training began in earnest on the doorstep of the Llano Estacado.

CHAPTER 3

A Neat Little Post

The installation of military bases in any territory influences that region's history, yet seldom to the degree that it did in New Mexico Territory. After being defeated by the United States in 1848, Mexico was forced to sign the Treaty of Guadalupe Hidalgo. This agreement affected societies from Veracruz to Santa Fe. Spanish-speaking New Mexicans were soon trying to communicate with strangers from the United States who embraced different concepts of land ownership, legal jurisprudence, and social justice. These Anglo-Americans spoke a different language, came from a different culture, and often perceived their new countrymen as subhuman. Urban and nomadic Indians also thrived in New Mexico in 1848. Many had warred with one another for centuries. In the mid-nineteenth century, sixty thousand New Mexicans and Puebloans lived in New Mexico Territory. Since the sixteenth century, the American Indians had been enmeshed in complicated alliances, rivalries, and economic relationships with their New Mexican neighbors. Anglo-American soldiers found these relationships difficult to decipher. Such confusion was reciprocal. Aside from charging the U.S. Army with protecting Anglo pioneers and the new government's officials, the Treaty of Guadalupe Hidalgo obligated these same troopers to stop Indians from raiding below the newly established border. The Southern Plains tribes, who had long considered the villages of Northern Mexico to be a resource domain, were confused by this twist in international diplomacy that saw the United States, recently at war with Mexico, suddenly become that country's demanding protector.[1]

New territories required a strong military presence because federal officials intended the first settlers and soldiers who traveled west to lay the groundwork for future entrepreneurs and other waves of immigrants. Many of the indigenous peoples who already lived in New Mexico were displeased with such plans. The United States' westward expansion meant the loss of land for many of New Mexico's earlier settlers, and it was these people, even if certain segments were miniscule, who fought encroachment in a variety of ways. Thus, for almost fifty years the United States was forced to maintain military bases up and down the length of the new territory as part of their overall plan to create the stability and security successful Euro-American expansion required.[2]

The acquisition of half of Mexico's claimed territory initiated a two-fold mission for the American conquerors. First, U.S. soldiers occupied the new territories at strategic locations to ensure locals would not disrupt government officials as they began to implement American policy. The second mission was more complicated because it included controlling the Southern Plains Indians. Both tasks proved more difficult than originally estimated. Although Mexico had ceded its northern territories as a result of the war, pronouncements of a "bloodless" New Mexican conquest did not ring true for many of the first American civilians charged with taking command there. In January 1847, within a year of annexation, enraged Puebloans, Apaches, and New Mexicans removed Charles Bent, the new territorial governor, from his Taos home and scalped and murdered him. Bent's disregard for warning signs of local resentment cost him and other civilians their lives. The revolt spread from Taos into the surrounding mountain communities. Troops stationed in Santa Fe and Las Vegas quickly quelled the rebellion, but not before American soldiers experienced their share of casualties. Regardless of its promise to Mexico to restrain aggressive Southern Plains Indians, for the United States the Taos Revolt highlighted the need for a strong military presence in New Mexico.[3]

In addition to stopping Indian raids into Northern Mexico, the second mission included halting the traditional wars that raged among Hispanos, Apaches, Comanches, and Navajos. This circle of violence had been ongoing for over a century. Part of stopping these wars of vengeance included policing a regional economy partially fueled by the slave trade, in which all societies in the region participated. The soldiers were also charged with creating a safe corridor for Anglo-American pioneer trains and merchant caravans traveling the Santa Fe Trail. Both missions were functions of conquest, empire, and expansion and required a substantial, long-term commitment by the U.S. military.[4]

Such an effort required the construction of a series of military posts across the western frontier. Shortly after the 1847 uprising, Camp Burgwin was established on the outskirts of Taos. By 1851 the federal government had grown weary of dealing with the social problems that came with maintaining Fort Marcy, a garrison near Santa Fe, and began to look for a location to replace it, seeking to distance soldiers from urban vices while still fulfilling the department's strategic requirements. Officials selected a site twenty-eight miles north Las Vegas, New Mexico, and in 1851 constructed one of the frontier army's most important nineteenth-century posts. Fort Union was built on the eastern face of the Sangre de Cristo range, where the Mountain and Cimarron routes of the Santa Fe Trail merged. Its location gave maximum protection to settlers and freighters and positioned it to serve as the main supply depot for future western garrisons. In 1854 Fort Craig was established about forty-five miles south of Socorro along the Rio Grande, and Fort Stanton was constructed on the banks of the Rio Bonito, about ten miles west of present-day Lincoln, New Mexico. Fort Craig's soldiers were charged with gaining control of the Gila and Mimbres Apaches, while Fort Stanton's troops sought to end Mescalero raids in southwestern New Mexico.[5]

Throughout the 1850s the federal government continued to establish posts at key locations, generally along New Mexico's main rivers and trade routes. Yet while military and territorial officials tried to implement policies that would create stronger links between New Mexico and eastern markets, Texas (first as the Republic of Texas [1836–46] and later as a state) sought recognition of its longstanding claim that at least half of this new territory was already within its boundaries. That claim began with the Texians' victory over Santa Ana at San Jacinto in 1836 and continued for almost a quarter century. In 1841 the president of the republic, Mirabeau Lamar, initiated a large-scale expedition to Santa Fe in hopes of establishing economic ties that would lead to the creation of a trade route similar to the Santa Fe Trail. Over three hundred well-armed men took part in this venture, leading some New Mexicans to believe Lamar had more on his mind

than trade. The Texas–Santa Fe Expedition was doomed from the out-
set by poor planning, poor logistics, and little water. The men struggled
across northwest Texas in the dead of summer. Indians stole some of
their horses. The expedition then got lost. When the straggling, disor-
ganized and dehydrated band finally wandered into northeastern New
Mexico, they were greeted not as trading partners but as invaders.
The Texians were arrested and eventually forced to march to Mexico
City, where they were imprisoned. Following the U.S.–Mexican War, the
Texas state legislature created two new counties within New Mexico
Territory and sent administrators north to establish a local govern-
ment. Despite indications to the contrary, Texans still believed that New
Mexicans would willingly become a part of Texas once Mexico lost
control of the region. When New Mexicans and the federal govern-
ment refused to recognize this scheme, Texas governor Peter H. Bell
issued a call to raise an army to put down the "rebellion" on land the
Lone Star State still claimed, but cooler heads eventually prevailed.
Because of a long history of such actions, most New Mexico Hispanos, like many Southern Plains Indians, considered the Texans to
be a greater enemy than the Apaches, Comanches, or the U.S. Army.[6]

Although New Mexicans did reserve a special hate in their hearts
for Texans, they also nourished a strong animosity toward other, closer
cultures. Because of this, the frontier army was fully engaged trying
to gain control of the territory while keeping the merchant lanes open
and safe. Events outside New Mexico often affected soldiers' ability
to carry out their mission. Government policies or military actions
north of the Arkansas or south of the Canadian River often affected
the lives of New Mexico Indians, which sometimes led to conflicts
with soldiers stationed in the territory. Incidents involving Arapahos
or Cheyennes along the Cimarron River were quickly communicated
across the southern prairies to Kiowa, Comanche, and Apache villages.
The Indians of the southern plains were not a homogenous group,
but they occasionally did unite in common cause, such as fighting perceived injustices by exacting revenge on the first Anglos they encountered. Military or political actions far from the Canadian River sometimes elicited unintended consequences in the Texas Panhandle and
New Mexico.[7]

As an example, during the 1850s many Texans were relentless in
their quest to eliminate Southern Plains tribes from their state. Despite

Maj. Robert S. Neighbors's earnest effort to establish a reservation system for Texas's Indians, by the late 1850s Comanches and Kiowas who did not want to settle in Indian Territory had few places where they could live as they always had. The one exception was the Llano Estacado. Southern Plains Indians found refuge along the Red and Canadian Rivers, centrally located between their old mountain trading partners in New Mexico and the Anglo settlements of northern and northwestern Texas. As the Comanches and Kiowas began to depend increasingly on the Comanchero trade to remain independent, the military in New Mexico was pressured to stop this exchange. The argument went that if the Comanches did not have a willing trading partner in New Mexico, raids and incursions would cease in Texas. In 1859 one Indian agent wrote of the Comanches' circumstances, "A smothered passion for revenge agitates these Indians." Even as military posts began to be abandoned in New Mexico and Texas at the start of the Civil War, a cumulative anger over broken treaties and land encroachment festered among the Comanches and Kiowas. When the War between the States began, the Southern Plains Indians once again found themselves in the middle of a confusing array of alliances, but sought to exploit the conflict, especially against the distracted and weakened Texans.[8]

In 1861, once Abraham Lincoln was sworn into office, the Lone Star State again turned its attention toward New Mexico. Shortly after Texas seceded from the Union, Ben McCulloch led a contingent of Texan volunteers into San Antonio and pressured the commander of its federal facilities, Gen. David E. Twiggs, to surrender all government property. Twiggs's capitulation gave the Texans reason to believe a similar success could soon be replicated in New Mexico.[9]

Letters from Mesilla Valley settlers and transplanted Texans in the northern part of the territory encouraged the newly minted Texas Confederates to move north. Robert P. Kelly, editor of the *Mesilla Times,* and James Magoffin, the merchant who preceded Brig. Gen. Stephen Watts Kearny into Santa Fe in 1846, intimated there would be little resistance to an occupation, implying that most New Mexicans sympathized with the South. As the war drums beat louder, adventurers, entrepreneurs, and leading Texas figures began to assemble a plan that envisioned a new southern nation that would expand into New

Mexico and points west, with the notion of someday incorporating San Francisco Bay and Northern Mexico's rich ore fields into their empire.[10]

Soon after the conflict began, two prominent Southern officers initiated the Confederate Army's invasion of New Mexico. After resigning from the U.S. Army in May 1861, Henry Hopkins Sibley left Taos and made his way southeast to San Antonio to confer with the Texans before traveling east to Richmond, Virginia. There, Sibley received a commission as brigadier general from Confederate President Jefferson Davis, who charged Sibley with securing New Mexico as he saw fit. While the new brigadier general was still in Richmond, Col. Earl Van Dorn, temporarily in charge of Confederate operations in Texas, ordered his troops in San Antonio to march toward present-day El Paso, the Mesilla Valley, and what would become Confederate Arizona. The man picked to lead this mission was adventurer, legislator, and Indian agent John R. Baylor. Baylor commanded six companies of the Second Texas Mounted Rifles. Upon his arrival in El Paso County, he and his men were escorted to the recently evacuated Fort Bliss, where they planted the Confederate flag. Just as Magoffin had promised, there was little opposition.[11]

In the meantime, Col. Edward R. S. Canby, in charge of Union forces in New Mexico, knew what the Texans were planning and was busy preparing for the anticipated assault. Most regular army companies had been transferred to the eastern theater or their men had left to join the Confederacy. Canby consolidated his remaining soldiers at Forts Craig, Fillmore, and Union, abandoning posts he could no longer adequately defend. In the summer of 1861, Canby, as the Department of New Mexico's commander, called up local militia and volunteer units to bolster his decimated ranks. The volunteers, mostly Hispanos, began to muster in late July and were subsequently sent to these three forts. These men—augmented by volunteers from Colorado Territory, many of whom would subsequently serve at Fort Bascom—were all that stood between the Confederacy and the conquest of New Mexico.[12]

On 21 October 1861 Brigadier General Sibley led thirty-two hundred Confederates up the Rio Grande, intent on moving quickly through New Mexico, capturing the North's main frontier supply depot at Fort Union, and then pushing into Colorado and seizing its goldfields. Sibley had convinced President Davis that this was an achievable goal, which, once accomplished, would position his army to march west and gain the Pacific Coast or to go north to Denver. Although fraught with delays and logistical issues, Sibley's army did make great gains, yet faced their greatest challenges after a hard winter descended in New Mexico.[13]

In late February 1862 Sibley's army fought Union troops to a stalemate at the Battle of Valverde. Afterward he continued north and captured the territorial capital, Santa Fe. Yet when the Confederate Army of New Mexico moved east toward Fort Union, it was repulsed in the Sangre de Cristo Mountains by regular army forces and the volunteer units from Colorado and New Mexico. These soldiers managed to fight the Confederates to a standstill at Glorieta Pass, but more important, in the process they destroyed the bulk of the Texans' supplies, which eventually forced the invaders back to Texas.[14]

The Civil War changed military dynamics within New Mexico Territory, both demographically and strategically. When the majority of regular troops were sent east, five regiments of New Mexico volunteers were enlisted to replenish the ranks. Volunteers from Colorado and California also played important roles in the defense of the territory. After the war, military dynamics continued to shift as officials transferred various companies of regulars and volunteers from post to post. The contributions from Anglo soldiers in the Civil War in the western territories and in the Indian wars have often overshadowed the actions of their Hispano brothers-in-arms. U.S. Army officers who fought with the New Mexico volunteers at the Battles of Valverde and Glorieta Pass later reported that New Mexicans did not fight well. Colonel Canby claimed that the army was better off without them. Such accounts were used by eastern newspapers—and later by public and academic historians—to craft histories that denigrated these men's role in repelling the Confederates and minimized their overall contributions to securing the Southwest. The New Mexico volunteers and their officers often disagreed with the characterizations. A thorough reading of official documents, when coupled with some contemporary accounts of the major battles, indicates that fear and panic, as well as steadfastness and bravery, were common experiences shared by all soldiers in New Mexico, regardless of ethnicity.

Debates over who fought at (and who fled from) the Battle of Valverde lingered long after General Sibley led his troops back to Texas.

When Hispano privates and their officers reenlisted after the war, negative opinions of their abilities and motives continued to haunt them. Some Eastern troopers believed locals' actions made army relations worse with Southern Plains Indians. Regular officers argued that because New Mexicans had violent histories with communities of Navajos, Utes, and Comanches, Hispano militia and volunteer units used their positions within the military to exact revenge on their longtime enemies for past grievances. Fort Bascom's first commander, West Point graduate Capt. Peter W. L. Plympton, expressed the general consensus of most regular army officers posted in New Mexico—scorn. The second commander of the post, Capt. Edward H. Bergmann, was a territorial volunteer and thus was the target of this disrespect. Originally Plympton's subordinate, Bergmann was also posted to Fort Bascom at its inception, and so his story is closely linked to that of the post.[15]

Many of the soldiers who occupied the frontier garrisons of New Mexico were veterans of the territory's bloody Civil War battles. Such was the case with Plympton and Bergmann. Both the regular army and volunteer companies brought raw memories of the conflict with them to the Canadian River post.[16]

The first two commanders of Fort Bascom were battle-tested leaders from completely different backgrounds, and they typified the differences between regular and volunteer officers. Captain Plympton was a career officer whose father had also been an army officer. Born in Missouri in 1827, Plympton graduated from West Point in 1847 and served in both the eastern and western divisions of the army prior to the war. Captain Bergmann was born in Prussia in 1832; his early life is unclear. He first appears in military records in July 1861 after joining Company C of the First New Mexico Volunteer Infantry as a first lieutenant. Plympton died on Galveston Island on 10 August 1866 of unknown causes while still in the service of his country. Bergmann retired from military service in 1867 with much of his life still in front of him. After attempting to run a ranching operation near the post, Bergmann directed the New Mexico State Penitentiary in Santa Fe and later ran a mining operation for Lucien Maxwell in Colfax County. He also operated a hotel and other businesses in Springer, New Mexico. He died in 1913 at the age of eighty-one.[17]

In 1861 Plympton just missed participating in one of the Union Army's most embarrassing episodes. In April, First Lieutenant Plympton,

Company B, Seventh Infantry, was stationed at Fort McLane, New Mexico Territory, under Maj. Isaac Lynde. After being promoted to captain of Company F, Plympton was reassigned to Fort Union on 26 May 1861. In July, Major Lynde took his six companies of Seventh Infantry to Fort Fillmore, near Mesilla. Lieutenant Colonel Baylor's Second Texas Mounted Rifles and other like-minded individuals from Arizona were already occupying the Mesilla Valley. Lynde's job was to prevent a Confederate advance up the Rio Grande. The same month that Lynde moved to Fort Fillmore, Plympton and Company F left Fort Union for Fort Craig, south of Socorro. Believing Baylor would scamper back to Fort Bliss in El Paso if confronted, Lynde moved south, but to his surprise he was repulsed by the Confederates. Stunned by this defeat, the major lost his nerve and retreated from Mesilla. After deciding (without real evidence) that he was being trailed by an overwhelming force, Lynde also abandoned Fort Fillmore. Having already lost many soldiers in the repulse, he ordered his remaining men to march toward Fort Stanton, but they never made it. In the midst of a hard country containing few streams, the exhausted Seventh Infantry was soon overtaken by the Confederates. Baylor ordered Lynde to surrender his force or face annihilation. Lynde did just that, only to find out afterwards that his troops far outnumbered Baylor's. It was a disgraceful showing by the Union Army and a great victory for Baylor. Each of the Seventh's captured companies was eventually forced to swear they would never again defend the Union in New Mexico Territory. Already reassigned to Fort Craig, Plympton and Company F escaped this humiliation.[18]

As happened elsewhere in the United States, New Mexico Territory became a chaotic place in the first months of the Civil War. As Union volunteers continued to muster in at Santa Fe and Fort Union, General Canby moved soldiers from post to post in an effort to maximize his defensive profile. While Baylor was making short work of Major Lynde's forces, units of New Mexico volunteers continued to organize and were dispersed to various forts throughout the territory. On 3 July 1861, about the same time Plympton was leaving Lynde's command for Fort Union, Bergmann was mustering into the First New Mexico Volunteer Infantry at Santa Fe. On 14 September, First Lieutenant Bergmann and his new company were also ordered to Fort Union. There Bergmann was detailed to the quartermaster department. By then Plympton had left this post with Company F and was on his way to Fort Craig. On 15 February 1862, just a few days before the Battle of Valverde, Capt. Santiago Valdez of Company H, First New Mexico Volunteer Infantry, resigned, and Bergmann was promoted to replace him. The new captain remained in charge of this company until May 1862, leading it against the Confederates in the Valverde Valley.[19]

In the lead up to this important battle, Brigadier General Sibley was unable to take advantage of Baylor's victory over Major Lynde's Seventh Infantry. Sibley had waited too long to get his so-called Army of New Mexico moving north. By February 1862 deep winter had settled on the region. When Sibley marched up the Rio Grande, both Plympton's Company F and Bergmann's Company H were within Fort Craig's walls, preparing for the Southwest's first major battle of the Civil War. On February 21 Sibley's men lingered on a mesa that overlooked this fort, daring the Union army to come out and fight. The Confederates were confident in their abilities, but low on supplies and almost desperate for the foodstuffs and other goods they knew were stocked behind Fort Craig's adobe walls. Union General Canby, protected from the elements, preferred to hold his position and force Sibley's hand. After feigning an attack, Confederate leaders realized the Union general was not going to engage, so they shifted their focus toward Santa Fe. No large Union force stood between Fort Craig and the capital. The Confederates anticipated that once they marched for Santa Fe, Canby would have no choice but to respond.[20]

Shortly after Sibley's forces started toward the capital, Canby ordered two battalions under Capt. Henry R. Selden to sally from Fort Craig and get ahead of Sibley's Army of New Mexico. Captains Plympton and Benjamin Wingate, Fifth U.S. Infantry, led these battalions toward the Valverde Valley. They were soon followed by all seven of Col. Kit Carson's volunteer companies, including Bergmann's. The battle soon commenced, with neither side gaining an advantage. When General Canby arrived on the scene about 3 P.M., he ordered Capt. Alexander McRae and his artillerymen to cross the Rio Grande and take a position on the Union left. Canby hoped that direct fire from McRae's battery would send the Confederates back to Mesilla. Plympton, commanding several regular army units, also crossed the stream. Shortly thereafter, Carson's troops followed. These volunteers were placed in the center

of the Union line that formed on the east side of the Rio Grande.
The Confederates, spotting the batteries, launched a fierce charge in
their direction. The New Mexicans released withering fire into this
first charge, forcing the Texans back. Union artillery began to blast
large holes in the Army of New Mexico's center. Suddenly Confederate
Col. Tom Green's regiment appeared from behind a series of large
sand hills and came crashing down on the Union left flank. A wild
melee ensued, with both sides battling for control of the big guns.
During fierce hand-to-hand combat, McRae was killed and the howitzers
were taken. This precipitated a ferocious Union counterattack. While
some federal troops still on the west side of the river moved toward the
fighting, others, volunteers and regulars alike, ran in the opposite direction. Efforts to regain the guns were unsuccessful. The captured howitzers were trained on the Union counterattack, forcing the remaining
volunteers and regulars to retreat. A hail of bullets followed them
across the river, resulting in additional casualties. Canby found his
position untenable and ordered his men back to Fort Craig.
Although Sibley had not destroyed the Union army, his force would
not be challenged again on their march to Santa Fe.[21]

In his report to headquarters, Plympton wrote that when Colonel
Green attacked, the New Mexico volunteers ran. He contended that
if they had stood their ground, McCrae would still be alive and the
Union would have prevailed, stopping Sibley's advance. Union commander Canby's report echoed Plympton's. These documents noted
that soldiers from the Seventh Infantry also fled during the engagement, yet both excused the regulars by explaining that when the volunteers broke for the rear, they started a general stampede. Contrary to
the claims in these reports, Colonel Carson's New Mexico volunteers,
including Company H under Captain Bergmann's command, had destroyed the first Confederate charge, yet neither Plympton nor Canby
noted their actions. Despite these reports, Bergmann later received
a promotion, in part because of his leadership during this battle.
Still, Canby had almost nothing good to say to his superiors concerning
the New Mexico volunteers. In fact he complained to Washington
that they were worthless; like Plympton, he blamed the Hispano soldiers
for his defeat. Certainly this damning criticism derived, at least in part,
from the disgrace and anger officers were grappling with just a couple

of days after the battle. Prejudice toward the Hispanic population, as well as a desire to protect their own careers, also played a role in how they crafted these reports.[22]

Regardless of their true motivations, the regular army would not soon forget the Battle of Valverde. Three federal outposts were named for commissioned officers who were killed in this engagement. When Green attacked McRae's battery, Captain Wingate, Fifth Infantry, led his men across the river to join the counterattack. During the attempt, he was hit in the leg by a Minié ball. Wingate's thighbone was shattered, and the captain soon died of his wound. (Fort Wingate was established on 22 October 1862.) As earlier noted, after the Texans surprised his battery, McRae was killed defending his guns. Fort McRae opened on 3 April 1863.[23]

Long before he was killed in this engagement, Capt. George Nicholas Bascom had distinguished himself militarily in the Southwest. In October 1860, while a second lieutenant in the Seventh U.S. Infantry stationed at Fort Buchanan, New Mexico Territory, Bascom was ordered to search for a boy, Felix Ward, believed to have been stolen by a band of Chiricahua Apaches led by Cochise. The hunt quickly degenerated into violence. As a result, some of Cochise's relatives were hanged, sparking a series of Chiricahuan raids and reprisals across the Southwest. Bascom led a contingent of the Seventh Infantry in several battles with the Apaches. During one battle, Bascom and his men became trapped by the Chiricahuas at Apache Pass in present-day Arizona. Army Surgeon Bernard J. D. Irwin led a group of volunteers to these soldiers' rescue, which resulted in Irwin receiving the Medal of Honor, in the earliest action to achieve this honor. That Bascom died fighting for his country at the Battle of Valverde would have come as no surprise to his peers. In his report, Plympton emphasized that along with various companies of the Seventh Infantry, Captain Bascom, commanding Company C of the Seventh, remained on the field when Green's men smashed into the Union left flank. At Valverde, Bascom was leading a company from his old regiment after having just been promoted to a captaincy in the Sixteenth U.S. Infantry. Plympton recalled that Bascom and his men continued to fight until the Union's own guns were turned on them. Captain Bascom was shot during the general retreat, Plympton recounted, as he waded back across the Rio

Figure 1. Lt. George Nicholas Bascom. In 1860, while serving as a second lieutenant in the Seventh U.S. Infantry, Bascom came into conflict with Cochise and the Chiricahua Apaches in an incident that later became known as the "Bascom Affair." As a result, these Apaches and the U.S. Army would remain at war for the next twenty years, long after Bascom's death. Shortly after being promoted to captain, he was transferred to the Sixteenth Infantry, where the twenty-five-year-old officer found himself in command of a company of his old regiment, the Seventh, at the Battle of Valverde. He was killed in this battle on 21 February 1862. *Courtesy of the Arizona Historical Society, photo no. 28642.*

Grande. So it was that on 15 August 1863 Captain Plympton of Company F raised the first U.S. flag over Fort Bascom, named for a fellow regular in the Seventh Infantry who fell in battle.[24]

A few weeks after the Battle of Valverde, the Confederate invasion was repulsed just east of Santa Fe at Glorieta Pass. In the middle of April, under Canby's command as a part of the Union army that harried Sibley's men back down the Rio Grande, Bergmann's Company H did scout duty in the Magdalena Mountains and harassed the enemy as they retreated south. They also participated in the Battle of Peralta, a minor engagement that ensured the Texans did not linger on the edges of the territory. By mid-April 1862 Bergmann's men were bereft of food or proper uniforms. He purchased both from local contractors, using his own funds. The following month, he was transferred to Company I, First New Mexico Volunteer Cavalry, where he also served as a commissary officer at the Las Lunas base camp. A year later, in 1863, Colonel Carson made a specific request for Bergmann to rejoin his command. Not long after, Bergmann was stationed at Fort Union, where he was soon leading scouts across the Canadian River Valley. During this period the new commander of the Department of New Mexico, Brig. Gen. James H. Carleton, ordered Bergmann to find the best location along this river for a new federal outpost.[25] Captain Plympton was Fort Bascom's first commander, but he did not remain there long. While serving together at the post, Plympton and Bergmann oversaw its construction and led scouts throughout the Eroded Plains. In December 1863 Plympton was reassigned to Santa Fe on a recruiting detail. Although Capt. Charles Rawn was put in charge of Company F, Seventh Infantry, it was the volunteer, Bergmann, who became the post commander. Company F remained on regular duty at Fort Bascom until May 1864. Plympton never returned. Bergmann led this post for the next two and a half years, only turning over command during scouts, major expeditions, and, during one odd case, for a few months after being promoted to major. No post commander spent more time at Fort Bascom than Bergmann.[26] In preparation for Company F's May 1864 departure, Company M of the First New Mexico Cavalry arrived in late April. Thus by 1 May 1864 only New Mexico volunteers were stationed at the post. This was not unusual. After the Confederate defeat, a number of the regular army units were ordered to the eastern theater. When the New Mexico volunteer infantry was mustered out, many of its soldiers were reconfigured into new volunteer cavalry companies and assembled as the First Battalion under Colonel Carson. Captain Bergmann was brevetted to lieutenant colonel. Along with the California Column, New Mexico's volunteers formed the main fighting force left to defend the territory against a possible second Confederate invasion and Indian incursions during the war.[27]

Despite driving the Confederates back to Texas, Union officers and territorial officials continued to believe another attack was imminent. The Canadian River began to appear in reports as a possible route for an invasion. Territorial delegate John Watts had often argued the strategic necessity of protecting this river from the Confederates. As Sibley's army approached Santa Fe, Watts wrote to Union Maj. Gen. Henry W. Halleck, commander of the Department of the Missouri, stating that if he would only "look at the map," he would see that after the Confederates sacked the capital, they would have a clear path to Missouri by following the Canadian River east. Although such a possibility was extinguished at Glorieta Pass, control of this river remained an object of military concern.[28]

Not long after the combined New Mexican–Coloradoan volunteer forces turned the Confederates back at Glorieta Pass, Brigadier General Carleton replaced Edward Canby as commander of the Department of New Mexico. Carleton had recently arrived after marching twenty companies of California volunteers to the territory. The new, forty-eight-year-old commander of the department was a twenty-year army veteran and had spent five years stationed in New Mexico prior to the war. The California Column remained in New Mexico for the duration of the war, and its men, like some of the Colorado volunteer companies, served at several frontier posts, including Fort Bascom. As Canby took his leave, he informed Carleton that if the Confederates invaded New Mexico a second time, he doubted it would be up the Rio Grande: "If our troops in the Southwest should meet with any serious reverses it may be by the Canadian." Thus, from Carleton's first days as department commander, he was warned of the possibility that the Canadian River might become the next Confederate entry point.[29]

Over the next few months Carleton dispatched to his field officers a series of orders and warnings that illustrated his concern. He ordered his acting inspector general, Maj. Henry Wallen Davies, to investigate all possible invasion routes and report his findings. While Davies believed it likely that any second attempt would also come up the Rio Grande, he could not completely rule out an advance up the Pecos or Canadian Rivers. Thus he recommended to Carleton that he place some "well mounted and rationed mountain men" somewhere close to the Llano Estacado.[30]

On 26 October 1862, Carleton directed Capt. William H. Backus and Company C of the Second Colorado Volunteer Infantry to move from Anton Chico, on the Pecos River, to a location near "the confluence of Utah Creek and the Canadian River northeast of Tucumcari Peak." This forward camp would act as an advance picket against a possible Confederate invasion from the Texas Panhandle. It was called Camp Easton. Soldiers dug cavities into the hillsides and used available logs, rocks, and branches to create living quarters that would serve them for the next several months. Besides watching for Confederates, Backus's troops would also escort the mail and military supply trains. General Carleton encouraged Backus to befriend the region's Comanches and employ them, if possible, as scouts. Yet it was Company C, not the Comanches, upon whom the department commander depended for critical information. Carleton ordered Backus and his men to "watch the road and the country toward Fort Smith and toward Texas, [and] to give *timely* notice of the advance of any force of rebels. . . . For this purpose you will keep scouts well down upon the Fort Smith road, and over toward the Llano Estacado." Carleton was specific in his instructions. He ordered Backus to shoot any rebel scouts his men spotted. He also instructed them to stampede the enemy's livestock and burn the prairie grass in front of any approaching force. He further ordered Backus's troops to shoot any male Mescalero Apaches or Navajos they encountered and to arrest any Anglos or Mexicans not carrying proper passes.[31]

A month later, in November 1862, Carleton informed Captain Plympton, then post commander of Fort Union, that he had ordered the Colorado volunteers (including Backus's Company C) to remain in New Mexico specifically because he was anticipating a second invasion. Carleton explained to Plympton that Col. Joseph R. West, commander of the Department of Arizona, had relayed information to him concerning rumors of the recently deposed Confederate governor of Arizona, John R. Baylor. Apparently Baylor was in Texas, just back from Virginia with orders to launch another attack into the territory.

According to Colonel West, Baylor was in San Antonio readying six thousand Texans for a second invasion. Carleton explained to Plympton that he believed the Texans would travel across the Texas Panhandle, follow the Canadian River west, turn north when the stream neared Tucumcari Peak, then move on to their intended target: Sibley's original goal, Fort Union. The general warned Plympton to prepare for such a circumstance by having the "artillery drill twice a day," continuing work on a new abattis, and ensuring that all soldiers carry out target practice three times a day.[32]

Camp Easton soon proved its value. On 1 November 1862, only six days after the camp was established, a group of Comanches approached a patrol led by Lt. George L. Shoup of Backus's Company C with information about a large wagon train traveling on the Fort Smith road toward Texas. The next day, assisted by the Comanches, Backus and his troops sought out and apprehended eighteen Confederate sympathizers and their families not far from Camp Easton. Green Russell, one of the prospectors who first found gold at Cherry Creek, in present-day Colorado, was the caravan's leader. Their last stop had been Las Vegas, New Mexico, where they had resupplied and prepared for the journey across the Texas Panhandle. Once Company C stopped the caravan, the Comanches demanded at least one of the travelers and half the party's possessions as reward for their assistance. Backus explained to the agitated Indians, including a "Chief Mowa" [Mowway], that he was willing to pay them for their services, but the prisoners would remain under his protection. Company C escorted the entire party to Fort Union. Twenty-eight thousand dollars was confiscated from the Confederate sympathizers, as well as several bags of gold dust. Released a few months later, Russell eventually showed up in Georgia, where he joined the Confederate Army and assembled a company to do battle.[33]

Over the winter and spring of 1862–63, similar patrols set out from Camp Easton, mainly in search of rebel invaders. Soldiers' reports were peppered with incidents of coming upon "mexicans" making their way onto the Llano Estacado with carts and wagons loaded with goods, prepared to trade with the Comanches. Sorting out who these traders were and what to do about them took up much of the army's time after the war ended. As the U.S. cavalry would soon learn, such travelers and traders knew the area much better than they did.[34]

By the summer of 1863, plans were being enacted for a more permanent Canadian River outpost. By then, Captain Bergmann, First New
Mexico Volunteer Cavalry, Company I, stationed at Fort Union, was
operating out of Camp Easton. In response to a request from Bergmann for some large trowels with which to fashion adobe bricks,
Carleton responded favorably, but he did not stop there: "Make a
plan for a compact (not too compact) post for two companies—with
stables, corrals, hospital, guard house, carpenter shop, saddle shop,
blacksmith shop, coal room, corral detached for hay, etc. The work
should be built on a square, face in. Have walls connect—logs holed—
and enfiladed by some sort of block house and diagonal corners.
Can you make the cavalry part?"[35]

Carleton was not the first officer determined to build a post closer
to the Llano Estacado. By the late 1850s, mounted patrols based out
of Fort Union (where Carleton was stationed at the time) had reduced
Indian incursions along the Santa Fe Trail and created widespread
confidence among merchants and pioneers moving west. The situation was different along the Fort Smith road, where Southern Plains
Indians still controlled much of the region. At the time, many officers lobbied for a new supply and command post farther south and
east from Fort Union, along either the Pecos or Canadian Rivers. Fort
Butler was approved on 12 March 1860 but was never built. Logistics,
costs, and the looming conflict in the east shelved plans for this garrison, which was to have been positioned along the Gallinas River at
the crossing of the Fort Smith road. That such plans were approved
indicates just how serious officials were about shifting their resources
closer to Texas. In the late 1850s, before the Confederacy was a cer-
tainty, the army's greatest regional concern was the Comanches and
Kiowas who controlled much of eastern New Mexico and northwest
Texas. Fort Butler's location would have addressed that concern by
creating a new supply post and operational base on the doorstep of
Comanchería. Yet it was not built.[36]

While Captain Backus and Company C of the Colorado Volunteers
were still building their makeshift shelters at Camp Easton, farther
south construction on another federal outpost began. Fort Sumner
was constructed along the Pecos River in November 1862, but unlike
Fort Butler it was never intended to supplant Fort Union. After the
Civil War began, thoughts of abandoning Fort Union or reducing its

workload evaporated, and it once again became one of the United States' most important western posts. It would remain so for decades to come. As for Fort Sumner, situated along another significant Comanchero trade route, it was soon charged with overseeing and controlling the American Indians who were confined to the new Bosque Redondo Indian Reservation. The same month construction began on Fort Sumner, General Carleton ordered Colonel Carson to capture the Mescalero Apaches who were harrying southern New Mexico. Carson and his First New Mexico Volunteer Cavalry accomplished this task, and then, on Carleton's orders, interred the Mescaleros at Bosque Redondo. Carleton envisioned an agricultural oasis emerging on this reservation. He believed Southern Plains Indians who were interred along the Pecos River would quickly learn Euro-American farming techniques perfected in Arkansas, Illinois, and Kentucky, resulting in abundant rows of corn and vegetables. The Department of New Mexico's commander was ignorant of the arid topsoils of the Pecos and Canadian River Valleys, which held little of the organic material needed to sustain crops.[37]

In 1864, not long after Colonel Carson and his New Mexico volunteers' mission against the Mescaleros, they received a similar, if much larger and more difficult task. That year Carleton ordered the former mountain man and his soldiers to remove the Navajos from their Canyon de Chelly homeland in what is now northeastern Arizona and relocate them to Bosque Redondo. Using scorch-and-burn tactics in the middle of winter, Carson and his men were successful. Soon, thousands of Navajos were being force-marched across New Mexico to Bosque Redondo. Once the Mescaleros realized the Navajos, their sworn enemies, were not only going to be their new neighbors, but also would outnumber them ten to one, they simply disappeared one night, never to return. The Navajos remained on the reservation for years. Over the next several months, thousands of Navajos who had heard of Carson's severe tactics in Canyon de Chelly began to assemble at Forts Canby and Wingate. From these posts, the military marched them to Fort Sumner and the reservation. The forced migration of these Indians created many problems for the soldiers stationed at Fort Bascom. By 1868 over eight thousand Navajos lived at the Bosque Redondo Indian Reservation. Starvation and disease, precipitated by crop failure, poor planning, and corrupt business practices, would eventually force the government to allow them to return to a portion of their homeland. Long before that happened, however, the Navajos of Bosque Redondo began to stream north through the Pecos and Canadian River Valleys, causing trouble for Fort Bascom's soldiers and its operations.[38]

Yet in the summer of 1863, before seeking the Navajos' internment, General Carleton had more pressing issues on his mind: the location of Colonel Baylor and the Confederate force he was rumored to be collecting around San Antonio. This apprehension explained his instructions to Captain Bergmann concerning the creation of another large-scale federal outpost. If Carleton's order to make a plan for a "compact (not too compact) post" appears ad hoc, that was simply how many frontier posts came to be in the nineteenth century. Much latitude was allowed each department's commanding officer regarding the specific location and design of such posts. Regulations regarding living quarters had to be followed, which included maintaining a certain number of square feet per soldier, but other specifications were either lacking or ignored. Aside from stipulations regarding living space, commanders retained much discretion regarding the construction of frontier facilities, and they were able to adapt their methods to fit the surrounding environment.[39]

The men who traveled to and from and inhabited such posts had concerns regarding their safety, regardless of whether a Texan or a Confederate ever set foot in New Mexico again. By 1863, the Canadian River Valley was being used quite heavily by soldiers traveling between Fort Union, Fort Sumner, and the various temporary base camps that were established in the Eroded Plains. In their travels and during patrols, the troopers understood that despite the emptiness that seemed to permeate the Canadian River Valley, it was a very dangerous place. On 22 July 1863, while headquarters was discussing plans to expand operations from a base camp to a full-fledged military outpost, the valley's "sublimity" turned into chaos. While herding cattle for the nearby troops, Sgt. José Lucero and Privates Juan F. Ortiz and José Banneras of Company I, First New Mexico Volunteer Cavalry, were attacked by a group of Navajo raiders at the junction of the Conchas and Canadian Rivers, at an old Comanchero rendezvous site, Conchas Springs. The Navajo wanted the cattle. Lucero, Ortiz, and Banneras became trapped near the springs, and a gun battle ensued that lasted until sundown. Eventually the soldiers were overwhelmed, and the raiders left the area with all the livestock. The three New Mexico troopers lay on the ground, riddled with arrows. One attacker, meaning to ensure his enemies were dead, used a rock to bash each Hispano over the head. Somehow, Private Banneras managed to survive this final assault. After the Navajos rode away, Banneras dumped his deceased compatriots' guns in Conchas Creek and walked back to camp with eight arrows protruding from his body. Captain Bergmann led several troopers from Company I in pursuit of these raiders. They eventually overtook the raiders, killing two and wounding several. Most of the cattle were lost. The volunteers returned to Camp Easton with three head.[40]

On 15 August 1863, three weeks after the attack on Lucero, Ortiz, and Banneras, Captain Plympton led Company F of the Seventh Infantry out of Fort Union to replace Camp Easton with a permanent outpost. Captain Bergmann's company of New Mexico volunteers was also placed under Captain Plympton's command, and together these two units, one regular army and one volunteer, became the first soldiers to occupy the new post. The recent attack was still a bitter memory to Company I as the men established themselves at the new location. It was Bergmann whom Carleton had originally called upon to develop a plan for the fort, and it was Bergmann who selected the site. He located it about fifteen miles farther west than Camp Easton, on the south side of the Canadian River where the river bent toward Texas. It stood about sixty miles west of the Texas border and eleven miles north of Tucumcari Peak, where the Fort Smith road passed. It is interesting to note that despite Carleton's obvious confidence in Bergmann, the post's first commander was a veteran of the regular army, Captain Plympton. As I note in this chapter and will explore in later chapters, both captains and companies had served at the Battle of Valverde.[41]

The fort was established in the middle of territorial delegate John Watts's land. A year earlier Watts had urged General Halleck to remember the strategic importance of the region. On 4 May 1865 Watts worked out a twenty-year lease agreement with the army for a two-square-mile reservation, which consisted of 2,360 acres. Watts, a lawyer by trade, inserted a stipulation in the lease that specified if the post was abandoned before the lease expired, all property, including buildings, reverted back to the owner.[42]

While headquarters had urged Captain Backus of the Colorado volunteers at Camp Easton to use the Comanches as lookouts against

Figure 2. Sketch of Fort Bascom, ca. 1865. The small letter designations on or above the buildings correlate with the 1865 ground plan shown in figure 7. In handwriting that is probably Capt. Edward H. Bergmann's, the following is noted on the back of this drawing: "Company for 400 men, stable for 100 horses, material of adobe and logs. Built May 10, 1864. About 130 miles from Santa Fe. Condition = very good." *Reservation File, Records of the Office of the Chief of Engineers, RG 77, DNM, entry 464, box 8, folder 38, NA, College Park, Md.*

a second Confederate invasion, the Army seldom trusted them. In General Orders No. 20, Acting Asst. Adj. Gen. Ben C. Cutler noted that Fort Bascom would be "an outpost to New Mexico during the present rebellion, its advanced pickets watching the roads from Arkansas and Texas." He added that it would be "of great importance in preventing the predatory incursion of the Comanche and Kiowa Indians." Thus while Carleton's concern regarding a second Confederate invasion prompted him to position soldiers along the Canadian on a full-time basis, their long-term service there was predicated on protecting New Mexicans from Indians.[43]

On paper, the creation of this post appears matter-of-fact and clearly representative of the origins of frontier posts throughout the West. Yet official descriptions of army posts seldom capture the reality imposed upon the men who served there. The open-ended attitude that most department commanders had to take regarding construction of such posts often led to less than optimum results. In the midst of a war, Carleton, like Canby before him, was forced to improvise and make choices he possibly could have avoided during peacetime. Throughout the war, the federal government devoted most of its resources to the east. This was especially true in the early years of the conflict. Secretary of War Edwin M. Stanton had more important responsibilities than determining how best to keep the Texans out of New Mexico or to protect the Santa Fe freighters. Gen. Robert E. Lee and the Army of Northern Virginia ensured that Carleton and his men were left to their own devices. This meant utilizing a creative construction process that involved numerous local civilians and army privates doing most of the work under the supervision of men trained in military tactics, not proper construction methods. While Captain Backus's Colorado volunteers had to cobble together Camp Easton on their own, the department's quartermaster did hire twenty civilians to help construct Fort Bascom, but much of the work was done by soldiers. The lack of timber, other than the cottonwoods that grew along the river, meant most of Fort Bascom's structures were made of adobe. All of the work was supervised by officers with no experience in construction matters. Lack of such knowledge complicated their ability to gain control of the frontier. Many of the problems regarding faulty construction were not unique to Fort Bascom, nor were they surprising. After the war,

Fort Sumner was authorized to hire ninety-nine civilians to continue work on that post.[44]

Captain Bergmann located Fort Bascom "on a plateau about 20 feet above the river bottom, and 500 yards from the bed of the river, which, [at that time was] . . . about 25 feet wide and 2 or 3 feet in depth. . . . On the opposite side of the stream [was] a bluff from 50 to 60 feet in height, beyond which the country is rolling and broken." The water was noted to be best from November to March, before the spring snowmelt. As water levels rose, the river became "muddy and loaded with organic matter." Bascom's position made it the easternmost garrison facing both Confederate Texas and the homeland of numerous bands of Comanche and Kiowa Indians. Fort Union, about 140 miles to the northwest, was a three-day ride. Fort Sumner was a day closer, about 90 miles to the south.[45]

Decisions regarding the construction of Fort Bascom involved more people than Captain Bergmann. In October, after Captain Plympton had taken command of the new site, he suggested to Carleton that the post be built of logs, not adobe. The department commander approved Plympton's change, yet for the most part, the post was still built with adobe bricks. Two exceptions were one wing of the hospital, which was built of cottonwood logs, and the officers' quarters, which were built with sandstone bricks. While the documents do not explain this divergence from Carleton's approved alterations, it is likely that Bergmann's original plan was the most plausible, if not the most desirable.[46]

Fort Bascom was built in a rectangle and centered on a plaza, or parade ground. To the east of the plaza stood the barracks. West of the plaza were the officers' quarters. To the north were the commissary and the hospital. Fort Bascom's original design included five buildings for officers' quarters, but only one was ever satisfactorily completed to serve that purpose. Additional buildings included a mess hall, storehouses, a guardhouse, a hospital, four barracks buildings large enough to house two full companies, quarters for laundresses that were situated west of the barracks, a kitchen, blacksmith and carpenter shops, and stables for the cavalry's horses. An adobe perimeter wall ran one thousand feet north to south and five hundred feet east to west around the garrison. Bastions were incorporated into the northeast and southwest

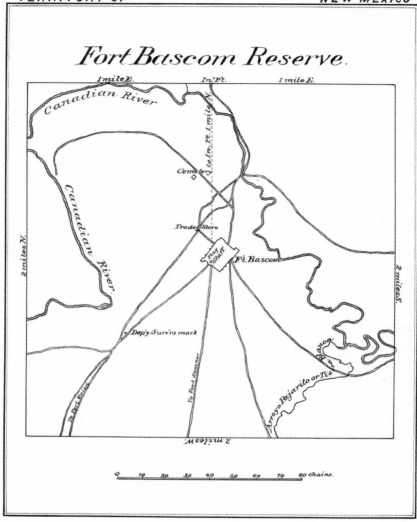

Figure 3. Survey of Fort Bascom military reservation. In 1868 deputy surveyor for New Mexico Territory John Lambert marked off and detailed the 2,360 acres that made up the two-square-mile reservation. *Reservation File, Records of the Office of the Chief of Engineers, RG 77, DNM, entry 464, box 8, folder 38, NA, College Park, Md.*

corners of these walls. A ten-foot-wide trench that encircled the post was dug beyond the perimeter wall. While deteriorating adobes caused problems from the beginning, Plympton's desire for a fort built solely of logs would have presented other issues. By 1870 the only building constructed completely of cottonwood logs, a hospital wing, had severe rotting problems.[47]

Officers stationed at Bascom to apprehend rebellious Indians and Comancheros were often occupied with contractors and construction issues. Rows of cottonwood logs, split and peeled, were also used to support the roofs, which were covered with planking and a final layer of sod. Because of water intrusion and rotting, some of these supports were eventually replaced with pine vigas. Regardless of which supports were used, the roofs still leaked. Water also penetrated the adobe walls. At Fort Sumner, the lack of organic matter in the soil was the most critical component of crop failure. At Bascom, this same soil caused the adobes to dissolve during prolonged weather events. Josiah Gregg had been right when he observed that the soils around the Canadian seemed to "melt" when touched by water. For the duration of its existence, the fort was plagued with roof leaks and water intrusions.[48]

Like most frontier garrisons, soldiers found little to like about Fort Bascom. The original design was meant to provide for four companies, but it never adequately housed more than two. The barracks were one hundred feet long and twenty feet wide. Each of the four barracks, built to withstand the valley's harsh winters, had hard-packed dirt floors and three fireplaces. With the fireplaces, thirteen-foot ceilings, and six windows per building, the enlisted men's quarters met the government's minimum standards regarding air flow and air return for each room. The partially completed officers' quarters stood across the parade ground, directly opposite the enlisted men's barracks. With the exception of the captain's quarters, the officers' quarters were very small— only fifteen by nine feet. Like most post buildings, their roofs leaked. Only a few years after the fort was built, post commander Maj. Andrew J. Alexander reported that water intrusion was ruining the officers' quarters, declaring that only two units were habitable. Yet despite what her husband wrote to headquarters, Eveline Alexander described Fort Bascom as "a neat little post . . . of some importance" with officers quarters that, although small, were quite comfortable.[49]

Building issues were not the only challenges that soldiers faced. Another problem concerned access to water. The fort's ground level stood twenty feet higher than the Canadian River, which prevented the soldiers from being able to dig an acequia; they could not easily access water for their gardens. The topography and the five-hundred-yard distance to the river led the soldiers to dig a well. This project failed. As a result, gardens had to be watered out of wooden casks hauled from the river. Capt. John Dubois of the Third Cavalry found he had not appreciated his previous posting at Fort Sumner as much as he should have. In a letter to his mother, he fondly recalled that Fort Sumner diverted enough water out of the Pecos River each year to fill its icehouse, a much more difficult task at Bascom, where the river was twenty feet below the fort's ground level. Thus Dubois longed for Fort Sumner's ice. Despite such inconveniences, most army personnel tried to make allowances. Perhaps Eveline Alexander found few negatives to write about the post because of officers like Captain Dubois, who tried to make the best of a bad situation. In a letter to his mother, he explained how he was able to make a "great show" of his military home while stationed at Fort Bascom with just a few books, pictures, and "scant" furniture.[50]

In those first winter months of 1863 and 1864, Captains Plympton of the Seventh Infantry and Bergmann of the First New Mexico Volunteer Cavalry were charged with dual missions: building the post and watching for both Confederate invaders and Southern Plains Indians. If the Confederates, mainly Texans, arrived from the east, they would probably follow the Canadian River west out of the Llano Estacado down the Fort Smith road. Comanches also roamed this valley, but Union forces were also concerned with various bands of Apaches and Navajos who remained threats to local villages, raiding along the river all the way north to Raton Pass. From the beginning, Fort Bascom was constantly sending out patrols in all directions, some missions lasting several weeks.

As would be the case for the next several years, it was the First New Mexico Volunteer Cavalry who performed most of these early scouts. On 29 August 1863 Captain Bergmann led Company I up the Canadian through the Narrows, a steep-walled canyon where red volcanic boulders seemed to be frozen in time as they spilled over its edges.

They moved past Conchas Springs, where two of their compatriots had been killed in the Navajo ambush just a few months earlier, and did not turn around until they reached the rim of Cañón Largo (near present-day Sabinoso, where the Canadian and Mora Rivers meet), sixty miles from the post. Cañón Largo, like Palo Duro Canyon, was known to harbor Indians who refused to submit to the federal government's plans to funnel them onto specific lands not of their choosing. Navajos fleeing Bosque Redondo, as well as Kiowas and Comanches, used this location to hide or position themselves for raids against local villages or isolated travelers. On 16 November 1863 Bergmann again patrolled north between Bascom and Fort Union, looking for raiders. As he scouted, remaining forces continued to work on post construction or to do duty as pickets along the Fort Smith road. About ten days after Bergmann's November scout, Lt. Juan Marqués led another mission, with fifteen days' rations, in search of "a party of Indians" who had rustled the fort's livestock. In January 1864 Captain Bergmann once again commanded Company I on a scout that took them to "Mesa Rica, Cañón Largo, and Corazon Mountain." Cerro de Corazón, part of the Canadian Escarpment, overlooks the Canadian River Valley, rising two thousand feet above the river. It is topped by the Las Vegas Plateau. This route leads to the town of Las Vegas, and beyond that, Fort Union. Over the next several years, the soldiers of Fort Bascom would become very familiar with the gutted topography of the Eroded Plains. Companies of volunteers and regulars followed Comanchero trails that led north, up the side of Corazon Mountain and across grassland prairies in search of escaping Navajo and Cheyenne raiders. To the east they scaled the Caprock and crisscrossed the Llano Estacado seeking out the Comanches and trying to disrupt the Comanchero trade. Small numbers of men from this post were scattered over large expanses of some of the harshest environments on the North America continent in search of people who did not want to be found. Fort Bascom troopers were charged first with alerting headquarters of an approaching invasion and second with placing themselves in the path of the invading army. Later, its soldiers engaged in the process of subduing the Southern Plains Indians and dismantling an economic culture that seemed as embedded in the Canadian River Valley as the "red bed" walls of the mesas that loomed over the garrison. Like most military missions in occupied territory, this duty was neither easy nor glorious and would take much longer than government officials believed necessary. When Captain Bergmann picked out the spot to the lay the foundation for this new post, he initiated a new chapter in the United States' conquest of the southern plains.[51]

CHAPTER 4

This Bean-Bellied Army

In pursuing their mission to gain control of the southern plains, Fort Bascom soldiers endured many challenges that had nothing to do with Comanches or Comancheros. A broad investigation into life at this post illuminates the difficulties experienced by many of the men and women who passed through the Canadian River Valley in the 1860s and early 1870s. Such a study includes looking at post life from a variety of angles. Construction problems, the search for supplies, social issues and demographics, how these troopers entertained themselves, health concerns, racism, and desertion rates all impacted the mission to subdue the Comanches and stop the Comancheros. Lack of fresh produce and beef, water concerns, and acquiring proper forage for horses and mules were challenges that constantly had to be addressed. Illuminating these challenges places Fort Bascom soldiers' ultimate mission within its proper context. Understanding their daily lives provides a basis from which to assess the patrols, scouts, and expeditions that originated from this post, and it also offers a compelling perspective on the challenges of the Canadian River Valley environment.

When Maj. Andrew Alexander arrived at Fort Bascom in December 1866, he and his wife were favorably impressed, yet within a month the new post commander had changed his mind. In both January and February 1867, he reported on the poor condition of the fort's buildings. Thus, a study of post life should begin with a look at Bascom's ongoing maintenance issues. Bad weather and poor accommodations bedeviled soldiers stationed in the Eroded Plains of New Mexico.[1]

Figure 4. Capt. Edward
Henry Bergmann. Brig. Gen.
James H. Carleton allowed
one of his most trusted officers
to choose where to build Fort
Bascom. Bergmann was also
instrumental in the post's
design and oversaw its early
construction. He was promoted
to major while serving as Fort
Bascom's post commander, a
position he held longer than
any other officer. *Title: Colonel
Edward H. Bergmann (1832–
1913). Courtesy Palace of the
Governors Photo Archives
(NMHM/DCA), no. 050350.*

Construction began in the fall of 1863 but was halted in January
1864 after Capt. William Shoemaker complained to General Carleton
about the fort's location. Shoemaker, the ordnance officer at Fort Union,
argued that Bascom should be located farther north, at Conchas Springs,
the confluence of the Conchas and Canadian Rivers. This ancient
crossing and campground had hosted Navajos, Kiowas, Comanches,
and Comancheros for generations. After receiving recommendation
from Shoemaker, Carleton apprised Captain Bergmann of its content.
By then Captain Plympton, the original post commander, had been
transferred to Santa Fe. It was Bergmann whom Carleton had relied
upon to determine where to build the post. Whatever concerns Carleton might have had regarding Shoemaker's recommendations, on
28 February he gave Bergmann permission to proceed with construction at the original location, closer to the Llano Estacado. In the same
letter, Carleton noted that he would visit Fort Bascom in March.[2]

Construction continued for the rest of 1864. The army contracted
one carpenter, eleven general laborers, and thirteen teamsters to help
build the post. Additionally, some of the 109 New Mexico volunteers
stationed at Bascom were ordered to help. When Col. Oscar M. Brown
took command in August 1865, construction was still not complete.
Apparently, soldiers were not the best construction workers. By then,

the carpenter Bergmann had hired was gone, as were the contract laborers. Brown pleaded with headquarters to send him at least one more carpenter and two masons so the officers' quarters and the hospital could be finished before the end of the year.[3]

Any discussion regarding everyday activities at Fort Bascom must consider these ongoing building projects. Construction issues affected the quality of life at the post. Heavy rains in the spring and summer of both 1864 and 1865 hampered construction. Sections of new walls and sod-covered roofs sprang leaks. Despite such problems, by August 1865, Bergmann reported that barracks for three companies were complete. He also wrote that there were plenty of storage facilities and made a point of noting that none of the rooms were leaking. Yet maintenance issues would not disappear.[4]

Just as challenging as leaks and other construction issues was the lack of good drinking water. Acquiring it involved soldiers riding down to the river in wagons where they filled large wooden casks. That water was often saturated with organic material or simply tasted bad due to its alkalinity. In 1867 post commander Capt. John Dubois sought suggestions from headquarters on how to purify it. Acting Asst. Adj. Gen. Cyrus H. De Forrest recommended he put charcoal in the bottom of the barrels to act as a filtering system. Such problems created both psychological and physical issues with the soldiers who lived on the post, for water extraction was dangerous and labor intensive, and at certain times of the year the river water was unhealthy to drink. Daily trips in water wagons exposed soldiers to the elements and to possible surprise attacks. A lack of water at certain times of the year also prevented laborers from making adobe bricks, which delayed construction. Oddly enough, when much-needed rain did appear, it brought with it another set of challenges. During the monsoons of July and August, when it stormed at noon every day for several weeks in a row, stacks of adobes remained exposed on unfinished walls, allowing water to intrude into half-finished buildings.[5]

Despite these water issues, Fort Bascom remained the center of operations for company after company of volunteers and army regulars from the mid-1860s to the mid-1870s. Each Sunday morning at seven A.M. troopers stood at dress parade on the plaza for battle inspections. During the week, life within this post was a regimented affair, with the trumpeter sounding reveille at five A.M. Fifteen minutes later, the soldiers stood at attention on the plaza awaiting roll call. If not posted to picket details or out on patrols, they were assigned "fatigue" duty. This included cleaning out the stables, making adobes, hauling wood and water, and peeling potatoes.[6]

Despite construction issues, the barracks were built to withstand New Mexico's extreme winters. Although no documents specifically describe the enlistees' bunking arrangements, it is reasonable to assume that they would resemble those found in nearby forts of the period. At Fort Craig, the barracks had single bedsteads. The men at Fort Stanton slept in single tiers of double beds. All of these beds consisted of a few simple pieces of iron framing that easily could be broken down and reassembled. Bed sacks stuffed with straw served as mattresses. Each soldier kept warm with a government-issued wool blanket that measured seven by five-and-a-half feet and weighed five pounds. These blankets were also carried on picket patrols and scouts. Some type of shelf usually ran along a wall of each barrack for the soldiers' personal items, but rifles were kept together in a rack in the middle of the room.[7]

Soldiers posted to New Mexico Territory stayed busy with a never-ending series of fatigue details and patrols, so they cherished the few hours they had at the end of each day to relax. Many made the most of these short respites by using their fireplaces and candles to light their surroundings. Candles were also taken on patrols. After a long day of fatigue duty or scouting through the Eroded Plains, privates and officers settled down and began to read newspapers and books, or to write letters to their loved ones, by candlelight. Candles were popular items because in 1869 the War Department outlawed the use of kerosene lamps on military posts due to their propensity for starting fires. Fires were a major concern at these frontier garrisons. In 1868 a fire destroyed the Fort Bascom cookhouse. When a soldier's candle ration ran out, he improvised by creating his own homemade illumination, called a slush-box. This device was made of a discarded sardine can, with a piece of rag used as its wick. The final touch was to pour a layer of old cooking grease on the rag wick. While on patrol, soldiers secured these improvised lamps to their tents' ridgepole with baling wire. When candles were available on these scouts, troopers were known to insert them into their rifles' bayonet sockets, which served as candle holders. In April 1871, after a long day in the saddle, Private Eddie

Matthews informed his parents that he would have to close his letter home because "It will be taps in a few moments, and my candle is just about to be a sixteenth past an inch long." Improvisation in the field and at the post, by both officers and enlistees, became the rule at Fort Bascom, for government-issued goods never met the demands of this territorial outpost.[8]

Establishing any garrison on the western frontier was fraught with logistical challenges, but none was greater than supplying its men with adequate food. Railroad lines were nonexistent in New Mexico Territory during the 1860s and early 1870s, so most supplies had to be freighted in by wagons or mules. Fort Bascom was approximately 140 miles from Fort Union, the army's main western supply depot. Yet the land between Union and Bascom was neither flat nor hospitable. Las Vegas, the only real town along the route, was ninety miles northwest of the Canadian River garrison. In winter, blizzardlike conditions could quickly roll off the Sangre de Cristo Mountains and blanket the Eroded Plains with several feet of snow. In summer, much of the route resembled a rock-strewn desert. Even so, monsoon rains were possible in both July and August. The Canadian was known to rise fifteen feet up its steep banks within twenty-four hours of such a deluge. These storms washed out roads, made crossing streams nearly impossible, and halted freighters in their tracks. The monsoon rains were also known to occasionally carry away supplies, animals, and soldiers. As a result, delivering government issues, both food and forage, was a challenge. Topography and weather were as dangerous as the Indians who raided along the Canadian River. Thus, the military looked to local New Mexicans to help supply its forts.[9]

The Department of New Mexico sought regional contractors to offset the lack of fresh food and the high costs of delivering goods from Missouri and points east. Yet dealing with such citizens produced its own set of challenges. Sometimes contracts between officials at the post and locals were not honored or the product delivered was of poor quality. In January 1866 Lt. Thomas Smith of the First New Mexico Volunteer Cavalry ordered the commissary of subsistence at Bascom to look elsewhere for fresh beef since the original contractor could not supply the fort's needs. He stated that if the post was required to break a contract, any difference in cost could be charged to the original contractor. A year later, problems procuring beef at reasonable prices remained a top priority. In 1867 post commander Major Alexander wrote to headquarters about the exorbitant price of fresh beef. With this correspondence Alexander inserted a proposal from William B. Stapp and Charles S. Hopkins, the post's sutlers, that offered beef for nine cents per pound, half of what the army had been paying. James Patterson was another local cattleman vying for the fort's business. As with any other market, scarcity and control shaped pricing in New Mexico. All frontier forts in the territory had similar problems. Maj. E. W. Eaton of Fort Wingate provides an even more illustrative example of problems procuring beef. In 1864 he noted that the only cattlemen he could make a deal with were Pueblo Indians. These Puebloans proved to be hard bargainers, only accepting silver or gold in exchange for their cattle. In discussing this issue with Chief Commissary of Subsistence A. F. Garrison, Eaton wrote that he hoped Garrison would "devise some means of having us supplied with good beef[,] which we have not had since I have been at the Post, and I am credibly informed that there has not been any beef here really fit for issue for a long time."[10]

Quartermaster officers were also charged with providing each post with the daily necessities. Soldiers were seldom supplied with enough vegetables because they often had spoiled before reaching the post. As a result, frontier garrisons depended on their own gardens for corn, tomatoes, and cabbage. Fort Bascom was no exception, yet issues with water made for poor crops. Commissary officers had better luck procuring beans, potatoes, corn, and bacon than they did beef.

Lack of trees around the post posed additional procurement problems. Available cottonwoods that grew along the Canadian were quickly consumed by the construction process, thus wood for lumber, cooking, and heating purposes was another sought-after resource that had to be purchased from nearby landowners. Small parties of soldiers with one or two wagons spent two to three days away from the post on such details. These assignments required them to chop and stack the wood and then haul it back to the fort. Such activities broke up the monotony of post life, yet like any journey away from the fort, they included a certain amount of danger. Small groups made the most inviting targets.[11]

While the commissary department worked to meet the needs of the frontier soldiers, it seldom provided enough good food. Fort Bascom soldiers' main diet consisted of bread, bacon, beans, and water. The bread was often too hard to eat. When not too hard, it was often laced with worms. Such staples were occasionally complimented by fresh beef and the meager pickings extracted from the post's garden. Fresh meat also came from afternoon hunts. Most troopers looked forward to the chance to bring down an antelope, bison, or the occasional bear to enhance the evening meal. Yet such excursions generally offered only momentary respites from typical army fare. Private Matthews expressed it best in 1874: "When I say we have had bean soup for dinner and baked beans for supper every day for the past month and that I have eaten heartily of them at every meal, and that I like them, I only tell the truth. Still when one has beans for about a thousand meals in succession the thing becomes monotonous and considerable on the order of sameness. And I have no doubt but that I would fight if any person said beans to me when I leave this bean bellied army. (Excuse the expression.)"[12]

Soldiers at Fort Bascom sought to incorporate fresh vegetables into their diet for more than the obvious reasons. It was well known throughout the army that vegetables provided protection against scurvy. Elliot Coues, Fort Whipple's post surgeon, recommended issuing extra rations of "molasses, vinegar, and desiccated vegetables and potatoes as antiscorbutics." While medical personnel were not quite sure what caused scurvy, they did know that providing vegetables to the troops helped to suppress it. There was a standing order for each post to grow their own vegetables or make efforts to procure produce from nearby villages. Since 1932 doctors have known that scurvy is caused by a lack of vitamin C, which is found in a variety of citrus fruits and vegetables such as tomatoes, potatoes, and cabbage. Scurvy is also a side effect of poor nutrition, something that afflicted most soldiers in New Mexico. Capt. John Dubois noted in 1866 that this "curse of the Army" was a serious issue at Fort Bascom. In a letter to Maj. Gen. A. B. Eaton, commissary general for the army, Dubois complained that his order for ten gallons of molasses had been "disallowed." He explained to Eaton that he had ordered the molasses because twenty Fort Bascom soldiers were afflicted with scurvy. In an obvious attempt to bypass the Department of New Mexico's subsistence officer, who had cancelled the shipment, Dubois (probably trying to anticipate any questions concerning whether someone at the post had a sweet tooth) noted that Henry Duane, the post's surgeon, had directed him to order the molasses.[13]

The sutlers' store also provided soldiers with the opportunity to purchase additional goods if they had the cash. Stapp and Hopkins's establishment was positioned about three hundred yards north of the post. As Robert W. Frazer explained in *Forts and Supplies: The Role of the Army in the Economy of the Southwest,* for a price civilians were more than happy to provide soldiers with whatever necessities the military could not, or would not. This included canned fruit, sardines, and crackers. These stores also sold glassware, shirts, pants, tobacco, candy, and liquor, but not necessarily in that order.[14]

In 1866, the last year Edward Bergmann, now a major, was stationed at Fort Bascom, he loaned John Watts (the New Mexico lawyer and politician who leased his land to the army for Bascom) three thousand dollars to build a military store. Watts's partner in this endeavor was his son-in-law, William V. B. Wardwell. Wardwell had arrived in New Mexico with the California Column during the Civil War and had become a successful merchant afterward, at least for a time. His connections with Watts probably helped. Like many veterans of the Column, he served at Fort Sumner prior to mustering out, so he would have been well acquainted with the area. Records show Wardwell also established a trading post at Fort Craig. According to court documents, Watts and Wardwell never paid Bergmann back. After he left the army Bergmann sued Wardwell. Represented by Thomas B. Catron and Stephen B. Elkins, two of New Mexico's most prominent lawyers and politicians, Bergmann finally received a settlement in 1872. Watts certainly took advantage of his position as the owner of the land that Bascom was built on. In addition to opening a nearby store, he sold cattle to the post through local contractor James Patterson and also sold the post tons of hay. Powerful and influential New Mexicans sought such opportunities at all the frontier outposts. Their involvement in all aspects of this trade illustrates just how lucrative it could be.[15]

Soldiers often frequented sutlers' stores and other nearby establishments operated by civilians because of the dietary challenges they faced on the western frontier. The cooks who fed the troops were generally pulled from the ranks and trained at the posts. Amateur cooks wasted food in a variety of ways, from burning to spoiling. Few knew their way around a large wood-burning stove or had the skills to feed hundreds of hungry men at one sitting. They knew even less about how to store food so it would not rot. Lack of knowledge in the kitchen led to a great deal of waste. The absence of an onsite granary was also a problem. Large amounts of corn and flour had to be stored, and much of it spoiled or became contaminated before it was consumed. A scarcity of eggs, milk, and butter also contributed to the monotonous character of most soldiers' meals.[16]

Once food was dished from the boiling cauldrons and onto tin plates, the men retired to the mess hall. Officers took their meals in the privacy of their quarters or together, away from the enlistees. Individual companies usually sat together at long wooden tables. Soldiers ate with iron knives and forks and drank from tin cups. While at the post, mealtimes were as regimented as reveille and taps. One of the few things officers and enlistees shared in the mess hall was their poor opinions of the food.[17]

Another key to better understanding the challenges the U.S. Army faced in their mission to subdue the Southern Plains Indians involves grasping how difficult it was for Fort Bascom's soldiers to keep enough hay on hand for their horses and mules. Procuring enough forage for their animals was just as crucial to supplying troopers with enough ammunition. Additionally, just as hungry men lacking proper nutrients made poor soldiers, ill-fed horses could not be counted on to perform as needed on the Eroded Plains or the Llano Estacado. Hay was the nineteenth-century equivalent of today's oil. Without proper forage, military operations in the West came to a standstill. In New Mexico, unlike the subhumid regions east of the Mississippi River, cavalry could not rely on native grasses to sustain their horses and mules throughout the year. This was certainly obvious in the fall, when snow often covered the ground for weeks. Quartermasters were constantly negotiating with local civilians for hay, oats, and other grains. Due to the unpredictable nature of the market, these officers preferred to secure prices far in advance of the post's needs. As with their experiences acquiring beef and produce, they were not always successful. Quartermasters were often caught between the department's edict not to buy above a certain price and local farmers' bottom line. Officers were pressured into securing contracts by early summer to ensure enough forage was available for winter. Hay-cutting season began in mid- to late July. Timing was crucial, as hay cut and stacked in June, or too early, would dry out before it was needed, eliminating the nutrients horses required to remain healthy all winter. Hay cut too late would not cure properly, which could bring on intestinal problems. One contract between Fort Bascom and James E. Whittemore of Gallinas Crossing (also known as Gallinas Springs) was very specific about what was required concerning the condition and type of hay to be delivered. It was to be cut by 30 July and delivered to Bascom's stables "on or before October 20, 1869." If such contracts were not executed on time and fulfilled as promised, winter patrols and expeditions would have to be curtailed, which hindered the military's overall operations in the region.[18]

In addition to selling the army beef, James Patterson also sold Fort Bascom tons of hay and corn. By 1868 Patterson was something of an entrepreneur-of-all-trades in northeastern New Mexico. Chief Commissary of Subsistence Charles McClure instructed his acting assistant quartermaster at Bascom, Lt. Adolph Luettwitz, to buy additional hay from Patterson because "Texas cattle will not eat corn." Perhaps McClure was unaware that Patterson's first venture in the territory involved driving thousands of these animals out of Texas and into New Mexico.[19]

Without ample forage, cavalry patrols could not venture far the post, so quartermaster officers were always working to acquire additional tons of oats, corn, and hay. Finding a place to safely store so much fodder was also a challenge. Quartermasters at Fort Bascom and at headquarters in Santa Fe were constantly finalizing contracts that would keep enough hay and grains on hand for winter. In early 1864 Chief Quartermaster for the Department of New Mexico Herbert M. Enos received a request from Bascom for two tons of hay to feed the "public animals." In 1867 Capt. George Letterman of the 125th U.S. Colored Infantry commanded the post. He requested that Enos authorize him to purchase more corn than was allowed by his contract because additional cavalry had recently been assigned to the post. In March Letterman asked if he could purchase twenty-two hundred tons of hay from John W. Dorsett, even though this local rancher's price was higher than the going rate. The captain explained to Enos that it was of excellent quality and there was no other hay available. In early 1868 Lt. Samuel Hildeburn of the Third Cavalry had to inform the new chief quartermaster of the district, Marshall I. Ludington, that the hay John Watts was selling him was of very poor quality. In response, Ludington assured Hildeburn that his agreement with Watts specified that only hay of "good quality" would be delivered to the post and if that was not the case, to cancel the contract and enter a new one with the same James Whittemore of Gallinas Crossing. As noted, Watts, a territorial delegate and owner of the land the Bascom military reservation resided on, continued to pursue every government contract he could acquire. In 1869 Lieutenant Luettwitz of the Third Cavalry also experienced problems with Fort Bascom contractors. Vicente Romero, one of the most prominent merchants in Mora County, agreed to deliver 400,000 pounds of corn to the post. The "light cotton sacks" the corn arrived in were not strong enough to hold their weight, and they ripped when removed from the wagons. Yet after eventually taking delivery of 200,000 pounds, Luettwitz ordered Romero to stop because he did not have the room to store the balance. After deliveries resumed several months later, Romero finally submitted his final bill for payment. Luettwitz informed Romero he was 690 pounds short of the total, so payment would have to wait until the contract amount was delivered.[20]

The specificity found in hay contracts as alluded to by Ludington, as well as in other correspondence concerning forage and grains, reveals some of the ongoing issues subsistence officers experienced while trying to meet Fort Bascom's needs. In one contract with Whittemore, 100 tons of "bottom grass," "free of dirt, sticks, and roots," were to be purchased at eighteen dollars per ton. Bottom grass was stipulated because, grown in New Mexico's river valleys, it created the most nutritious hay. This agreement also called for Whittemore to produce and deliver 225 tons of feed grains at twenty-five dollars per ton. Once these goods arrived at the post, they were weighed and tabulated. The stipulation regarding dirt and sticks was important to insert in these contracts. The absence of such materials not only improved the quality of the forage, but also affected the total weight being tabulated and thus costs. A contractor might occasionally try to undermine this process by hiding fifty pounds of sand or stone under his hay.[21]

Military policy concerning how much forage horses needed changed with the circumstances. During the Civil War, the standard for both Union and Confederate horses, most of which were east of the Mississippi River, was between twenty-six and twenty-nine pounds of some combination of oats, barley, corn, and hay for each horse per day. Additionally, the average daily water ration for a cavalry horse was ten gallons per day. Such a policy was seldom attainable west of the Mississippi River. By 1868 that standard had been reduced to "half rations," yet such reductions were in practice always more than half. In New Mexico Territory and Texas, horses were reduced to around six pounds of grain, hay, and available pasturage per day. Officers in New Mexico were left to apply a fuzzy sort of math. Such reductions in forage helps to explain why horses and mules alike suffered on campaigns across the Eroded Plains and the Llano Estacado.[22]

The post–Civil War military was forced to cut costs everywhere, which also made it hard for commanders to provide enough forage to keep their troops on horseback. In the winter of 1867, a frustrated Captain Dubois informed the quartermaster in Santa Fe that his horses had gone without adequate rations of hay and grain since summer because headquarters had not allowed him to purchase hay above a certain price. Dubois explained to Lt. Edward Hunter that "no one could sell at those prices." Pricing policies often played as significant a role in gaining control of the region as troop reductions, tactics, or the scarcity of resources. Transactions between civilians and the military were as much a competition as a partnership, which resulted in a steady undercurrent of tension. Yet friction between the two factions was not restricted to issues of pricing and quality or contracting for hay and beef.[23]

The sale of liquor also promoted discord on the base. In 1864 General Orders No. 51 specified that the establishment operated by sutlers Stapp and Hopkins could only open between the hours of seven and eleven A.M. and one to four-thirty P.M. This order also declared that no soldier could buy liquor without the written approval of post commander Bergmann. Five years later, in 1869, Capt. Louis Morris of the Thirty-Seventh U.S. Infantry forbade the sale of spirits at Bascom at any time. In May 1870 Capt. Horace Jewett informed post trader William Florsheim that "selling Liquors to enlisted men" in pint and quart bottles would immediately cease. He further warned that "post traders are particularly cautioned about giving credit to enlisted men. No claims will be allowed to be collected at the Pay table that are not approved by the company commanders." Such edicts did not occur in a vacuum. Officers were prompted to issue such measures and warnings as a result of past experiences.[24]

Orders denying men access to whiskey often proved problematic. The sutlers' desire to make a profit and the soldiers' desire to quench their thirst conflicted with the post commanders' intent to maintain order. Privates detailed to water wagons were required to replenish the sutlers' casks before returning to the fort. One hot June day in 1866, while laboring at this task some soldiers developed a thirst for something more powerful than Canadian River water. After rolling up to Stapp and Hopkins's store, they informed Hopkins that he would get his water after he sold them whiskey. As Hopkins explained it later, he ignored the rule about written permission and sold them a "small amount" of liquor. Yet this small amount was enough to inebriate these privates, who in turn created a disturbance of some kind outside the walls of the post that eventually led to their military arrest and incarceration. Speaking for the post commander, Lt. Thomas Smith gave a blistering rebuke to Hopkins for knowingly breaking the rules. Smith did not want to hear any excuses about how the men had blackmailed Hopkins into selling them whiskey. He made it clear that disobeying Captain Bergmann's rules was unacceptable and that future violations would jeopardize their business standing.[25]

As I noted earlier, Captain Dubois characterized scurvy as the "curse of the army," but alcohol was another curse that haunted the frontier forts. Soldiers fell victim to alcohol-related injuries more often than they did from battles with the Comanches. Captain Morris reported that one mail carrier's fondness for drink was detrimental to good communications, noting that it had become his habit to become inebriated somewhere between Crouch's Ranch and Fort Bascom. Such problems affected all military ranks. Reports often noted officers' involvement in drunken brawls from Mesilla to Fort Sumner. Alcohol-related accidents were as common as bar fights. The two were often related. In a letter home, Private Matthews reported that a trooper from Company M, Eighth Cavalry, riding in rough country about twelve miles north of the post, fell from his horse and later died. The following year, he related that this same troop experienced another, similar fatality. Having left Fort Union to return to Bascom, Company M stopped for the night at Taylor's Ranch, a midpoint of sorts below the Canadian Escarpment. While at this location, they "got drunk and as a natural consequence fought among themselves and in the melee that followed one of the party, a young man named McCaffery, was shot in the head and instantly killed." Disgusted, Matthews continued, "It is too bad that a young man should be killed in that manner, but nearly all deaths of any Soldier on the frontier occur in this manner." In 1872 Capt.

Ranald S. Mackenzie stopped at Fort Bascom to resupply his Fourth Cavalry companies after scouring the Llano Estacado for Comancheros and Comanches. According to scout Henry Strong, some of these troopers got so drunk during this respite that they "wallowed around in the mud like hogs in a mud-hole." Thus the concerns of Bergmann and Morris regarding the purchase of liquor were well founded.[26]

Commanding generals and post commanders alike often found themselves at odds with the sutlers for the reasons described above. Therefore, while such concessions could prove to be very lucrative, they were seldom long-lasting. In the summer of 1869 post commander Louis Morris was ordered to stop trading with Stapp and Hopkins. When Morris requested that the soldiers first be allowed to purchase all the "necessary articles" that were still in stock, explaining that the next closest facility was 145 miles away, district commander Col. George W. Getty relented. In reply to Morris's request, Getty's assistant wrote, "Sir: Mr. Stapp and Hopkins will close there [sic] establishment and business as sutler and traders at Fort Bascom within sixty days after receipt of this communication at your post." Shortly thereafter William Florsheim was selling merchandise at Fort Bascom.[27]

A town of sorts, Liberty, sprang up about six miles south of Fort Bascom. Its name derived from the soldiers' phrase for time off. Liberty sported the mandatory saloons, as well as a hardware store and few other businesses found in any fledgling frontier town. Merchants seeking business with the federal government also gravitated toward the only settlement near the post. Certainly soldiers with a little money in their pockets also ventured into town on occasion seeking to forget about fatigue duty for a little while.[28]

Soldiers at Fort Bascom also found ways to entertain themselves that did not include whiskey. After fatigue duties were complete, soldiers had several free hours to occupy themselves before taps. Troopers spent the remainder of their day reading and rereading letters from home by candlelight, playing cards, or perhaps having a smoke or chew of tobacco. They also read old newspapers and books. If not reading, many were penning replies to their loved ones. Communication with friends and family, especially after the mid 1860s, was a key source of entertainment for soldiers posted far from home. Before a prolonged scout, some troopers would write several letters because they did not know when they would get another opportunity. A few kept journals of their experiences on scouts and then mailed them east after returning to the post. Stacks of letters often awaited their return. Soldiers like Private Matthews of the Eighth Cavalry and Captain Dubois of the Third Cavalry often spent their first hours back at Fort Bascom catching up on what was happening with their families. They returned the favor by penning replies to family and friends about their experiences in the Canadian River Valley. Fort Bascom received its mail from Santa Fe (barring delays due to inebriation or some other malady) every week or two. Yet there was more than family correspondence to occupy a soldier's free time. Matthews bragged to his father that "ours was a very literary troop, when any ten cent novels are to be had." While stationed at Fort Bascom, he read *The House of Seven Gables* and noted that all the New York papers, as well as the *Democratic Advocate,* circulated among the men. Reading materials helped to pass the time, yet their acquisition also held an intrinsic value. As noted earlier, Captain Dubois related to his mother that with just a few books, pictures, and minimal furniture, he was able to make a "great show" of his quarters at Fort Bascom. Such items, including newspapers and dime novels, were both links to the world from which they came and intellectual status symbols among their peers. In November 1869 Lt. Wilson Hartz, Fifteenth Infantry, acting in the role of post treasurer, placed an order for several books and volumes with D. Appleton and Company of New York. The titles included *Arabian Nights,* Burns's *Poetical Works,* all available publications by Anthony Trollop, and the *Reveries of a Bachelor,* by Ik Marvel (Donald Grant Mitchell). Whatever the topic, such media proved to be both informative and transformative, allowing the lonely trooper the opportunity to escape the isolation he associated with the Eroded Plains environment.[29]

Longer stretches of off-duty time allowed soldiers to participate in events organized for larger groups or everyone at the post. During such events the barriers between officers and enlisted men melted away. On weekends or special occasions like the Fourth of July or Christmas, horse racing, shooting competitions, and footraces were held on the parade grounds, as were picnics and musical presentations. Baseball had taken the nation by storm by the 1870s, and Fort Bascom was not an exception. The Eighth Cavalry brought the game to the Canadian River Valley. Matthews noted that along with additional rations and ammunition, Company L brought along their bats and balls on one particular scout. Imagine the puzzlement, or possible envy, of a party of Kwahadi Comanches upon stumbling onto a game taking place on the banks of the Canadian River.[30]

Women also lived at Fort Bascom. Officers' wives often traveled west with their husbands, lending an outsiders' perspective to military life on the southern plains. Perhaps Martha Summerhayes, stationed in Arizona with her husband, characterized a soldier's life best when she called it a "glittering misery." As to Fort Bascom, the few women who did live there represented opposite ends of the social spectrum. Along with officers' wives, it was not unusual to find a private's wife living on the post, earning her keep as a washerwoman or performing other menial chores. As a result of their presence, either at the post or in the towns that sprang up nearby, prostitution was also a concern.[31]

While many of the women who worked at Fort Bascom helped officers and enlisted men deal with some of the daily drudgeries of post life, a percentage acquired reputations as prostitutes, using their job as laundresses as fronts to procure additional income. Because of this possibility, single females were seldom hired at military installations, yet an enlistee's wife was able to live on, or near, the base in return for washing clothes, cleaning officers' quarters, and doing some cooking. Finding single women on the base was unusual, but it did occur. Marian Sloan worked as a cook with her mother at Fort Union. But the great majority of women at the frontier forts were married. Once hired, they were provided a food ration, a stipulation that helped feed families, for many times women brought their children with them. At Fort Bascom in the early 1860s, these positions were filled by Hispanic women since their husbands manned the fort. Wives followed their men out of the mountain villages of San Miguel and Mora Counties, about a week's journey away. The significance of laundresses to military operations is highlighted by the construction of quarters for them at most frontier posts. Laundress quarters at Fort Bascom were positioned directly behind the soldiers' barracks.[32]

Headquarters suspected the requirement that such women workers be married was often circumvented by enterprising enlistees. Some Anglo soldiers, lonely and sick of the post's mundane tasks, sought out local girls for companionship. When these soldiers mustered out, many of them abandoned the women and their offspring. Entrepreneurial sorts, both Anglo and Hispanic, more interested in money than companionship, sometimes offered their wives to other soldiers for a price. As a result, Special Orders No. 4 was issued at Fort Bascom on 22 January 1865 by Captain Bergmann. It read: "All women living at this post not lawfully married, or other than servants to officers will leave today with the Government train for Chapiarita [Chaperito] and in the future no one at the post will be allowed to harbor any woman without permission." A similar order was issued throughout New Mexico. Officers had to establish the legality of any soldier's marriage by reviewing the actual certificate. If there was no certificate, the woman could not remain on the post. Captain Bergmann explained to his superiors that on the surface such an order made perfect sense—if it was issued in Missouri or Illinois. It did not make much sense in New Mexico. To explain his reasoning, he offered up the case of Sgt. Antonio Sandoval of Company I, First New Mexico Cavalry. Sandoval had joined the Union cause in 1861. After his tour ended, he reenlisted in 1863 and at the time of Bergmann's letter was a soldier at Fort Bascom. When Bergmann noted that Sandoval joined to defend the United States against the Confederate invasion, he did so with his family. The post commander explained that the Sandovals had two children, ages three and twelve, but no marriage certificate. Mrs. Sandoval worked at Fort Bascom as a laundress, and if she lost her ration because they could not provide a marriage certificate, this family would not be able to properly support their children. That same month, Lieutenant Colonel Brown took temporary command of the post and immediately wrote a similar letter. A legal certificate of marriage, Brown explained, came with a price most New Mexicans could not afford. The Catholic priests required fifty cents for an official marriage license, so most locals did without. Brown argued that Bergmann had already vouched for the woman, and "in a court of law, one living witness is worth a dozen certificates." The new commander "respectfully [recommended] that the Department Commander be induced to reconsider his actions and modify his orders" for this specific case. Although women were rare at Fort Bascom, post life did include a few, and their presence reveals how orders from headquarters were often disconnected from reality.[33]

Eveline Alexander's journal illustrates how officers' wives stood at the center of the social functions that enlivened frontier posts throughout the West. They organized large holiday parties and coordinated entertainment events such as musicals and plays. These women also occasionally provided the officer corps with delicious alternatives to government-issued beans and beef. Their physical presence softened the atmosphere for all soldiers on the base; they were a welcome relief to the emptiness and isolation found on the southern plains.[34]

Upon Mrs. Alexander's arrival at Fort Bascom in December 1866, she noted that a few women already lived there. Maj. Nicolás Quintana of the New Mexico Volunteer Infantry, temporarily in command when she arrived, gave the Alexanders a warm greeting and subsequently introduced his wife. Mrs. Alexander noted this greeting, yet had nothing positive to say about the "Mexican" woman. Conversely, she spoke highly of the Anglo post surgeon's spouse. She found pleasure in Mrs. J. N. De Weisse's company, noting this woman's mastery of Spanish, which she evidently had learned in a short period. Alexander couched this accomplishment as an indication of Mrs. De Weisse's talents, yet failed to address why such a task was worthwhile. It seems clear that learning Spanish afforded Mrs. De Weisse the opportunity to converse with Mrs. Quintana, one of the few women of equal social standing on the post. While social interaction, regardless of ethnicity, seems to have been the driving force, Mrs. Alexander failed to grasp this concept. While many frontier soldiers were drawn to women of any ethnicity, some were especially fascinated with any Anglo woman who ventured west. Young soldiers sought their company for a variety of reasons, including polite conversation. Officers' wives seldom interacted with the enlistees, yet they were still regarded as military royalty, someone to admire from a distance. Engaging the opposite sex in conversation reminded soldiers of their own girlfriends, mothers, and sisters.[35]

On rare occasions, the soldiers sought more meaningful relationships. For example, in 1866 Richard D. Russell, an officer in the California Column, spotted young Marion Sloan working as a cook with her mother at Fort Union. Russell pursued Ms. Sloan for several months, even following her back to Santa Fe after she quit her job at Fort Union. He courted her and convinced her to marry him. Russell mustered out of the California Column and joined the New Mexico volunteers, becoming a first lieutenant for Company E, First New Mexico Infantry. When he was transferred to Fort Bascom, his new bride, Marion Sloan Russell, accompanied him. Mrs. Russell, like Eveline Alexander, kept a journal of her experiences on the frontier that was eventually published in book form. While neither woman met with physical harm in New Mexico, the possibility of sudden tragedy was never far away. Not long after arriving at Fort Bascom, the Russells' three-month-old son fell ill and died. What role isolation, the environment, or the hardship of moving to the Canadian River Valley played in the infant's death is unknown. For parents to question their own actions after suffering such a devastating blow is quite natural. The Russells certainly would have ruminated about their transfer to this post and what relationship it might have had to the death of their son, the only child ever buried in the Fort Bascom cemetery.[36]

The Canadian River Valley, always a dangerous place for soldiers, was doubly so for women. Maj. A. H. Pfeiffer surely thought of these dangers when he was transferred to Fort Bascom in February 1866. Three years earlier, this frontiersman's wife had been slain in an attack near Hot Springs (now Truth or Consequences), New Mexico. They had been traveling with a small party to Pfeiffer's new posting at Fort Wingate. While violent death and assault were rarities, when they came, it was usually without warning. On 15 June 1870 a female employee of William B. Stapp, no longer the post sutler but still raising cattle near Bascom, was attacked by a small group of Arapahos and Cheyennes as she slept in her bed. Capt. Horace Jewett reported that they broke into this New Mexican woman's house at one A.M., stabbed and scalped her, and then stole three horses. The raiders subsequently invaded the post and stole a few horses before being driven away. Captain Jewett admitted the injured woman to the post hospital where she was treated by assistant army surgeon W. Michler. The captain also allowed her mother onto the post to help care for her. Due to their "inadequate circumstances," Jewett provided both a ration during the daughter's convalescence. Despite such dangers, women always remained a presence throughout Fort Bascom's history.[37]

The 1870 census reveals that several women and their children lived at the post. Some were connected to the officers who ran the garrison. Like Eveline Alexander, thirty-six-year-old Harriet Jewett followed her husband Horace to Fort Bascom. Their three-year-old daughter, Elizabeth, and their black cook, Emma Billingly, also made the trip. Corp. Ernest Nown of Württemberg, Germany, met his future wife, Teresa,

after entering the Territory. The Nowns lived on the Fort Bascom
Military Reservation with their three-year-old son. Teresa listed her
occupation as housekeeper, as did Mary Ann Dorsett, the thirty-one-
year-old wife of John Dorsett, a farmer who worked for Stapp, the post
sutler. The 1870 census notes that fourteen adult women were either
living within the post or on the military grounds, which encompassed
two square miles. Twenty children of various ages also lived there.
Seven of these women and one sixteen-year-old female were New Mexicans, but Teresa Nown was not the only local that was married to an
immigrant soldier. Felícita Kelly's husband, Private Thomas Kelly, originated from Newfoundland. Conversely, not all of the post's laundresses
and washerwomen hailed from New Mexico. They came from as far as
New York, Pennsylvania, and Ireland.[38]

Such diversity among the female population hints at the demographics found in Fort Bascom's muster rolls. Many of the Anglo–New
Mexicans who joined the Union army in the early 1860s were mustered
in as officers while Hispanos made up the majority who filled the ranks
of volunteer companies from 1862 to mid-1866. Several of the officers
were first- and second-generation immigrants. Captain Bergmann was
born in Prussia. Lieutenants Thomas Henderson and Michael Cronin,
who both served at Fort Bascom in 1864, were second-generation
Irishmen. Officers Saturnino Baca and Nicolás Quintana, native New
Mexicans, were the exception, not the rule. Yet early on, the typical
Fort Bascom enlistee was of Hispanic origin: men like Antonio Sandoval, José Lucero, and Juan F. Ortiz. Sandoval rose through the ranks
and served as a sergeant at Fort Bascom in 1865. Both Captain Bergmann and Colonel Brown vouched for this soldier's integrity and
loyalty. Sgt. José Lucero and Private Juan Ortiz were killed by Navajos
in 1863. In *One Blanket and Ten Days Rations,* historians Charles and
Jacqueline Meketa argue that New Mexicans have seldom received
recognition for their role in fighting Southern Plains Indians and
Confederates, yet the Union could not have functioned in the territory
without them.[39]

As the threat of another Confederate invasion diminished and regular army companies transferred east to help in the western and eastern
theaters, federal officials authorized a robust recruiting effort in the
territory to replace them. Military recruiters stationed at frontier posts
offered one-hundred-dollar bounties to enlistees. These bounties, over

and above the soldiers' monthly salaries, would be paid after the enlistee had honorably served for at least two years. The recruiters were veteran officers assigned to seek out young men in nearby villages. An additional two-dollar bonus was paid to those who joined of their own volition. Such income in cash-poor mountain communities had the desired effect—bolstering enlistments. This bonus was also offered to officers who procured new enlistees. In 1864 Lt. Thomas Henderson was Fort Bascom's recruiter. The muster rolls note that Cruz Aragón enlisted as a musician on 15 February 1864 for twelve dollars per month. This was the standard salary for a musician in the frontier army. Yet Aragón could not have enlisted without Henderson's help. A note in Henderson's hand attached to the muster roll acknowledged that he was the fifteen-year-old Aragón's legal guardian. Acting as both recruiting agent and guardian, the lieutenant certified that he had "freely consented to Aragón's volunteering as a soldier in the Army of the United States for a period of three years." The note did not indicate who received the two-dollar bonus or how young Aragón's bounty or salary was to be distributed.[40]

Regular army units returned to the frontier after the Civil War ended, and the New Mexican volunteers began to muster out. On 22 August 1866 Major Bergmann led the last of these men out of Fort Bascom. They were replaced by a company of the Third U.S. Cavalry and three companies of the Fifty-Seventh U.S. Colored Infantry. Black soldiers would serve periodically at this post until its official closure in 1870. Many white officers looked upon African American soldiers, like the Hispanics they replaced, as unwanted necessities. Disdain rooted in racism shaded officers' and outsiders' comments.[41]

The correspondence regarding black troops does not praise their service, but officers' comments still illustrate the unique challenges these soldiers faced in the Canadian River Valley. In referencing men of Company K, 125th Colored Infantry, who were posted to Fort Bascom in April 1867, Captain Dubois, Third Cavalry, wrote, "Besides my company I have a company of niggers. They are poor soldiers and very stupid [,] but then I manage them very well." This officer seems to confirm that the men of Company K obeyed orders, but he took the credit for anything positive that could be derived from their activities. In an equally devastating characterization, in 1867 Eveline Alexander, the wife of post commander Maj. Andrew Alexander, described members of the Fifty-Seventh Colored Infantry as "hideous blacks," which perhaps indicated Major Alexander's own views. It is also possible that Captain Dubois's distaste for black soldiers shaped his opinions on how the military should operate in New Mexico. In one message to headquarters, he noted: "The Comanches will not come in to talk. The last reports say they [the Comanches] believe this post in charge of negroe [*sic*] troops only. The Comanches will not kill negroes, they have many negroes among them. In consequence this is a bad place to use negro troops." In contrast to Dubois's reluctance to be associated with black soldiers, the Comanches, whom many army officers respected for their tactics and bravery, seemed to have held a different opinion, at least according to this captain. Another report concerning "colored" men seen riding with both Comanches and Comancheros indicates that such soldiers sometimes chose to desert and take their chances on the Llano Estacado instead of remaining under the command of men like Dubois.[42]

Over its history, Fort Bascom soldiers represented a variety of nationalities and ethnicities. In addition to African Americans, Hispanos, Germans, and Irishmen, Americans from all regions of the country were posted to this garrison. First- and second-generation Irishmen had a particularly strong presence in New Mexico both during and after the war. From Capt. William Brady and Lieutenant Henderson in 1864 to Sgt. John Welsh and Private Martin Shea in 1870, Irishmen at Fort Bascom served the federal government's efforts to gain control of the southern plains. David M. Emmons notes that by 1870, Irish immigrants made up about a fourth of the entire frontier army, so it is not surprising to find them scattered throughout the documents concerning Bascom.[43]

As did African Americans, immigrants joined the army because less desirable options restricted them to low-paying, menial jobs that no one else wanted. Enlisting gave both groups a means of escaping overcrowded slums and majority populations that were unwilling to accept them as anything more than subservient classes. The army guaranteed meals and board and offered an escape from urban decay and the cotton economy. There was also the possibility that once their military obligations were fulfilled, former soldiers might put down roots in a region more accepting of different nationalities and ethnicities. Yet

as Captain Dubois indicated, not everyone who joined the army fulfilled those obligations. Some deserted.

Soldiers deserted for a variety reasons. Fighting Indians and Comancheros along the Canadian River was not why many of the early enlistees
had signed up. They had joined to shoot Confederates. They also had
been enticed by cash bounties paid for enlisting. Once mustered into
the service, most soon realized that a soldier's life was 98 percent
boring and 2 percent dangerous. As noted above, the food was bad
and the work was hard. Privates spent a lot of time stacking adobes,
chopping wood, shoveling horse manure, and hauling water—all within
an area most considered an isolated wasteland. Even the water, when
it was available, often had to be purged of organic material before it
could be consumed. Enlistees found themselves at the beck and call
of frustrated, alcoholic officers who felt as trapped as they did. Poor
nutrition and bad water often led to sickness and misery. Soldiers
feared cholera more than Comanches, for the medical personnel and
their facilities were often subpar. For these reasons, 33 percent of
enlisted men deserted their posts.[44]

The post returns indicate desertions affected all regiments and
companies. In July 1867 four enlistees of Company E, Third Cavalry,
deserted. In August another cavalryman from this troop disappeared.
In September three more troopers from Company E deserted. Before
the year was out, two more would also melt into the Eroded Plains. Men
from Company K, 125th Colored Infantry, also deserted during this
period. Private Matthews estimated that over a three-year span, one
hundred men of Company L, Eighth Cavalry, deserted. He explained
to his family that "small and inferior rations, too much work, and rough
treatment" by superior officers drove men to flee the army.[45]

Some of these desertions may have been in response to outbreaks
of disease or the dangers associated with the more mundane tasks of
being stationed at such a post. In June 1867 Lt. John D. Lee died of
typhoid fever. Two more soldiers died in August: Private John Hendricks
of Company E, Third Cavalry, drowned after falling off his mount while
"herding horses across to cross [sic] the Canadian River." Private John
Taylor, Company K, 125th Colored Infantry, died from undisclosed
"wounds." A second trooper from Company E, Third Cavalry, died in
September, yet his name was not listed, nor was his cause of death.

Clues as to what was killing soldiers can be gleaned from a compilation of illnesses made in 1868. Bascom's "mean strength," or monthly
average of troop strength, that year was 133 soldiers. During this same
year, medical personnel reported 112 cases of diarrhea, 22 cases of
malarial fever, 23 cases of venereal disease, and 32 cases of rheuma-
tism. Typhoid was not mentioned. Yet the records make clear that poor
water quality and a lack of vegetables diminished the health of soldiers
serving at Fort Bascom and created conditions some might have thought
warranted desertion. As I note above, prostitution, while never expli-
citly identified as having occurred at this post, was certainly a concern,
and the cases of syphilis recorded in 1868 offer circumstantial proof
of its presence. Each post in the territory was assigned a surgeon to
address the various maladies and injuries associated with army life.
The quality of care varied. Distance from the states and a lack of funding occasionally required the army to hire civilian doctors to fill the
voids. Eveline Alexander noted that J. N. De Weisse was the civilian
doctor who attended the post in 1867. Regular army doctor Henry
Duane served at Fort Bascom for parts of 1868 and 1869. While stationed
at Bascom in the summer of 1873, Private Matthews, sick with a sore
throat, was diagnosed as suffering from an "ulcerated throat . . . The
doctor burnt my throat with caustic this morning." Ten days later Matthews noted he was feeling better, yet not everyone recovered from
the illnesses they contracted while stationed along the Canadian.[46]

While Henry Duane was the post's surgeon in 1868, he wasn't always
there, as Lt. John K. Sullivan of the Thirty-Seventh Infantry communicated to the assistant quartermaster on 27 October 1868. One of
the privates from Company I, Thirty-Seventh Infantry, had been shot
in the stomach and hand by another soldier. Sullivan explained, "[Since]
neither surgeon or Hospital Steward is at this post to attend to his case,
you will at once send an Expressman to Las Vegas and direct him to
have the enclosed message telegraphed to the Commanding Officer
at Fort Union, N.M. in order that a Surgeon may be sent from that post
as soon as possible." In his haste to get this message out, the lieutenant
did not identify the soldier or explain the circumstances of the shooting. Las Vegas was ninety miles away. It is unknown if the wounded
man survived.

In the fall of 1869 Lt. Wilson T. Hartz reported that seventeen enlisted
men and one child were buried at Fort Bascom. The child was surely

the infant son of Lt. Richard Russell and his wife, Marion, who had died of some unknown illness shortly after his parents arrived in the Canadian River Valley. Soldiers buried there had died of a variety of causes, including typhoid fever, drowning, and accidents. Hartz, with an endorsement from post commander Horace Jewett, informed head-quarters of the cemetery's poor condition and requested funds to build a wall around the graves. If funding was not possible, he suggested that their remains be taken to another military cemetery.[47]

Unfortunately, Lieutenant Hartz did not forward a list of the sol-diers who were buried at Fort Bascom with his request. The quarter-master general's office published a list in 1869, yet it contained only seven names. Post returns and other official correspondence note three additional soldiers who died at this post, yet the list remains incom-plete. In 1972 the superintendent of the Fort Leavenworth National Cemetery reported that thirty-one people who were originally buried at the Fort Bascom cemetery were reinterred at Fort Leavenworth. He noted that eighteen of the deceased were soldiers but did not include their names. Still, the names and regiments of the men on the incom-plete list, compiled below, have historical implications. While no publi-cation references their role at Fort Bascom, the burial of African Americans in the post cemetery signifies these men were just as active in the Canadian River Valley as the Third Cavalry troopers and His-pano volunteers historians have recognized. Their role at Fort Bascom is obscure and deserves further study.

Pvt. Michael Smith	Seventh Infantry	September 1863 (D)
Pvt. Antonio Hernández	First New Mexico Cavalry	July 1866 (D)
Sgt. Thomas Craddick	Third Cavalry	October 1866 (D)
Corp. Aaron Cooper	125th Colored Troops	November 1866 (D)
Pvt. Thomas Smith	125th Colored Troops	November 1866 (D)
Bugler Isaac Hammond	125th Colored Troops	March 1867 (D)
2nd Lt. John D. Lee	Third Cavalry	June 1867 (R)
Pvt. John Taylor	125th Colored Troops	August 1867 (D)
Pvt. John Hendricks	Third Cavalry	August 1868 (R)
Lt. Robert Carrick	Eighth Cavalry	August 1870 (A)[48]

While Fort Bascom soldiers were not constantly in danger, bad water, poor food, harsh environmental conditions, and isolation all contri-buted to mental and physical stresses on their bodies. Captain Berg-mann's optimistic assessment of progress regarding repairs was only temporary. In February 1867 Major Alexander described Bascom as "not fit for dogs to live in." In April of following year, ex-soldier William H. Ayres of Albuquerque received a contract to ship and install 250,000 adobe bricks to the post. These adobes would be used for repairs and the completion of the officers' quarters. Evidently, Alexander's harsh characterization, which was sent to headquarters, opened the federal coffers a bit, for other contractors began to deliver building materials as well. Pedro Martínez sold 84,000 feet of lumber to Fort Bascom. Around this time Samuel Gorham, who lived just north of Anton Chico, shipped 610 vigas, used as roof beams, to the post. Yet even as work was approved and ongoing at Fort Bascom, every officer charged with overseeing repairs and new construction was haunted by the civilian contractors' inability to fulfill their obligations. Ayres was unable to deliver the adobes, so Lt. Adolph Luettwitz was forced to look for other contractors. Chief Quartermaster Ludington finally worked out a deal with Salvador Armijo, also of Albuquerque, to finish what Ayres had started.[49]

Despite the setback, headquarters in Santa Fe continued to approve new work at the fort. On 14 March 1870 entrepreneur James Patterson signed a contract to provide extensive repairs to the hospital and replace the existing flat roofs on the storeroom buildings of the quartermaster and commissary with pitched, shingle roofs. Long after the deadline to complete this work had passed (25 April), the roofs were only half-installed. As summer approached, Lt. Wilson Hartz, in charge of overseeing this construction, and Major Jewett, his post commander, communicated their concern to the new chief quartermaster of the District of New Mexico, Augustus G. Robinson. They explained that the monsoon rains appear in New Mexico each July and August like clockwork, drenching the river valleys and arid plains alike with much-needed moisture. If Patterson had met the deadline of April 25th, the weather would not have been an issue, but as of 14 May 1870 a third of the roofs were still not completed. Patterson's excuse was that he had run out of shingles, but he promised that a new subcontractor, James Whittemore of Gallinas Crossing, was on his way with several more wagonloads. In the meantime, Lieutenant Hartz told Chief Quartermaster Robinson that he was thinking about moving supplies that were in the commissary building to one of the barracks. The only problem, Hartz admitted, was that the barracks also leaked. "If Mr. Patterson cannot or does not intend to complete the Contract," he wrote to the chief quartermaster, "there are parties willing to take it on." A second option was to stop work on the existing commissary and hospital buildings and purchase post trader William Florsheim's store and utilize it. Although it stood outside the perimeter walls of the post, Florsheim's store was quite large and, most important, did not leak. As to Hartz's statement regarding other locals willing to take on an uncompleted job, throughout the fort's history, many Fort Bascom officers had entertained similar offers that seldom ended well.[50]

As concern mounted regarding whether or not the roofs could be completed before the rains began, Major Jewett faced issues more in keeping with his stated mission at Fort Bascom. On 12 May 1870 between eighty and one hundred Indians of unknown affiliation swept through the Pecos River Valley and made off with twelve hundred of Mariano Jurisarro's sheep. Almost a week passed before Jewett was notified. With such a head start for the rustlers, he doubted his men could catch them. The raiders had brought several pack mules, which meant they could have butchered the sheep, packed the wool and meat, and made a quick getaway. He believed they were headed toward the Rio Grande. Jewett hoped that headquarters could get word to Fort Craig, where soldiers would have a better chance of apprehending the marauders.[51]

Construction issues surely complicated Fort Bascom officers' ability to carry out their regular duties. The day after Jewett informed head-quarters about the Pecos River Valley raid, he wrote a scathing letter to J. Clark, Patterson's agent in Santa Fe. The roofs were still open on some of the buildings because the four-by-four lumber needed for the rafters had not been delivered. Perhaps Patterson knew more about cattle than construction. With the monsoon rains ready to make their annual appearance, Hartz asked Jewett if he could use enlisted men to help finish the roof repairs. By mid-July another Las Vegas citizen, Louis Leroux, was hired to complete the buildings, yet when he later submitted his bill, the lieutenant refused to pay him. Hartz explained to Leroux that the work was not complete.[52]

Surprisingly, in spite of these delays, Chief Quartermaster Robinson pushed forward with additional contracts to totally renovate Fort Bascom. Las Vegas businessman Frank C. Ogden now entered the picture, having been approved to finish up all the work started by others as well as being awarded contracts for completely new buildings. These buildings included new officers' quarters, a guardhouse, and an elaborate granary to properly store the hundreds of tons of oats and corn an active frontier post needed to adequately feed its horses and mules. Ogden's men began working in August 1870. Hartz busied himself making sketches of the proposed granary and guardhouse, as well as overseeing the ongoing repairs of the existing hospital and commissary.[53]

It should be clear that even before the army granted the new contract to Ogden, Fort Bascom was a very busy base. Yet throughout the summer of 1870, Brig. Gen. John Pope, the new commander of the Department of the Missouri, of which the District of New Mexico was then a part, was contriving a new strategy that would govern Fort Bascom's future. General Pope took command of the Department of the Missouri on 3 May 1870. Maintaining frontier posts was an expensive proposition on many levels, which was certainly on Pope's mind as he contemplated reorganizing his command. In early September, Major Jewett received stunning new orders. All work on the post was to cease immediately. Pope had decided that Bascom would no longer operate as a full-time fort. Once Jewett received his orders, he informed headquarters that Frank Ogden had thirty men at the post working on a variety of projects. In light of his new orders and due to the delicacy of the situation, Jewett recommended to Ogden that he go directly to Santa Fe to get all of his questions answered. Work stopped. Bills continued to trickle in over the next couple of months, yet after 1870 the U.S. Army would never again expend money on Fort Bascom's upkeep. Despite the finality of such an order, this fort's position on the doorstep of Comanchería meant it would continue to operate as a seasonal base for military operations over the next four years.[54]

Ongoing logistical issues coupled with the boredom of daily drudgery provide the context surrounding which the U.S. Army sought to wrest control of the Llano Estacado from the Comanches and Kiowas who called the Canadian River Valley home. In contrast, the Indians were not bored with their surroundings, burdened by a sense of isolation, or hampered by leaking roofs and walls. The Eroded Plains and the Llano Estacado were part of their homeland, not wastelands. In spite of the daily challenges Fort Bascom soldiers faced, their greatest challenge remained finding a way to enforce U.S. Army control over the Southern Plains Indians of the Canadian River Valley.

CHAPTER 5

Hundreds of Days and Hundreds of Miles

New Mexico volunteers operated out of Fort Bascom from 15 August 1863 to 22 August 1866. Capt. Peter Plympton planted the first post flag south of the Canadian River while Col. Kit Carson was making plans to venture into Canyon de Chelly to force the Navajos onto the Bosque Redondo Reservation. Even before Colonel Carson and his men started this operation in January 1864, isolated bands of Navajos were escaping into the Canadian River Valley and points farther south and west. By mid-1864 thousands of Navajos had been relocated to the reservation, about ninety miles south of Bascom. As a result of this demographic shift, the region between the Sangre de Cristo Mountains and the Texas border became much more volatile. Concurrently, with most of the regular army east of the Mississippi River, raids along the Santa Fe Trail increased. Brig. Gen. James Carleton was worried that isolated incidents over such a widespread area had the potential to develop into a full-blown war if the region's Utes, Comanches, Kiowas, Apaches, and Navajos formed a stronger alliance. No frontier post was closer to Comanchería, where many of the raiders lived, than Fort Bascom. During the post's first three years, the volunteers played a major role in efforts to stop raids, return runaway Navajos to the Bosque Redondo, and circumvent the illegal trade between the Comanches and Comancheros. Troopers spent untold hours in the saddle riding hundreds of miles in all directions to accomplish these tasks. Their patrols took them through much of New Mexico and the Texas Panhandle. In 1864 the U.S. Army launched its first major expedition from Fort Bascom against the Southern Plains Indians who lived in the Canadian River Valley. What the New Mexico volunteers learned in this battle would be passed on to commanders in the future who took the same route, on similar missions, in search of the same enemy.

Before the first adobe bricks were laid at the new fort in 1863, General Carleton ordered post commander Plympton to send Lt. William Brady into the field on a scout with twenty-two troopers from Company I, First New Mexico Cavalry. Brady led these men up the Canadian River to, as Carleton put it, "hunt up and destroy any parties of Navajoes [sic] or Apaches which may be found." The forced relocation of both Mescalero Apaches and Navajos to the Bosque Redondo became a launching point for desperate Indians who could not abide their new confines. Many escapees followed the Pecos and Canadian Rivers north toward the Sangre de Cristo Mountains. Such trajectories sent them through Fort Bascom's domain. Carleton's directive made it clear that patrols were not to "destroy" women or children, just the adult males.[1]

As Lieutenant Brady moved north, the landscape grew more rugged. Hispanos called this region Las Angosturas (the Narrows). Here, the river cut a winding path through the valley. Red-and-orange boulders as large as houses overlooked the river. Rust-colored lava beds, frozen in time, fell down the canyon's walls and into sunken arroyos. Outcrops and crevices hid the stream—and anyone who did not want to be found. Company I moved toward Conchas Springs, where a month earlier Sgt. José Lucero and Private Juan F. Ortiz were killed by a band of Navajos. Brady's ultimate destination was Cañón Largo, an Indian rendezvous of sorts situated between the Llano Estacado and the Sangre de Cristo Mountains. Here, on its descent into the valley, the river cuts a huge swath out of the Canadian Escarpment. Comanches, Kiowas, Navajos, and Apaches were known to congregate at this point after raiding along major crossings on the Cimarron route of the Santa Fe Trail. Brady and Company I remained in the field for thirty days, ascending the escarpment, venturing across the Las Vegas Plateau, and scouting into Cañon Largo. The lieutenant also made notes on the best location to place a military road that could connect Union and Bascom. Such scouts had multiple goals. All officers throughout the Department of New Mexico had orders to execute any off-reservation male Indians on the spot. This directive was distributed at the Bosque Redondo to force Navajos to reconsider leaving the reservation. Additionally, such patrols were meant to signal a new, more permanent presence in the valley for the U.S. Army. Such a presence could not be ignored by Confederate Texans, Southern Plains Indians, or Comancheros.[2]

While the impetus for building the post derived from concern over a second Confederate invasion, the need to protect local citizens from Indian raids quickly became the volunteers' main focus. Ranchers and other civilians who lived or traveled between Forts Union and Bascom were often the preferred targets of native aggression. Livestock, particularly sheep, were continually being stolen. As 1863 came to a close, Capt. Edward Bergmann and Lt. Juan Marqués both pursued raiders who were operating in the region. Lieutenant Marqués's company hauled enough rations and ammunition to remain in the field for two weeks. Mesa Rica, the massive formation to the west of the post, provided the perfect shield for these raiders, often Navajos who had just slipped away from the reservation. By the time such thefts were reported to the post, the perpetrators were riding along the western face of the mesa or hiding within one of its deep folds. By the end of December, Captain Plympton was reassigned to Santa Fe, and Bergmann became the post's commander. The scouts continued.[3]

In early January 1864, as Colonel Carson guided his forces into Canyon de Chelly, Lt. Thomas Henderson of the First New Mexico Volunteer Cavalry led twenty-two privates and a train of pack mules atop Mesa Rica on another search-and-destroy mission. After traversing the mesa's summit they continued north to Corazon Mountain. Corazon, more a two-thousand-foot wall than a mountain, rises above the valley where the river bends to the east. The troopers followed a winding, ancient footpath to the top of the Canadian Escarpment. Ahead of them, to the north, was a rolling prairie, the Las Vegas Plateau. At their backs was the Eroded Plains, dissected by mesas and arroyos that stretched all the way back to the post. They had traveled forty miles as the crow flies, yet their meandering search encompassed much more than just miles traveled. As instructed, Lieutenant Henderson kept the troopers moving northeast, avoiding local villages as they made their way to Cañón Largo. From this point, they descended into the valley once again and struck the river. From there they began the trek back to Fort Bascom. They were gone twenty-five days.[4]

Between such excursions, troopers pitched in with Fort Bascom's construction. Company F, Seventh U.S. Infantry, remained through the spring of 1864. In May, Capt. Charles Rawn led them back to Fort Union. They were replaced by Company M, First New Mexico Volunteer Cavalry. The regular army would not return to this garrison for two years.[5]

The volunteers were left to conduct all operations in the region. Certainly the Indians were aware that the regulars were gone. By the summer of 1864 they were raiding army supply wagons, stage lines, and merchant caravans along the Santa Fe Trail. These raids were particularly devastating along the Cimarron route, a portion of the Santa Fe Trail that followed the Cimarron River southwest through Kansas and Indian Territory. Here bands of Comanches and Kiowas regularly attacked caravans as they crossed the Lower and Middle Crossings of the river in Kansas. Travelers were also vulnerable at the Upper Crossing, near present-day Boise City, Oklahoma. Captain Bergmann was ordered to intercept one such band in June. Carleton ordered him to take a "party of the best men at your post to endeavor to cut this trail in case the robbers have gone south, and if the party finds the trail to follow it up and either capture or destroy them. The general prefers that you go in command of this party."[6]

Territorial Governor Henry Connelly informed headquarters that some of these raiders were Anglo-Americans. On 20 May 1864 a large band of "Americans" moving south with approximately seventy mules came upon Ygnacio Esquibal and Félix García's trade caravan in Texas near Palo Duro Canyon. According to Connelly, after killing the herders, the raiders stole the group's provisions, took their horses and mules, and then continued southwest, possibly to Franklin, Texas. The governor suggested that Carleton get word to troops to be on the lookout for men trying to sell a large herd of mules in El Paso.[7]

Continual attacks on wagon trains between Fort Larned, Kansas, and Fort Union throughout the summer spurred Carleton to send Capt. Nicholas Davis on a fact-finding expedition up the Cimarron route to help determine a future course of action. Davis was gone forty days. The captain later reported that on 7 August 1864 about seventy Comanches and Kiowas had attacked a civilian wagon train that was camped at Lower Cimarron Spring in Kansas, killing five American teamsters. Three days later thirty Indians of unknown origin absconded with 135 mules from a caravan that was camped on the Upper Crossing in Indian Territory. A few days after that incident, mules were stolen from another civilian train that was camped at this same crossing. On 17 August Kiowas and Comanches were blamed for a major raid along the "Dry Route" (the Cimarron route), where "240 head of oxen" were taken. The wagon master, a man Captain Davis noted only as Blanchard, was killed in this attack. About the same time, Indians made off with much of the livestock that grazed next to Fort Larned. Davis also reported that a July attack at Walnut Creek, Kansas, left ten Americans dead. Two boys, who had been scalped, survived their ordeal. Additionally, two teamsters were killed near Cow Creek. On 23 August Davis and his patrol reached the camp on the Lower Cimarron in Kansas where the 7 August attack had occurred. They "gathered up and buried" the scattered remains of the five Americans. Some Hispano teamsters who had been in this wagon train were spared. The Comanches gave these men a "yoke of oxen and a wagon" and told them to return to their homes. According to Davis's report, the Comanches told these survivors that they had no quarrel with New Mexicans, but that they "would kill every white man that came on the road." This message was particularly galling to Carleton. He believed that most of his problems with Southern Plains Indians were related to an unspoken alliance between Comanches and New Mexicans, specifically the Comancheros.[8]

Even before he received Davis's report, the general was implementing a plan to stop the Santa Fe Trail attacks. This plan involved sending large patrols to stake out key river crossings and campgrounds in both Kansas and Indian Territory. Fort Bascom's Captain Bergmann was again ordered to the region, this time to the general vicinity of Upper Cimarron Spring, in present-day Oklahoma, one of the most volatile points on the trail. Carleton ordered Bergmann to take the post's guide, Frank de Lisle. De Lisle, of French Canadian descent, originally came west with Ceran St. Vrain and Charles Bent. By 1864 he was one of the Army's most experienced frontier scouts, having led patrols and expeditions across the southern plains for eighteen years. Carleton left it up to Bergmann as to exactly where to establish their camp, yet he was very specific as to the actions his captain was to take once he was in the area.[9]

Capt. Charles Deus, a fellow German immigrant and veteran of the volunteer service, became Bascom's temporary post commander. Bergmann left Capt. Deus with multiple orders to carry out while he was gone: "You are to continue with the erection of the buildings at the post, for which purpose all the mechanics are left at your disposal. Finish the company quarters as soon as you can and commence then with the hospital. You will find the plan of the Post in the Quartermaster's office." If that wasn't enough for a soldier with no construction experience, Bergmann ordered Deus to send a patrol down the Canadian River in search of Comanches. He closed with a warning. If his men contacted "hostile" Indians, "you are to send at once to Fort Sumner, so as to get help from that post." On that note Bergmann led fifty men out of Bascom to Fort Union, where they were fitted out for a fifty-day scout. He also picked up an additional thirty troopers and then rode for Indian Territory. Bergmann's campground near Cold Spring (in what is now the Oklahoma Panhandle) was approximately 140 miles from Bascom.[10]

Carleton assigned two other large patrols to other key points along this portion of the trail. Maj. Joseph Updegraff and one hundred soldiers were ordered to the Lower Cimarron Spring (also called Wagonbed Spring) in Kansas, about a two-day ride from Captain Davis, who had moved from the Upper Spring to just inside New Mexico Territory near the rocky outcrops known as Rabbit Ears. Carleton ordered Davis to inform civilians that the military was operating in the area and that trade along all the routes was safe. Any other possibility was detrimental to the regional economy. This economy was centered in Santa Fe, which was also Carleton's headquarters. Such raids, whether against civilians or military trains, tarnished the general's reputation. Continued violence along the Santa Fe Trail meant both the War Department and Congress would keep their attention focused in his direction. The significance of the region Bergmann and his men were protecting was highlighted the following May when Colonel Carson returned with one company of First California Volunteer Cavalry and two companies of First New Mexico Volunteer Cavalry to establish Camp Nichols. But before that would occur, General Carleton had other plans for the Colonel Carson.[11]

As the summer of 1864 turned into fall, the southern plains grew more violent. Not long after Carleton had dispatched hundreds of men to protect the Cimarron route, he received information that prompted him to launch a much larger military operation. Rancher Lucien Maxwell informed the commander that the Ute Indians were interested in taking part in any future war against their blood enemies, the Kiowas and the Comanches. Maxwell lived in Cimarron, in northern New Mexico Territory, not far from the Utes' village. Carleton wanted to take advantage of this news. The commanding general began to formulate a plan. He wrote to Carson at his home in Taos and ordered him to ride to Maxwell's Ranch to confer with the Utes. Many of the Ute males had recently served with Carson at Canyon de Chelly. If Maxwell's information was correct, Carleton instructed Carson to convince as many of the Utes as possible to join him on a mission into the Texas Panhandle. A strike into their common enemy's homeland would provide an opportunity to extract a rich bounty of bison robes and livestock to all who were interested. Carleton informed the veteran Indian fighter that three patrols, including Bergmann's, were to his northeast and were at his disposal for any reason he might need.[12]

This time Carleton had more in mind than a police action. He ordered Carson to meet with the Utes because he feared that other groups of Southern Plains Indians were interested in forming some kind of grand alliance while much of the regular army remained east of the Mississippi River fighting the Confederates. Before any such scheme by the Indians could bear fruit, he wanted Carson to get the Utes involved in a fight against the Comanches and the Kiowas. Carleton believed a joint attack into Comanchería, even a minor engagement, would help scuttle any future Southern Plains Indian confederation. If the various tribes were fighting each other, they were less likely to mount a combined effort against a weakened western army during the Civil War. He had a similar idea regarding the Navajos at the Bosque Redondo. He hoped to include a contingent of Navajos and volunteer cavalry from Fort Sumner who would head east and join forces with Carson's group somewhere down the Fort Smith road. Such an action would surely destroy any future alliance between Indians in New Mexico Territory and Comanches and Kiowas in Texas.[13]

About the time Carleton began devising this plan, he received a dispatch from Captain Deus, in command of Fort Bascom while Bergmann operated in Indian Territory. Deus informed the general that several chiefs were camped outside the fort and were talking peace. Comanche Chief Paruasemen, also known as Ten Bears, was apparently their spokesman, communicating that they were ready to end hostilities. In reply, Carleton warned Deus to be on his guard. He believed that this might be the same group that had absconded with Fort Larned's livestock just a few weeks earlier. He instructed the captain to inform the chief that the only way there could be peace was if his people immediately produced all the livestock they had stolen over the last several months and brought the animals forthwith to Fort Bascom. He told Deus to make sure Paruasemen knew that Carleton considered him his enemy and would continue to believe so until all the animals were returned. He also informed the captain that Maj. J. Francisco Cháves was on his way to take command of Bascom. He warned Deus that once he delivered this message to the Indians, the post might be attacked, so he should prepare his men to do battle. It took several days for Carleton's reply to get back to Fort Bascom. By then the Comanche chief and his followers were gone. Carleton believed this confirmed his suspicions about Paruasemen's original intentions, which were to take an inventory of the post's stock and see how easy or difficult it would be to steal it.[14]

Major Cháves refused to take command of Fort Bascom. Once Carleton received this surprise, he quickly explained to the major that the assignment was never meant to be permanent. Captain Deus was not able to run the garrison, and he only needed someone to command it until Bergmann returned from Indian Territory. Almost apologizing, Carleton issued Major Cháves new orders, sending him to Los Pinos on a recruiting detail instead. In his place, Carleton ordered Lt. Col. Francisco P. Abreu of the First New Mexico Volunteer Infantry to take command of Fort Bascom until Bergmann returned. Some of Cháves's connections were with persons loosely linked to the Comanchero trade. It is possible that he did not want to serve on a post so close to Comanchería. Regardless, Carleton's unusual deference to this man also had something to do with his family connection. Territorial Governor Henry Connelly was his stepfather.[15]

Carleton's plans for a large military expedition continued to evolve as September gave way to October. Carson informed Carleton that he planned to leave Taos for Cimarron on 8 October. In this same correspondence, he requested of his commander to "please don't forget to remember Captain E. H. Bergmann in the appointment for majorship [sic], as I consider him fully entitled to the position." At the time of the letter Bergmann was still using Cold Spring as a base camp and patrolling the Cimarron route near Upper Cimarron Spring. On 9 October Abreu arrived at Fort Bascom and notified Carleton that there were sixty-nine soldiers at the post. These men "could be well mounted for any service required." Abreu also reported that some Hispano traders had seen a large group of Indians, as many as three thousand, "about two hundred miles from the post." This encampment was northeast of Palo Duro Canyon, along the Canadian River. Carleton discounted the Hispanos' estimate as a gross exaggeration and awaited the outcome of his most able officer's meeting with the Utes. Carson arrived at Lucien Maxwell's ranch in Cimarron on 10 October 1864. He met with several veterans of the Canyon de Chelly campaign, including the Ute's leader, Kan-ni-at-ze. Afterward he reported to Carleton that they were willing to participate in an expedition, but they needed rations for both themselves and their families. The colonel also requested a hundred rifles, ammunition, and blankets for the men.[16]

October communications from headquarters reveal the logistical and tactical wheels that whirled within Carleton's head as he formulated his strategy. In addition to Carson and the Utes, it involved the three patrols along the Santa Fe Trail that were currently in Kansas and Indian Territory. These groups would converge at Fort Bascom, where they would prepare for the expedition into the Texas Panhandle. A separate column of Navajo auxiliaries would leave Fort Sumner at the same time. Additionally, Carleton contacted Maj. Gen. James G. Blunt of Fort Leavenworth with another idea. Blunt was already pursuing the Kiowas and Comanches who had raided the area around Fort Larned. Carleton informed the major general that he was sending "a force of three hundred volunteer troops . . . and, say, one hundred Ute and Apache Indians . . . all, under Colonel Christopher Carson, to attack the Kiowas and Comanches." He hoped Blunt could meet Carson somewhere near Palo Duro Canyon, so "a blow may be struck which those two treacherous tribes will remember." On 14 October Carleton informed Carson that he could not provide beef and bread to the Utes' families. He explained that these provisions were the responsibility of the Department of Indian Affairs. Rifles and other supplies for the Indian auxilliaries would be available at Fort Union, and they could acquire sugar and coffee rations when they arrived at Fort Bascom. He urged Carson to move his forces south as soon as possible. As winter approached, orders continued to fly out of Santa Fe.[17]

The expedition continued to evolve as weather, logistics, and realities reshaped Carleton's plans. Once apprised of the goal, Carson told Carleton that to accomplish the mission he needed at least three

Figure 5. Edward H. Bergmann among his contemporaries at a meeting of the Masonic Lodge in Santa Fe on 26 December 1866. *Standing, from left to right:* Major Bergmann; New Mexico territorial delegate C. P. Clever; Assistant Inspector General Col. Nelson H. Davis; Chief Quartermaster of the Department of New Mexico Maj. Herbert M. Enos; surgeon Basil Norris; Deputy Quartermaster General Lt. Col. James C. McFerran. *Seated, from left to right:* Assistant Quartermaster General Col. Daniel C. Rucker; Col. Kit Carson; Commander of the Department of New Mexico Brig. Gen. James H. Carleton. Such a photo reveals Bergmann's standing among leading figures in New Mexico Territory and U.S. history. Both Colonel Rucker and surgeon Norris had been drawn into a dark chapter of the nation's past when President Abraham Lincoln was assassinated. Colonel Rucker was with the dying president when he was taken to the Peterson house, and he ordered the pine coffin Lincoln was placed in. On the same night, Dr. Norris, the attending physician for presidents Andrew Johnson and Ulysses S. Grant, was sent to give aid to Secretary of State William Seward after he was attacked by one of John Wilkes Booth's co-conspirators. Photographer: Nicholas Brown. Date: 1866. *Courtesy Palace of the Governors Photo Archives (NMHM/DCA), no. 09826.*

hundred volunteers, as well an additional two hundred Indian auxiliaries. Even as Carson struggled to keep the Utes committed to the plan, the commanding general disappointed him by scaling back the expedition. He again told Carson that he could not feed the Utes' families while they were gone. He also admitted that the entire column, including

Indian auxiliaries, would not amount to more than three hundred men. Bosque Redondo's Navajos refused to play a role in any type of attack. On 22 October Carleton's plan changed again. Bergmann's cavalrymen and mounts had returned from Indian Territory too worn to take part in another prolonged excursion away from the post. Captain Deus and Company M of Fort Bascom would take their place, becoming the largest force to take part in the upcoming expedition.[18]

On 23 October, the day after Carleton suggested to Major General Blunt that they coordinate their attacks, he sent a copy of General Orders No. 32, Carson's order of battle, to Blunt's superior, Maj. Gen. Samuel R. Curtis. Carleton attached a note to this order that implied Carson and Blunt had agreed to work together to "put a stop to the Comanche and Kiowa depredations." This was a coy attempt on Carleton's part to gain Curtis's approval without asking for it. A positive response from Curtis could be copied and delivered to Blunt, almost forcing him to move south and join Carson somewhere near Palo Duro Canyon.[19]

Michael Steck, the superintendent of Indian affairs in New Mexico, soon caught wind of the impending expedition. He immediately wrote Carleton, explaining that the Texas Comanches had nothing to do with the recent Santa Fe Trail attacks. Steck's proof was information gained from Hispano traders. In Carleton's reply, the reader can almost hear the ink sizzling across the page. Incident by incident, Carleton detailed for Steck the eyewitness accounts that identified the Comanches and Kiowas as the culprits. He was "not surprised" at the denials of the Hispanos because these same traders "desire[d] to control the trade . . . with the Comanches." In other words, Carleton told the superintendent that he was wrong and that his letter would have no effect on the general's plans.[20]

In early November, as winter descended on the Sangre de Cristo Mountains, Carleton formulated his final plan. Cavalry and infantry units from Forts Bascom, Sumner, and Union would participate in the mission. Although the Navajos had refused to make war on the Comanches, a few Mescalero Apaches from the Bosque Redondo were willing to join the expedition. Despite Carleton's unwillingness to provide additional supplies for the Utes' families, Carson had managed to keep them interested with promises of Comanche livestock and buffalo robes. A four-day snowstorm blew in at the end of October, almost cancelling the expedition. The skies finally cleared on 3 November, and Carson led the Utes south. He sent one more request to his commander as he left Cimarron, urging him once again to find a way to provide for the families of the eighty Indians who had agreed to join him. After moving down the northern Canadian River, they stopped at Fort Union to acquire rifles and ammunition and then continued on to Fort Bascom.[21]

Having left Fort Union a few days before Carson arrived, Maj. William McCleave, First Calvary, California Volunteers, led several companies of the California Column into Bascom on 4 November. Companies K and M, First California Cavalry; Company K, First California Infantry; Company A, First California Veteran Volunteer Infantry; and Company D, First New Mexico Cavalry also filed in and began making preparations for the mission. Carson arrived a few days later with the Utes. As Carleton directed, Captain Deus and Company M, First New Mexico Volunteer Cavalry, composed the balance of the expeditionary force. Ammunition, food, and other accouterments of war were loaded into twenty-seven supply wagons. The goods they took with them, along with a small herd of cattle for beef, would have to sustain them for several weeks. After quickly organizing the column, Carson prepared to move out. On 12 November 1864, 321 volunteer soldiers, 14 officers, 72 Utes and Apaches, and the wagon train left the post for Confederate Texas. Lt. George H. Pettis of Company K, First California Infantry, was put in charge of the post's two mountain howitzers. Carson placed Bascom's Lt. Charles Haberkorn in charge of the Indian auxiliaries. Bergmann and his fifty men remained behind, but his longtime guide, Frank de Lisle, traveled east with Carson down the Canadian River in search of the Comanches.[22]

The war of words between the commander of the Department of New Mexico and superintendent Steck continued. Just as the expedition was about to leave, Steck informed Carleton that he had no authority to instigate a war between the Utes and the Comanches. All interactions between the U.S. government and Southern Plains Indians must be approved through his office. Carleton replied that it was clearly evident that Indian coalitions were afoot, and he felt it was in the army's best interest to get the "savages of the mountains" on its side while that was still possible. He reminded the superintendent that as commander of the Department of New Mexico, it was his duty to protect civilians by any means necessary.[23]

About a week after the expedition left Fort Bascom, Major General Curtis replied to Carleton's sly attempt to add another military prong to his plan. Curtis began by noting that he assumed Carleton knew that events in Missouri and Kansas had forced him to cancel Blunt's own expedition against the Kiowas and Comanches. The presence of Confederate cavalry in those states required Blunt's men to help in a Union repulse. Curtis urged Carleton to demand that telegraph lines be installed "in the direction of your country." He believed that if communications had been available, an earlier plan of attack might have resulted in the serious blow they were all looking for.[24]

To further complicate Carleton's plans, an event involving military volunteers in Colorado Territory was about to take place that, when combined with Carson's expedition, would blight relations between Southern Plains Indians and the U.S. Army for the next decade. Just to the west of Blunt's forces, near Cedar Bluffs, Colorado Territory, the First Colorado Volunteers were involved in locating and eliminating Arapaho and Cheyenne bands accused of raiding settlements north of New Mexico Territory. As encroachment onto Indian lands increased, so did regional violence. On 29 November 1864, a few days after Carson's expedition neared its target in Texas, Col. John M. Chivington led his Colorado volunteers into the villages of a large group of Arapahos and Cheyennes who were camped on Sand Creek, about forty miles from Fort Lyon. While it is possible that some of the Indians camped there had taken part in recent raids, their leader, Black Kettle, had come to Fort Lyon to negotiate peace with the U.S government. Yet despite his earnest intentions, the entire party was attacked by Chivington's volunteers. In the ensuing battle, many women and children were killed. This action became known as the Sand Creek Massacre, and it would forever sear into the psyches of the Southern Plains Indians that the American army could not be trusted.[25]

By then, far to the south, Carson was deep into the Texas Panhandle in search of the Comanches. Carleton's instructions, written 22 October, explained that he expected the old Indian fighter to engage the enemy:

> You know where to find the Indians; you know how to punish them. The means and men are placed at your disposal to do it, and now all the rest is left with you. . . . women and children will not be killed—only men who bear arms. Of course, I know that in

attacking a village, women and children are liable to be killed, and this cannot, in the rush and confusion of a fight, particularly at night, be avoided; but let none be killed willfully and wantonly.[26]

Fourteen years later, Lt. George Pettis's experiences during this expedition were published. Add to this Colonel Carson's official report, a published reminiscence by Dr. George S. Courtright (posted to the expedition by Carleton), and a recent archeological history of the expedition by Alvin Lynn, and we can construct a fair account of what happened to these men and the Indians they encountered. When the column left Bascom, it moved south for about four miles, where it passed "Bergmann's ranch." From this point the expedition angled east across Carros Creek, then turned north, crossing the Canadian River. The military followed an "old Comanchero trail" on the north side of the river until they were deep into Texas. After crossing the Canadian, they spent the next several days moving through the Eroded Plains, first camping on Ute Creek and Red River Springs. Winter followed them. As they penetrated Confederate Texas, northern winds cut across the prairies and through their ranks. They passed Salinas Lake, Hay, Romero Creek, and an old Comanchero campground where Punta de Agua and Rita Blanca Creeks came together. Occasional snow fell, slowing the march. Adding to the bitter winds and snowy conditions, Pettis complained that the men had a hard time getting any sleep because the Utes, in preparation for war, remained up half the night singing and dancing. When the troops began to pack up each morning, some of these same Indians were already miles ahead, searching for the first signs of Comanche and Kiowa villages.[27]

Those first signs illustrate just what a foreign world the U.S. Army was operating in, and why the subjugation of the Southern Plains Indians would take much longer than the defeat of the Confederate Army. On 24 November, after following an old Indian trail for eighteen miles, Carson called a halt to the day's march. They were about sixty miles north of, and slightly east of, present-day Amarillo. The soldiers dismounted and began to pitch camp at a place called Mule Springs. Pettis explained that just as everyone finished and began to relax, the Utes, already at rest, jumped up as one and began to talk excitedly among themselves. The soldiers looked around in confusion but saw nothing on the horizon that would cause this commotion. After a lengthy translation, the news spread that two of Carson's scouts had spotted the enemy about ten miles distant. Pettis and the other soldiers continued to stare across the Llano Estacado, yet they could see nothing. Writing from a perspective that contained both awe and confusion, Lt. Pettis recalled that even after some of these Indians pointed to a distant spot across the prairie, neither he nor his men could see any movement. Additionally, Pettis was mystified as to how these men were aware of the scouts' arrival long before the soldiers were. After a while, the soldiers did see two distant specks moving toward them. Twenty years earlier, Josiah Gregg had been similarly stunned by Comanche Tábba-quena's ability to scratch out a map of the entire Southwest using only memory as a reference. In 1864 the U.S. Army was only beginning to understand that the Plains Indians had a deep connection with the land. This connection seemed to make little distinction between the animate and inanimate, and it apparently gave them the advantage of a sixth sense. This would bode well for the Indians who preferred to remain on prairies far from the reservation. Carson's recent victories over the Mescalero Apaches and the Navajos had made him confident that he could replicate those successes in Comanchería, yet he was about to receive a stern reminder of why he had originally informed Carleton that he needed a much larger force for any such mission.[28]

Shortly thereafter, the two scouts arrived in camp and met with Carson. A large Indian village lay just a few miles to the east. The colonel brought his officers together and organized a plan of attack. He ordered Colonel Abreu and one of the infantry companies to remain behind with the supply wagons. They were to catch up with the rest of the column later. Carson was concerned about the noise twenty-seven wagons would make bumping along on an old Indian trail, and he did not want the added distraction of having to protect the supplies during a battle. The cavalry, artillery unit, and Indian auxiliaries mounted up and followed Carson east. Around midnight they descended from the rim of the valley to the Canadian River bottom. The ground was cut up from hooves, lodge poles, and foot traffic. Carson ordered his men to dismount, stand in silence, and hold their horses by their bridles until morning. Cigars and pipes were forbidden. From midnight until daybreak, the volunteers stood as silent sentinels in the middle of Comanchería, a heavy frost coating their uniforms.[29]

At the first hint of dawn, 25 November, they were ordered to mount up. Pettis recalled that as Carson led them east, the Utes and Apaches, completely covered in bison skins and robes, were scattered in "no regular order," around the colonel. Half the cavalry rode behind Carson and the Indians, trailed by the howitzers secured in a "prairie carriage." The remaining troopers followed the artillery. It did not take long for the column to spot a few Comanches on the south side of the river. Carson ordered Major McCleave, Captain Deus, and Company M to cross the river and attack. The Ute and Apache auxiliaries bolted into a stand of tall grass, discarded their robes, and then chased after Company M, their bare skin covered in war paint.[30]

Carson and the rest of the column followed, the sound of gunshots echoing across the valley. The colonel rode up on a bluff that overlooked Mustang Creek (now Moore and Bugbee Creeks) and spied an Indian village about five miles away. Carson then led the rest of the men down into the Canadian River Valley. Dr. Courtright recalled that when they crossed the Canadian, the water came "about midway up our saddle skirts." After crossing, they traveled about five miles and then moved through the recently abandoned Kiowa village. At this point, Carson ordered the rest of the cavalry to charge toward the sound of the guns. He remained behind with Lieutenant Pettis's two howitzers. Ahead, McCleave, Deus, and the various cavalry units were engaged against hundreds of Kiowas. These Indians were led by Chief Dohäson (also known as Little Mountain), one of the Kiowas' most prominent leaders for three decades. Under his direction the Indians performed a screening action that allowed their families to flee in the opposite direction. By the time Carson and Pettis passed through the Kiowa village, Utes were already rounding up loose cattle and horses. The lieutenant had an odd thought when he first spied the village, wondering how the Kiowas had accumulated so many Sibley tents. Carson explained to Pettis that he had mistaken the gleaming white bison hides that covered the village's teepees for military issue. Carson and Pettis continued through the encampment toward the battle. The old Indian fighter was confident the battle would conclude before they got there. For one of the few times in his fighting career, Carson was wrong.[31]

The colonel and the artillery battery caught up with the rest of the column around ten in the morning. The men were dismounted, their horses corralled behind the crumbling ruins of Bent's old adobe fort.

The soldiers had created a defensive perimeter, and everyone faced east. In their front, just out of rifle range, about two hundred Indians sat on their horses staring back. McCleave informed Carson that the cavalrymen had already repulsed several charges. Pettis's attention was drawn to what loomed behind these warriors. In the distance, he could see approximately twelve hundred Indians standing in front of another, larger village. The lieutenant later estimated 350 lodges were a part of this community. Here was the heart of Comanchería.[32]

After a moment's pause, Carson ordered Pettis to unlimber one of the howitzers. Within seconds of the first shot, all of the Indians dispersed. Instead of pursuing, the colonel ordered his men to break out their haversacks and have a quick lunch of bacon and hardtack. The horses were allowed to drink from a stream behind the old adobe fort. Carson allowed his men to relax because he believed the howitzers had performed their service for the day. Based on prior experience, he was sure that the enemy was in retreat and would not seriously challenge him again. At that point the colonel began to plan his approach to the huge Comanche village in the distance. But Carson was wrong. The Comanches and Kiowas soon returned, rimming the horizon. Over the next hour, the Indians charged from different vantage points, trying to break through the cavalrymen's defensive perimeter. The mountain howitzers were brought back into action, proving to be the great equalizer in the face of an overwhelming adversary. Still, the warriors refused to leave. Carson later reported that he feared that once night fell, the Kiowas would return to their village (the one the expedition had passed through earlier) to retrieve their winter supplies. He did not want that to happen. One of the main goals of the expedition was to destroy as much of the Indians' winter supplies as possible. Additionally, the colonel voiced concern regarding Colonel Abreu and the infantry, whom he had not seen since morning. According to Pettis, against the wishes of many of his officers Carson made the decision to fall back, destroy the Kiowa village, and rejoin the infantry somewhere along the way. Carson assured his men that once this was accomplished, they would regroup and mount a full assault on the Comanche village.[33]

Retreat in the face of the enemy, regardless of the century, is never easy. On this late November day in 1864, Carson faced an almost impossible situation. The column was outnumbered at least three to one. He ordered Capt. Emil Fritz and thirty men from Company B, First

California Cavalry, to dismount and guard the right flank of the retreat. Fort Bascom's Company M, First New Mexico Cavalry, was deployed on both the right flank and in the rear. Once the Comanches realized the column was on the move, they set fire to the prairie. As fire and smoke roiled over the valley, the troopers faced the full ramification of having ventured into Comanchería. When the column made it back to the Kiowa village, it was full of warriors trying to salvage their goods. While Deus's and Fritz's men continued to defend the flanks and the rear, Carson ordered the rest of his troops to attack the village. Once the Kiowas scattered, he gave the order to set it on fire. Now smoke from the lodges mixed with smoke from the prairies as the fifteen-acre camp burned to the ground. Between 150 and 170 lodges, along with large amounts of dried meat and berries and numerous bison robes, were either taken or destroyed. In addition to robes, Alvin Lynn has noted that it took twelve to fourteen bison hides to cover one lodge. At that rate, between fifteen hundred and two thousand hides were destroyed. Similarly, it took around twenty lodge poles to build the frame for one teepee. This meant around three thousand lodge poles in a land with few trees were destroyed by Carson's men. After setting fire to the village, the soldiers kept moving west and the battle subsided. As evening approached, Carson met Abreu and the infantry about five miles west of the old adobe fort. His earlier promise to launch another attack after connecting with the infantry was not fulfilled. Instead, he ordered the entire column west, toward New Mexico. The First Battle of Adobe Walls and the expedition were over.[34]

On 4 December, while camped at Rito Blanco, about one hundred miles east of Fort Bascom, Carson reported that he was returning to the post because his horses were exhausted and the column was low on ammunition. The expedition had left Fort Bascom on 12 November and had fought both the harsh topography and bitter elements for fourteen days before making contact with the enemy. On 14 December, while camped just outside of Fort Bascom, he glossed over the expedition's realities by listing the types and amounts of winter goods his men had destroyed. He also expounded on the fact that they had discovered a large cache of "powder, lead, [and] caps." Carson explained to Carleton that Comancheros had reached the Indian camp about ten days ahead of the expedition and alerted the Comanches. Because of this, two of his men were dead and ten were wounded. Yet, despite this declaration, he saved most of his wrath for Michael Steck. The colonel claimed that Steck had given these traders the passes that allowed them into Comanchería, where they warned the Comanches of the expedition's approach.[35]

After his scout in the Indian Territory, Captain Bergmann had been unable to accompany Carson on the expedition because of the depleted condition of his men and mounts. While Carson was in Texas, the captain immediately became embroiled in a war of words with headquarters. The subject was also Comancheros. Just prior to Carson's battle, one of Bergmann's Fort Bascom patrols had apprehended José Costillo and José Anaya, of Anton Chico, loaded with trade goods on their way to Texas. Costillo and Anaya were taken to Fort Bascom. Unknown to Bergmann, these men's employers, two merchants from Anton Chico, "Martínez and Hornberger," must have immediately discovered their arrest, because within a couple of days they were in Santa Fe complaining to both Superintendent of Indian Affairs Michael Steck and Territorial Governor Henry Connelly. Someone must have contacted General Carleton, because he sent a quick order to Bergmann to release the traders after they posted bond for the goods they were carrying. Bergmann's report on their arrest reached Carleton's desk on 26 November. Bergmann probably received Carleton's orders to release his prisoners about the same time headquarters received his report. Once Carleton read Bergmann's report, he must have felt some guilt about his order to release the Comancheros. In a later missive, Carleton wrote, "You are directed to arrest and hold all other parties who may be trading with the Comanches, or, may endeavor to go into this country for that purpose, no matter what source they derive their authority for such traffic." Clearly Carleton was still aggravated by what he considered civilian interference in military affairs.[36]

It is at least conceivable that the New Mexican merchants who supplied the goods for the Comanchero trade also supported the political elite within the territory. Such politicians, even Governor Connelly, were evidently quick to come to the aid of merchants who supported their political careers. Another letter from Bergmann reached Santa Fe after Carleton left the capital on other business. The general's chief of staff, Col. James C. McFerran, learned that Bergmann still held the traders, but his explanation for doing so was much more detailed. In his reply McFerran was sympathetic, but explained that since Carleton was not there to countermand previous orders, the captain had to release the prisoners. Yet McFerran admitted that Bergmann's follow-up put "a different, and very criminal aspect, upon the course pursued by your traders." He then encouraged the captain to gain any knowledge he could regarding distances traveled, who the traders met along the way, and whether they had ever encountered any white females among the Comanches when they traded. Only after such questioning was he to release them. On the same day, McFerran wrote a letter of apology to Martínez and Hornberger, assuring them that their men would soon be released. This series of communications illustrates why Carleton and Carson were so frustrated with government officials over the Comanchero trade.[37]

In the aftermath of the Canadian River Expedition, while still at Fort Bascom, Carson wrote a second letter to Carleton. The colonel believed a victory against the Comanches was still possible, yet he made the prediction with cautious caveats. Certain conditions had to be met before any such attempt was made. First, his horses and mules needed at least six weeks of rest and good forage. Second, he needed at least a thousand men for a second expedition. Third, they would need two more artillery pieces. Clearly Carson was shaken. Carleton had neither the means nor the men to carry out such an operation. Carson knew this. Deus and Company M remained at Fort Bascom. The other units rode back to Fort Union and Fort Sumner. Carson spent Christmas with Bergmann and his men. Four years would pass before another serious attempt would be made to defeat the Southern Plains Indians. By then, the task belonged to the regular army. One of Carleton's goals, however, was accomplished as 1864 came to a close: Steck lost his job as superintendent of Indian affairs in New Mexico.[38]

The Sand Creek Massacre in Colorado Territory and Carson's expedition into the Texas Panhandle occurred almost simultaneously. Southern Plains Indians immediately linked the two operations. The execution of Cheyenne women and children at Sand Creek and Carleton's orders to Carson to strip the Indians of their food and shelter make such a linkage understandable. The Kiowas and Comanches of the Texas Panhandle believed their fierce defense of their Canadian River homeland had allowed them to escape a fate similar to the Cheyennes at Sand Creek. While such warfare was not completely incompatible with their own methods, the timing of these two battles convinced many Southern Plains Indians that the Anglos meant to exterminate them. As a result, some immediately sought peace while others prepared to battle to the death. One party of Comanches traveled to Fort Bascom to seek an audience with General Carleton. The commander credited Carson's efforts in Texas with this response and hoped the colonel would find time away from Taos to join him at Bascom if an agreement could be worked out. A small, hard-core minority forged a band of resistance fighters who would remain active for the next ten years.[39]

In the first months of 1865 word spread that this second group held the soldiers of Fort Bascom responsible for the destruction of the Kiowa village and planned to exact retribution. Arthur Morrison delivered such a message to Carleton after returning from Texas. Morrison, a former officer at Bascom, had remained in the region after the war to seek his best opportunity, like so many other veterans. Morrison had become a mercantilist whose clientele were often Indians. After gaining some knowledge of the location of several captive Anglo women and children, he traveled to Texas loaded with several wagons of supplies, seeking their release. He failed, but while he was never allowed to enter the Comanches' main camp, he did converse with some of the Indians stationed on the perimeter. Upon returning to Santa Fe, he reported that he had heard a rumor that obstinate Confederates were urging the Comanches to take their revenge on Fort Bascom and nearby Hispanic villages for what had happened in the Texas Panhandle and Sand Creek. Some of Bergmann's local contacts had supplied him with similar information. In early March he requested additional men to protect the fort. Carleton complied, shuttling regular army and volunteer units in and out of the post in April. At different times during the month, four companies of the First New Mexico Volunteer Cavalry were supported by Company E, Fifth U.S. Infantry, and Company F, Seventh U.S. Infantry. By the spring of 1865, of the fourteen posts Carleton had under his command, Fort Bascom housed the third largest force. He also had some specific instruction for the post commander.[40]

Carleton warned the newly promoted Major Bergmann to prepare for an attack. He reminded him to protect the post's animals, as horses and cattle were especially vulnerable while out grazing. He ordered him to alert the herders between the Pecos and Canadian Rivers to be on their guard and wrote, "Have a party of men under a careful officer drilled in the use of the howitzers." He finished this directive with a reminder: "You will not have much ammunition to expend in practice." Even though there were obvious supply issues, Carleton wanted Bergmann battle-ready in the aftermath of the expedition.[41]

Such an attack did not occur, yet Carleton's reallocation of men to the Canadian River Valley might have helped dissuade any Indians who considered it possible. Raids of this nature were not uncommon. As a detail of soldiers and drovers watched over a large herd of cattle grazing outside of Fort Larned in Kansas, a company of Union cavalry appeared—or that is what the herders took them for. In reality, they were Comanches wearing army-issue blue overcoats. The trick worked. Before the fort could react, the Indians had absconded with the cattle. Such were the conditions under which most frontier posts operated. Given the right conditions, Indians often invaded the military's space. Several such raids also occurred on the Fort Bascom military reservation.[42]

Morrison's information about a Confederate-Comanche alliance was accurate, for as the Civil War was ending the Texans were making an earnest attempt to create one. The reality was that Southern Plains Indians seldom maintained an alliance of any sort with Anglo-Americans. This latest attempt by the Lone Star State was as much an effort to stop attacks on its own people as any grand plan to form an Anglo-Indian alliance. During the war, Comanches and Kiowas were more likely to raid frontier Texans than a Union fort. In late 1864, to quell such attacks, Texas's frontier defense forces had attempted their own invasion of Indian Territory, in a mission similar in purpose and scope to Colonel Carson's. Maj. Charles Roff of the Border Regiment was ordered into the Wichita Mountains with four hundred men to find and eradicate the Comanches responsible for frontier attacks. This group had even less success than Carson, returning after ten days because of bad weather and a general lack of will. This failure and the subsequent desperation it generated led to the Confederates' final attempt to forge an alliance. On 15 May 1865, unaware that the war was over, Texas Brig. Gen. James W. Throckmorton met with some Comanche and Kiowa bands in Oklahoma. Gifts and captives were exchanged. Throckmorton returned to Decatur, Texas, believing progress had been made. Yet such progress went for naught because the government that executed the meeting was no longer in existence. This gave Canadian River Indians one more reason never to put faith in a white man's promise.[43]

After the war, patrols out of Fort Bascom continued, focusing on three main areas: Mesa Rica, Cañón Largo, and the Fort Smith road into Texas. Bergmann was ordered to post pickets and send patrols down this road. In April Lt. Richard Russell led a scout around Mesa Rica, and Lt. Cornelius Daley camped with a picket detail at Cañón Largo. The following month, Capt. Patrick Healy of the First New Mexico Volunteer Infantry led seventeen men back to Mesa Rica, and Lieutenant Daley returned to Cañón Largo with another group of First New Mexico Volunteer Cavalry. In response to reported raids in the area, General Carleton ordered Bergmann to personally oversee these two scouts. He directed the captain to meet with both officers in the field and specify where they were to set up pickets. The two patrols were to remain in the field and "destroy all Navajoe [*sic*] and Apache Indians (*men*)" who did not have passports. Bergmann then followed Healy's party and placed a picket on the southeast side of the mesa. Afterward he spent three days searching "that Mesa," but he never found Navajos or Apaches. With Capt. Charles M. Hubbell of the First New Mexico Cavalry at his side, Bergmann rode down the north face of Mesa Rica and continued in that direction. Near don Francisco López's ranch, he met Capt. B. F. Fox and men from the First Colorado Volunteers, who had just made their way from Cañón Largo. Fox was also searching for raiders but had not seen any. Bergmann retraced Fox's journey and positioned Lieutenant Daley and his cavalrymen in the canyon. He then returned to Fort Bascom, having been gone a total of eight days.[44]

Meanwhile, Captain Emil Fritz, First California Cavalry, was dispatched with a company of troopers out of Fort Sumner to scout up the Pecos River. His mission was also to round up escaping Navajos and bring them back to the Bosque Redondo. Captain Fritz was more successful, finding Indians on the west side of Mesa Rica along the Conchas River between the Pecos and the Canadian. Now part of a wagon route that connected Fort Union and Fort Bascom, this trail had been used by Comancheros and Indians long before the arrival of the Anglo-Americans. Fritz ordered the rebellious Indians south.[45]

That same month, May 1865, the post was informed that Abraham Lincoln had been assassinated five days after Lee surrendered his army at Appomattox Court House. Work at Fort Bascom was suspended for the day and flags were flown at half-mast. Major Bergmann reported that in honor of "that Great and Good man," all soldiers would wear black armbands for thirty days.[46]

In June 1865 the commanding general ordered Bascom's post commander to report to Fort Sumner with fifty volunteer cavalry and Company E, Fifth U.S. Infantry. Bergmann and his men were to continue hunting Navajos who escaped the Bosque Redondo. Captain William Ayres was left in charge of Bascom. There was a sense of urgency in Carleton's order, as Bergmann was told to leave at once with the cavalry and allow the infantry to catch up later. He was reminded to "take a good supply of ammunition and be prompt."[47]

One specific piece of correspondence makes it obvious that Major Bergmann occasionally found his commander's orders very frustrating. He was somewhat defensive in his response to Carleton's directive to take personal command of the scout around Mesa Rica. Clearly Carleton's orders stemmed from accusations that Bergmann was ignoring the pleas of local citizens for protection. Bergmann explained to his commander that on numerous occasions he had responded to the "almost daily" reports of outrages by sending scouts, but they had never found a trace of the supposed pillagers. The major informed Carleton that in recent weeks he had come to the conclusion that many of the reports that crossed his desk were "invented." He contended that such inventions were a part of a larger plan to distract him from illegal traders who continued to slip down the Canadian River toward the Llano Estacado. Certainly this would have been in keeping with Colonel Carson's belief that the Comancheros, possibly some of these very ranchers reporting Indian sightings to Bergmann, were in fact working in conjunction with the supposed perpetrators.[48]

In August 1865 several volunteer cavalrymen from Fort Bascom escorted a herd of cattle to the newly established Camp Nichols in Indian Territory, which was located in the same general area along the Cimarron route where Captain Bergmann and his soldiers had patrolled the previous year. Captain Hubbell and twenty troopers protected the herd as they journeyed across some of the most desolate land in New Mexico Territory. Traveling in the dead of summer, several of the pack mules that hauled the soldiers' supplies died along this stretch of the trail. Even the most mundane duties became complicated and difficult in this region.[49]

While Bergmann defended his reluctance to send patrols to chase after what he perceived to be disingenuous claims, occasional events reminded everyone in the army why they were posted in the Canadian and Pecos River Valleys. In May 1866 a report noted that the express man who had just left Fort Bascom with the mail did not reach his next destination, Hatch's Ranch, an old military post located near Chaperito, about seventy miles east of Bascom. Some herders from the area informed Bergmann that they had seen an unknown group of Indians waylay the carrier on "the Chaperito Road." This road followed the same trail along the Conchas River that Luis Griego had described to Surveyor General William Pelham in 1857. When Lt. Antonio Abeyta arrived back at Fort Bascom from a patrol, he delivered a different version of the attack. He informed Bergmann that the express man, whose last name was Chambers, had been attacked near Conchas Springs, "about 12 [miles] E of Hatch's Ranch." Conchas Springs was one of a number of old Comanchero rendezvous sites. Bergmann ordered Captain Hubbell to scout the region north and west of Mesa Rica for the body and the mailbag. While the post commander emphasized the importance of finding Chamber's remains, he seemed just as concerned about the mail. In correspondence with both Fort Union's quartermaster and Carleton, Bergmann expressed that he was "astonished to learn that my A. A. Q. M. has never kept a record of the waybills since he was placed in that position." The waybill was a record of all the mail Chambers carried. This was a particularly embarrassing event that indicated proper procedures were not being followed at Fort Bascom. Neither the mailman nor the mail was found. It would not be the only time questions were posed concerning proper recordkeeping at Bascom.[50]

On 25 July 1866 Major Bergmann led his last significant mission from Fort Bascom. Carleton ordered him deep into Texas to negotiate the release of several white captives. While on this mission he was to watch for livestock that had been stolen from the Bosque Redondo Reservation and Fort Sumner. Much of the impetus for the rescue mission surrounded the story of ten-year-old Rudolph Fisher of Fredericksburg, Texas. In 1860, on a raid into the Texas Hill Country, the Comanches had stolen the boy from his family. Five years later he remained in their possession, living the life of a herder. Gottlieb Fisher, the boy's father, never gave up hope of retrieving his son and sent a constant stream of requests to officials across the country. One plea went directly to President Andrew Johnson. Fisher was constantly badgering Texas and New Mexico military officials to do something. When General

Carleton received concrete information of Rudolph's whereabouts, he acted. Trader Marcus Goldbaum had seen this boy and twenty other white captives with a large band of Kwahadi Comanches "near the Texas settlements." Carleton ordered Bergmann to venture into Texas, far from his command, and attempt to negotiate their release.[51]

Bergmann rode out of Fort Bascom on 10 July 1866. He was not looking for a fight and took only eight troopers and "two citizens" with him. The lack of firepower was intentional, as the major wanted to communicate to the Comanches that he was not a threat. Goldbaum and Diego Morales were the citizens who accompanied the troopers. According to Bergmann, Goldbaum and Morales were men "who have been acquainted with these Indians for many years and who are enjoying their confidence." As traders, they were very possibly associated with Comancheros. Goldbaum had recently spoken with a young man named Rudolph while bartering goods in Texas. The fellow knew German, as did Goldbaum. When this trader returned to New Mexico, he communicated this information to Carleton, which initiated the mission. Goldbaum volunteered to accompany Bergmann, another immigrant from Prussia, back into Comanchería to seek the boy's release.[52]

This journey took Bergmann and his men across trade routes that had been in existence for generations. On their departure, they passed the Canadian River's Comanchero Trail, a route used by mountain and plains people for centuries. Moving south through a land of rolling prairies and isolated mesas, they passed the Quitaque Trail, about 50 miles from the post. To the west this path ran beyond the Tucumcari Peak until it hit the Pecos River. Here, it turned north, following the river all the way to the Sangre de Cristos. To the east, this trail eventually ended in Palo Duro Canyon. While Bergmann reported that they traveled to the southeast for about 250 miles, it is more likely that it was closer to 300. His trajectory would have led them across Río de Tierra Blanca and Agua Fría, two thin streams that followed the Las Escarbadas Trail. This Comanchero route originated fifty to seventy miles east of the Bosque Redondo Reservation, which at the time was the home of eight thousand Navajos. For generations, mountain traders had followed the Pecos River south. Some turned east where the Gallinas River joined the Pecos (west of Fort Bascom), while others continued a few miles farther south until they crossed Esteros Creek (Lt. Charles Morrison called this tributary Hurrah Creek), where they also turned eastward. Long before Fort Sumner or the reservation was established, some of the Comancheros who filed out of the villages of Las Vegas, La Cuesta, and Anton Chico stayed with the Pecos, not stopping until they reached the Bosque Redondo campsite. From Bosque Redondo, the traders' route depended on their final destination. In earlier times, they waited there until the Comanches came to them. By the 1850s the Comanches were powerful enough to demand the traders meet them closer to home. By 1866, when Bergmann left Fort Bascom, most transactions were occurring deep within the Texas.[53]

Although Bergmann's exact route is unknown, his trajectory would have led him down the last great Comanchero trail, La Pista de Vida Agua (The Trail of Living Water). This route was popular because water was almost always available. About thirty miles southeast of present-day Lubbock, the North Fork of the Double Mountain Fork of the Brazos River gouges a two-hundred-foot-deep rift below the plains, creating a five- to six-mile-wide canyon. Here was another well-known rendezvous site, Cañón del Rescate. Called Ransom Canyon by Anglos, it was a place where captives of all ethnicities were bartered—as viable a human market as any found in antebellum South Carolina. Mexicans, Anglos, African Americans, Mescalero Apaches, and Navajos were all exchanged for weapons, food, and livestock. It was possible that Bergmann would find who he was looking for within this canyon's steep yellow walls, but the distance he traveled indicates he kept riding to the southeast, deeper into Texas.[54]

Averaging approximately thirty miles per day, Bergmann and his companions began to see signs, including abandoned campsites, that confirmed they were nearing their goal. Bergmann sent Goldbaum and Morales ahead to make contact and assure the Comanches that they meant no harm. He wanted the traders to arrange a meeting between himself and their leaders. Yet the Comanches and Kiowas were skeptical. They feared that Bergmann's group could be the advance guard of a much larger force, similar to the one Carson had brought into the Texas Panhandle in 1864. Goldbaum and Morales returned empty-handed, but on 31 July the expedition stumbled onto two Hispanics who were working for the Indians as spies. Bergmann convinced or forced these men to show him where the village was.[55]

Now around 250 miles from Fort Bascom, the eight New Mexico cavalrymen and two citizen traders made their final approach toward a very large Southern Plains Indian community. Their route put them somewhere between Muchaque and present-day Jayton, Texas, on the eastern edge of the Llano Estacado. Both of these locations were well-known Comanche/Comanchero rendezvous sites. The major's report to Carleton contains an additional clue as to their location. He noted that the Comanches were "very close to the Texas settlements." In 1866 a 250-mile journey would have landed him about 100 miles from such settlements.[56]

At this point the troopers knew they were being followed. At first isolated scouts were seen on the horizon, yet after a while the soldiers spotted Indians "at elevated points in [on] the prairie." Bergmann was not dissuaded and continued on the course the two Hispanics indicated. An advance team of Indians finally approached, a verification that Bergmann was headed in the right direction. The major later recalled that as soon as he informed them of his intentions, this information, as well as how many were in his party, was quickly delivered back to the village, about twelve miles away, via an "ingenious" method of signals and relays. Bergmann likened the speed of the reply to that of a telegraphic message. "Bring them in," it began. "You are welcome."

Bergmann counted 160 lodges on the ride into this village, which was located on what he called the "Arroyo de Nuez." As noted, the major had been unable to accompany Colonel Carson on his expedition in 1864 because he had just returned from an extended mission in Indian Territory. In August 1866, under completely different circumstances, he became one of the few, if not the only, U.S. Army officers to ride into the heart of a Comanche stronghold while hostilities remained at a boil. His report of his experiences provides a glimpse into a world that few Americans ever lived to describe.[57]

Rage was the word Bergmann used to describe the emotions emanating from the people he passed when riding into the village. All the men were well armed, carrying pistols, rifles, and plenty of ammunition: "All of these Indians are splendidly mounted and well provided (by the traders) with arms. I have seen not one Indian without a revolver, [a] great many were even armed with two of them and all of them handle this formidable weapon admirably." At other places in the report he called them "savages," but later explained that he understood why they were so angry. Bergmann wrote of a recently broken "flag of truce." This could have been a reference to the Sand Creek Massacre or to

Carleton's refusal to seek a peace with the Comanches both prior to and after Carson's expedition. Bergmann explained that the Indians felt disrespected and were exacting revenge upon the perpetrators of this broken truce. Such animosity confirms the level of interconnectedness the Southern Plains Indians felt with one another and the extent to which Chivington's and Carson's strikes were on their minds. Despite this animosity, his characterizations of the people he found there were both complimentary and disparaging. Kiowas, Comanches, and Hispanos populated the village. He made a point of reserving his most negative comments for the Hispanos he saw there:

> These vagabonds are very dangerous and by far worse than the real Indians. Some of them, partly acquainted with the English language[,] are constantly employed as decoys and spies and it are [sic] these wretches who understand so well [how] to throw travelers off their guards. They delight in narrating their outrages and triumphantly show how they betrayed and entrapped and then afterwards butchered poor white men, who were foolish enough to believe these monsters.[58]

Bergmann was met by five chiefs: three Comanches and two Kiowas. For the next two days he attempted to negotiate the release of Rudolph Fisher and several other white children. Comanche Chief Quajipe led the discussions for both tribes. Comanches Sheerkenakwaugh and Paruaquahip, as well as Kiowas Toche and Pi-ti-tis-che, also took part. In his report to headquarters, Bergmann reminded Carleton that he had met Sheerkenakwaugh at Fort Bascom in May of 1865. This was probably the future meeting between Carleton and a Comanche chief that he was referring to in his correspondence to Col. Carson after the first Battle of Adobe Walls.[59]

The major offered money, supplies, horses, and mules for the return of Fisher and the other captives, to no avail. On 2 August, he gave up. Bitter and disgusted, as he prepared to leave he contemplated taking them by force, yet he knew such an attempt was little more than suicide. He related to Carleton that in his negotiations, he had first tried kindness. When kindness did not work, he resorted to threats. Neither worked. He likened the negotiations to talking to "blocks of granite." Bergmann described the chiefs as a cocky lot, men who did not seem to care one way or another about what the army did. The Indians were confident that they could repulse any attack, just as they had on the Canadian River. In fact, they informed Bergmann that the U.S. Army needed to prepare for future operations in New Mexico, because they had already robbed the Texans of anything of value and it was time to look to the northwest.[60]

Finally, Bergmann's quest to locate a large cache of stolen New Mexico horses and mules also bore no fruit. He did find five animals that belonged to Fort Sumner, and he took them back to their owners. While the mission was not a success, the journey these ten men had undertaken required equal amounts of courage and fortitude, not uncommon traits of New Mexico volunteer soldiers. Their efforts seldom garnered more than a sentence or a footnote in the histories of the region. When assessing how the United States ultimately exerted control over the Southwest, the historian should reflect on the subtle influence Bergmann's foray into Comanchería had on future military strategy and operations. Knowledge gained by the volunteers was passed along to officers in the regular army. Their official reports detailing distances to water holes, available forage, and the size and temperament of the enemy would all be used by the soldiers who served after them.[61]

Major Bergmann left Fort Bascom for the last time in an official capacity just eleven days after he had returned from this mission. General Sherman's push to replace the volunteer forces with regular army units was almost complete. On 22 August 1866, 141 New Mexico volunteers followed Bergman to Fort Union and mustered out. The new regular army units would soon discover what the volunteers had long known. Experiences gained in the conflict between the Union and Confederate armies in Virginia or Missouri had little value in New Mexico Territory, where the mission was not so straightforward. Loyalties among locals regarding stopping the Comanchero trade and defeating the Comanches were ambiguous at best. Defeating an enemy in their homeland, when the invaders perceived that there was a lack of water or proper forage within that homeland, made becoming familiar with New Mexico's climate and geography vital to military strategy. Such circumstances, where the distances between streams were so important, created the perception of isolation and emptiness for many of the eastern soldiers posted to Fort Bascom. Like Sherman, some considered the Canadian River Valley of New Mexico an awful country. Yet the Indians of Llano Estacado did not believe their homeland was isolated, empty, or awful. Southern Plains Indians were current on events in the Texas Panhandle, the Sangre de Cristo Mountains, the plains of Kansas, and Colorado Territory. Information flowed east and west along Comanchero trails and north and south down the Pecos River and the northern portion of the Canadian River. Bergmann knew this, and the regular army would soon learn it. In the process, they would often rely on the experiences of the volunteer soldiers stationed at Fort Bascom from 1863 to 1866.

CHAPTER 6

Between Comancheros
and Comanchería

In 1866 Major Generals William T. Sherman and Philip Sheridan knew more about prosecuting war than anyone west of the Mississippi River, yet this knowledge was acquired against enemies in gray who spoke the same language, often read the same newspapers, and, to a certain degree, possessed the same worldviews. They would use the same techniques that defeated the Confederates to subdue the Southern Plains Indians, but victory would take twice as long. One reason was that defining the enemy was more complicated on the southern plains. The twenty-year-old privates from Kentucky and Indiana who manned the frontier forts had difficulty understanding the complicated alliances that often existed between the U.S. government and local populations. At times the Comanches were to be treated as friends, while escaping Navajo men were to be shot on sight. At other times any Comanche was to be shot if he attacked a Navajo who lived at the Bosque Redondo Reservation. The Navajos hated the reservation and were constantly escaping, closing the circle. To add to the confusion, Pueblo and Hispano traders who participated in the Comanchero trade often dressed and looked like Comanches. This chapter details the regular army's insertion into the Canadian River Valley, illustrates its impact on the region, and reveals how some of its first officers came to grips with Brig. Gen. James H. Carleton's shoot-to-kill orders. It also explores the deeps roots this black market economy had in the region and details how its pull enticed ex-military officers from Fort Bascom and elsewhere to participate. Finally, this chapter looks at the role this post's soldiers played in prosecuting the War Department's strategy to subdue the Comanches and Kiowas who were raiding in Texas between 1866 and 1868.

The regular army took command of Fort Bascom in the last week of August 1866. General Sherman believed these soldiers were better fit to serve on the frontier than the volunteers because they had less history with the Southern Plains Indians. That was certainly true of the regiment that replaced Bergmann's men, the Fifty-Seventh U.S. Colored Infantry. Not long after they arrived, Lt. Col. Silas M. Hunter led thirty of these soldiers about sixty miles east to extract salt from a dry lake bed. After about a week of laboring in the August sun, they loaded eleven thousand pounds of salt onto their wagons and hauled it back to the post. They also performed the normal scouts and fatigue duty while stationed there. Sherman argued that the insertion of soldiers who did not hold personal grudges against the Comanches and Kiowas for past injustices, nor the Indians against the newcomers, automatically eliminated tension in the region. Under the command of Lieutenant Colonel Hunter, three companies of the Fifty-Seventh remained at the post through September.[1]

In October, they were replaced by Capt. William Hawley and Company A, Third U.S. Cavalry. Captain Hawley and his troopers were immediately busy chasing down the stream of Navajos who failed to appreciate the Bosque Redondo Reservation in the manner General Carleton envisioned. Instead, they rode into the path of Hawley's patrols, stealing ranchers' livestock along the way. Company A engaged these escapees in firefights, yet the captain was never satisfied with the results, as more often than not the Navajos eluded capture. Many of Hawley's reports noted that the Navajos were disappearing across a large mesa to his west. In correspondence that must have seemed all-too-familiar to Carleton, Hawley explained that his attempts to apprehend these Indians had failed because of the "impassable nature" of Mesa Rica. Yet Carleton must have wondered if Mesa Rica was so "impassable," how did the Navajos manage to use it so effectively as an escape route?[2]

At the bottom of one such report, Hawley brought up the order to shoot any adult male Navajo found off the reservation. While this directive might have become a matter of course for the New Mexican volunteers, it was a new concept for the regular army. Hawley related to Carleton that when he arrived at the post he was informed of this order, but he could not find anything in writing. Probably as much to cover

Map 3. Many of the military roads that connected Fort Bascom to the rest of New Mexico Territory were originally trails that had tied mountain and plains cultures together for centuries. Copyright © 2016 The University of Oklahoma Press, Publishing Division of the University. All rights reserved.

himself as any desire for clarification, the captain requested such a document. The department commander replied by special express to Hawley and to Maj. George Sykes, commander of Fort Sumner. Sykes was to make the Navajos at Bosque Redondo aware of this message. It read, in part: "The Commanding officer at Fort Bascom will destroy every Navajoe [*sic*] man able to bear arms [who leaves the reservation without a pass]."[3]

Post command and personnel changed again over November and December 1866. These changes included posting black soldiers to Fort Bascom for the second time. Lt. George Letterman and Company K, 125th U.S. Colored Infantry, joined the Third Cavalry at Bascom in November. Lieutenant Letterman and his soldiers remained at the post for a little over a year. In late December, Maj. Andrew Alexander—slated to become commander of the Ninth U.S. Cavalry—and Company G of the Third Cavalry joined the garrison. In December, eleven recruits from the Tenth Cavalry also arrived at the post, as did a few more in January. They remained until April, being outfitted, armed, and trained in frontier tactics before being sent back to Fort Leavenworth where they rejoined their regiment. Alexander relieved Captain Hawley, becoming the third post commander since Maj. Edward H. Bergmann's departure in August 1866. Incoming officers continued to seek clarification regarding shoot-on-sight orders.[4]

Carleton ordered his new commander to patrol the Eroded Plains from Fort Bascom to Fort Sumner, ninety miles to the southwest. Just before he left to do so, Alexander informed Major Sykes of his intentions. He also explained to Sykes that "My instructions . . . [are to] . . . kill every Indian [Navajo] capable of bearing arms." The Comanches were to be informed of these instructions so they would remain clear of the area. With perhaps a touch of irony, Alexander told Sykes that he was to warn these Indians that the Navajos were under his protection. Yet this protection evaporated if these same Navajos strayed from the reservation, in which case they would be shot. The next day, Alexander sent a similar letter to Charles M. Hubbell, a retired New Mexico volunteer whom Captain Letterman had recently employed as both a "guide and spy." Hubbell had served at Fort Bascom under Captain Bergmann. Like many veterans, he established a cattle ranch after he left the army. His ranch lay about fifty miles southwest of Fort Bascom. In addition to making extra money as a guide, Hubbell quickly established a business relationship with federal forces that allowed him to sell beef to the post. Alexander admitted to Hubbell that his men, new to the area, could not tell a Comanche from a Navajo. He told Hubbell to warn the Comanches to keep their distance. The new post commander did not want an accidental shooting of a Comanche to lead to new outbreak of hostilities. A newcomer such as Alexander was probably a little confused as to frontier subtleties regarding gaining control of the region. On 7 January 1867 he left on his first patrol across the region.[5]

Alexander first rode to Hubbell's Ranch, coincidently (or not) located near Comanche Springs, an old Comanchero campground. This campground was situated about halfway between Fort Bascom and Fort Sumner. After bivouacking there for the night, he divided his men into two units. He sent Lt. Lambert L. Mulford of the Third Cavalry with half the troopers west toward Alamogordo Creek, located about twenty miles north of Fort Sumner. The major headed east with the rest of the troopers, scouting the high plains along the Texas border. He noted that cattle had recently moved through the area, heading west. After circling back toward New Mexico, Alexander's group struck a fresh Indian trail. They pursued it until they found a small band of Navajos led by Chief Manuelito. Alexander fired his pistol in the air to get the Indians to stop. When it had the opposite effect, the cavalrymen raced across the valley in pursuit. At one point during the chase the Navajos set the prairie grass on fire. This created a formidable screen that Alexander and his men had to ride through. Manuelito's tactic worked. The major reported that the Indians disappeared into a "deep rock arroyo." He searched this defile and the surrounding countryside but could not find them. Lieutenant Mulford's group had even less success. Despite being accompanied by the post guide (whom Alexander later characterized as worthless), they got lost on their way to Alamogordo Creek and wandered across the Eroded Plains without water for fifty-two hours.[6]

Major Alexander refused to give up. While camped near the arroyo where he had lost Manuelito's trail, he came up with a plan that revealed his true feelings toward Carleton's shoot-to-kill policy. He sent a friendly Navajo in the chief's direction, wanting him to innocently leak the information to this group that all males who had escaped the reservation faced death if they were caught. Once he was sure they had this information, he allowed them to escape, certain they would return to the Bosque Redondo on their own. With the soldiers literally turning their backs, these Navajos did return to the reservation. In this manner Alexander ensured Carleton's harsh order was distributed among the escapees without having to kill anyone.[7]

The major's first patrol out of Fort Bascom was important for several reasons. Alexander established the regular army's presence in the Canadian River Valley. He also connected his command with Fort Sumner's.

Additionally, his discovery of the cattle trail that linked Texas to New Mexico revealed the vitality of this illegal barter. Hearing about the trade was different than experiencing it firsthand and having to grasp the difficulty of enforcing the law across such an immense territory. During this same scout, Alexander and his men came across several groups of Pueblo "Indian Traders," all with passes signed by their agent, John D. Henderson. In Alexander's report to his superiors, he asked what he was supposed do about them.[8]

Clearly the War Department paid particular attention to Major Alexander's correspondence. This was surely due his personal ties with Generals Ulysses S. Grant, Sherman, and Philip Sheridan. After the war, the army was reorganized, and the Department of New Mexico became the District of New Mexico and fell under the jurisdiction of the Military Division of the Missouri, which was first commanded by Sherman. Not long after Alexander's report of his scout reached Sherman at Fort Leavenworth, Kansas, the division commander recommended that all civilians who wished to trade with the Southern Plains Indians report to Fort Bascom on their way to the plains. General Carleton, the District of New Mexico's commander, explained to Sherman that he did not have the manpower to enforce such an edict, and even if he did, he had little faith in the willingness of New Mexican courts to prosecute anyone who refused to follow it.[9]

Here again Alexander's presence in New Mexico elicited new information, this time in Carleton's response to Sherman's suggestion on how to deal with traders. The top commanders within the War Department would have found the response interesting on two levels. First, Carleton seemed to lack interest in any serious attempt to stop the trade. If that was the case, was he really the man the army wanted running the District of New Mexico? Second, did Carleton's explanation as to why he made such a comment point the War Department toward a larger problem? If it was true that the territorial courts in New Mexico were not prosecuting illegal traders, what did that say about the trade in general? It had taken a couple of years after the Civil War for the U.S. Army to refocus its attention on the Southern Plains Indians. Carleton's response illustrated that there was more to the "Indian problem" than just rounding up defiant Comanches. Illegal trade connected Indians and American citizens, whether those citizens were Hispano or Anglo. American Indians such as the Puebloan people were also connected to this economic activity. If the territorial court system would not prosecute lawbreakers, a deeper and more systemic problem, one that involved more than trading liquor for cattle, lay at the root of the Comanchero trade. Borderlands by their very nature are economic hotspots. Within those hotspots, regardless of their location, black market economies thrive. When a borderland connects two disparate cultures that are in conflict, such markets act as profit centers and as sources of funds for resistance movements. The illegal trade that Alexander stumbled upon was doing both.[10]

After Grant dispatched Alexander to inspect the rest of the posts in the territory, interesting revelations concerning this trade began to come to light. On 18 April 1867 Captain Letterman, 125th Colored Infantry, was in command of Fort Bascom when some of the post's cattle were stolen. A fresh trail was found and Letterman ordered Lt. John D. Lee, Third Cavalry, and six troopers from Company E to pursue. After tracking the absconded herd for about forty miles, the soldiers found the rustlers about eight miles west of Hubbell's Ranch. After spotting Lieutenant Lee and his men, the thieves fled. Sam Smith, one of Hubbell's hired hands, informed Lieutenant Lee that Hubbell had "arrived a short time previous and immediately left." Captain Letterman made clear in his report to headquarters that Hubbell was his prime suspect. Subsequent reports reveal the military believed this man was trading weapons and whiskey for stolen livestock. As it turned out, Hubbell—veteran of the New Mexico Volunteer Cavalry, spy, guide, and rancher—was not only selling the army cattle from Texas but their own cattle as well. Not surprisingly, Hubbell never returned. Alexander realized that his ranch, located at an old Comanchero camp, was a good location to establish a permanent picket detail. The army took over the abandoned ranch.[11]

Evidence that incriminated ex-soldiers in the Comanchero trade, when coupled with the territorial courts' unwillingness to prosecute illegal traders, illustrates just how systemic and deep-seated this black market economy was. Pekka Hämäläinen's eloquent portrayal of Comanche dominance in the region notes the participation of the New Mexican traders in this illegal market, but he barely touches upon the Comancheros' impact. Bartering for agricultural and manufactured products was legal and ongoing, which made stopping illegal transactions more difficult. It was almost impossible for the pickets stationed along the Fort Smith road (the main highway between the Llano Estacado and the Sangre de Cristos) to ensure only authorized traders used it. Like Carleton and Carson, Alexander protested that far too many permits were being issued. The War Department sought help from the Office of Indian Affairs, complaining that too many Indians from the Rio Grande Pueblo communities were also getting passes. Finally, the superintendent of Indian affairs in New Mexico, A. B. Norton, was ordered to stop giving passes to the Puebloans. He responded by pointing out that General Carleton had been freely handing out passes of his own to Hispano traders. Superintendent Norton explained that if Washington officials were serious about stopping illegal trade, the District of New Mexico's commander needed to stop issuing passes as well.[12]

In the midst of these evolving concerns, in July 1867 General Carleton was removed from command. Early on, the Bosque Redondo disaster reflected badly on his skills as a department commander. After the war, he had been slow to muster out the volunteers, and he seemed reluctant to listen to new ideas regarding how best to address the Comanchero problem. During the war, no such accusations were made because Carleton was constantly issuing orders to halt the trade. It is true that during the war his superiors gave him free rein, and that was not the case in 1867. It is possible that Carleton was dragging his feet because he resented Sherman and Sheridan's interference. But Carleton believed Major Alexander's damning report on the conditions of the frontier posts was behind his removal. He defended himself, noting the lack of funds, manpower, and resources as the culprits behind the disrepair and reported neglect. Whether Alexander's report was the sole cause or just a convenient excuse is unknown, but in July 1867, Col. George Washington Getty became the new commander of the District of New Mexico.[13]

Southwestern Indians were oblivious to such changes. Like Anglo-Americans, they continued to seek out their best opportunity to improve their lives. Sometimes that meant stealing livestock that they could use or trade for something better. On 30 August, about ten miles east of Fort Bascom, where Ute Creek joins the Canadian, a hay-cutting crew employed by William Stapp and Charles Hopkins was attacked by Indian raiders. Although the men were not hurt, four mules and one horse were stolen. Captain Letterman received this information about noon on

31 August. He immediately ordered ten men of Company E, Third
Cavalry, into the field with six days' rations. They arrived at the hay
camp that evening. Charles Hopkins believed the marauders had about
a twenty-six-hour head start. The next morning, accompanied by Hopkins and a guide, the cavalry gave chase, following tracks northeast
over a "high sandy prairie," a feat that could have killed their horses
and surely tested every man's stamina. With good reason, as the landscape they were traversing had been depicted by many easterners as
the "Great American Desert."[14]

They stopped after finding an abandoned campsite. They were sure
it had been used the night before by the Indians they were chasing.
The next day they rode an additional twenty-five miles, noting at the
end of the day the remains of a recently cooked antelope. The following morning they continued northeast, toward a large round-topped
mountain that appeared on the horizon. Rabbit Ear Mountain, or
Rabbit Ears, loomed over the nearby Santa Fe Trail and was one of
the few landmarks travelers used to determine their location after
leaving Lower Cimarron Spring. The soldiers rode another eight miles,
following a fresh trail down into a canyon described as near the "junction of Rabbit Ear and Beaver Creeks." This was a known hideout,
where raiders often waited for the next merchant caravan. The troopers
trapped the Indians in the canyon, forcing them to abandon the stolen
livestock and escape on foot. Although the perpetrators got away, the
soldiers, Hopkins, and the guide returned to Fort Bascom with the
stolen stock.[15]

Such an event illustrates how seriously these men took their jobs.
As soon as Letterman was informed of the theft, he issued orders to
apprehend the culprits. Although the captain did not receive this message until noon, the Third Cavalry was on the scene of the crime by
late evening, interviewing the victims and preparing a strategy. Even
though the raiders had more than a day's head start, the troopers were
determined to catch them, and drove their mounts quickly across the
llano to do just that. Within three days, after traveling about one hundred miles, they retrieved Stapp and Hopkins's four mules and one
horse and returned to their post.

Colonel Getty's ascension to the command of the District of New
Mexico was but one of many changes that would impact the Comanchero trade, and thus Fort Bascom's operations, during this period.

Change can usher in renewed vigor and positive results, but it can also bring confusion. In 1866, about the same time the New Mexico volunteers began to muster out, the superintendent of the Department of Indian Affairs in New Mexico, Felipe Delgado, was replaced by Norton. Norton ordered the Pueblo Indians to stop trading in Texas, as well as with other New Mexicans. The military also stopped issuing passes. These changes created an opening for Anglo-American traders, at least for a while.[16]

Anglo-American civilian traders were not new to the Eroded Plains or the Texas Panhandle, but the insertion of a military post along the Canadian River altered trade dynamics, at least for a while. Situated between the Comanches and the Comancheros, soldiers were keenly aware of the large volume of goods that flowed east and west along the Comanchero trails. Exploring how some of the District of New Mexico's officers, including some who served at Fort Bascom, tried to insert themselves into this trade illustrates just how enticing it could be. Thirty years after the fact, one such trader, José Piedad Tafoya, claimed that Maj. Edward Bergmann hired him to trade with the Indians in 1864. It was true that Bergmann kept a ranch about four miles south of the post, and he did sell cattle to the U.S. Army for a short period of time. It is also true that he applied to Commissioner of Indian Affairs Nathaniel G. Taylor for a license in 1868, yet no contemporary account verifies that the government granted his request. Possibly, he was a silent partner in John Watts and William V. B. Wardwell's earlier attempt to establish a store near Fort Bascom, since he loaned Watts money to build it. That failed enterprise might have prompted him to try one of his own two years later. Whatever plans he may have had regarding trading with the Indians, legitimate or otherwise, they would have been short-lived because by 1870 Bergmann was working in Colfax County, New Mexico, running Lucien Maxwell's mining operation.[17]

Captain Bergmann was not the only soldier who had dealings with Tafoya. A longtime resident of Gallinas Spring, this Comanchero's name is sprinkled throughout the historical record of postwar San Miguel County. He knew several officers for a variety of reasons, from doing business with them to acting as translator, scout, and guide for the army. One particular instance illustrates his value to the U.S. Army's Department of New Mexico. Oddly enough, it begins in 1864 with Tafoya serving time in the Fort Sumner stockade for absconding with a pair of military boots. When post commander H. B. Bristol learned that a band of Indians were approaching the fort, he felt compelled to release Tafoya before he had served out his sentence. He explained to headquarters: "I could not find nobody who could speak the Comanche language but him, and sent him with the party, in order that should the Comanches be met, and be friendly, he would interpret." Tafoya's knowledge of the Eroded Plains and the Llano Estacado, when coupled with his Southern Plains Indian contacts, made him uniquely suited to act as a middle-man between the United States and Comanchería.[18]

The records do show that Major Bergmann did act when he unearthed a fellow officer's scheme to trade government property for profit. In March 1866 he ordered Capt. Charles Deus and Company M, First New Mexico Cavalry, veterans of the Battle of Adobe Walls, to escort a supply train back "to the states." In this case the state was Fort Larned, Kansas. Bergmann directed Captain Deus to box up and label supplies the company would not be taking with it. He also ordered Deus to create a list of those goods. Once Deus was on his way, Bergmann compared the list with materials stored in the boxes and found that several old rifles were missing. During an inquiry into the matter, Deus and his sergeant, A. W. Branch, claimed the guns had been stolen. In a letter to headquarters, Bergmann was clearly disgusted with Deus. As far as he was concerned, Deus was probably trading the rifles for profit.[19]

As noted above, once the government began to restrict Hispano and Pueblo passes to trade with the Comanches and Kiowas, a small group of officers who had just mustered out saw an opportunity to profit by filling the void. Prior to mustering out, one of these men, Capt. Patrick Healy of the First New Mexico Infantry, was a member of Fort Bascom's Council of Administration. This council broke down the costs of supplies for the post on a per-man basis. In January 1866 this group also included post quartermaster Lt. Charles T. Jennings and the soon-to-be infamous Capt. Charles M. Hubbell. As an example, the council determined that the cost for flour in January, as recorded by Captain Healy, was fourteen cents per man. The council also determined that the cumulative average cost for all goods purchased for the post in January was ten cents per man. In this manner these officers kept track of the cost of doing business on the frontier with the contractors who supplied goods to the military. After mustering out of the volunteers in August 1866, Healy and Jennings formed a partnership with two other officers, Captains Rufus C. Vose and Erastus W. Wood. They made their headquarters at Hatch's Ranch, not far from Gallinas Spring. These men had all served together at Fort Sumner in the previous year. Lieutenant Jennings's last job at this post was doing special duty "superintending Indian issues" at the Bosque Redondo. Erastus Wood was once Carleton's adjutant in Santa Fe. This Hatch's Ranch faction sought to impose a monopoly on the Indian trade.[20]

After mustering out in 1866, Healy traveled to Washington, D.C., to meet with Commissioner of Indian Affairs D. N. Cooley. His goal was to win the approval of the Washington bureaucrats. Healy convinced Cooley that cleaning up the illegal barter in New Mexico required the elimination of Hispano middlemen and the establishment of trade between Anglo-Americans and the Southern Plains Indians. Such an exchange, Healy argued, would ensure that the Comanches and Kiowas would be provided with food and clothing, not whiskey and weapons. Additionally, if he and his partners were in charge of the trade, the flow of stolen livestock would cease, because he would not accept contraband in any form for his goods. Cooley was certainly looking for a new way to address the problem and agreed to supply Healy and his partners with trading permits.[21]

Healy returned to New Mexico believing the trade was his, yet he underestimated the entrepreneurial spirit of his main competitors, the Comancheros. At first, his trip to Washington seemed to have worked just as he had envisioned. General Carleton and superintendent A. B. Norton received messages from their superiors to stop Hispanos and Pueblo Indians from traveling to Texas. This appeared to present unbridled opportunity for Healy and his partners. Yet Puebloan and Hispano traders had seldom paid heed to authority, whether it was Spanish, Mexican, or American. To Healy's dismay, this was still the case in late 1866 and early 1867. The Puebloans managed to extract passes from their agent, John D. Henderson, and the Hispanos who lived in the Sangre de Cristo Mountains continued to slip by authorities and make their exchanges anyway. Within weeks Healy was in deep financial trouble, for not only had his scheme failed to corner the market, his competitors were flooding that same market with their own goods. Unable to compete, Healy and his partners tried to salvage their investments.[22]

While it is not clear if the four men remained partners, it is obvious that they all went into business with local Comancheros. Jennings continued to maintain his trading post at Hatch's Ranch. It was situated within the Comancheros' heartland, located southeast of San Miguel, just to the east of both La Cuesta (Villanueva) and Anton Chico, a few miles south of Chaperito, and north of Alamogordo. From Hatch's Ranch, Jennings did business with José Tafoya. Rufus C. Vose made deals with Comanchero Manuel Chávez. After coming to terms with the ex-soldiers, these Hispano traders struck deals of their own with other Hispano traders. Thus Healy, Jennings, Vose, and Wood, in an effort to unload their goods and then sit back and wait for the profits to roll in, actually sparked a new wave of illegal trading in the Canadian River Valley. Comanches and Kiowas, aware of a new influx of goods, began to round up the barter needed to make successful trades. By the time Colonel Getty replaced General Carleton in the summer of 1867, this black market economy was in full bloom across the Llano Estacado. In one instance a Fort Bascom officer reported that he had stopped "Sub. traders . . . scoundrels who succeed frequently in smuggling contraband goods." These "Sub. traders" had papers signed by Charles T. Jennings. As it turned out, Patrick Healy, who initiated this disaster, was later charged with facilitating the same illegal barter that he had promised Commissioner Cooley he would stop, if only given the chance. Getty revoked Healy's trading license on 12 September 1867, declaring that this "Indian Trader" had violated regulations by sending Hispanos into "Comanche country." Getty also ordered Healy's remaining merchandise confiscated and taken to Fort Bascom.[23]

Soldiers who served at Fort Bascom were not the only ex-army personnel or Anglo civilians to make their homes along the Pecos River. By 1860 James E. Whittemore and his family lived above the Pecos River on the Gallinas River. Juan Esteban Pino once grazed sheep in the same location. During the war, Whittemore had profited as a foraging agent for both Forts Bascom and Sumner. He was also involved in the construction work at Bascom. Preston Beck was another ex-soldier who settled in the area. After mustering out, Beck developed his own ranch on his substantial land grant farther down the Pecos. Lorenzo Labadie was not a soldier, but he was the Apache Indian agent at the Bosque Redondo Reservation for part of 1864 and 1865. Labadie owned property at Agua Negra, a few miles southwest of present-day Santa Rosa. Labadie's ranch was sixty miles north of Sumner. He lost his position as Indian agent in March 1865 after seventy-seven of the fort's oxen were found grazing very near, or on, his Agua Negra property. Oxen were generally used to haul freight. Labadie's most prominent neighbor in Agua Negra was James M. Giddings, who came to New Mexico on the heels of the U.S. Army in the late 1840s. Originally a Missouri trader, he became a Santa Fe merchant of some renown before moving to Agua Negra. He later helped to found the town of Santa Rosa.[24]

Fort Sumner was a common thread that linked many of these ex-Army officials to the region where they began to make a living as traders, mercantilists, and military contractors. Capt. Lawrence G. Murphy was at Sumner at the same time as fellow officers Vose, Woods, and Jennings. Murphy replaced Lorenzo Labadie as a special agent to the Apache Indians. He did this as an officer, not as a civilian. After mustering out, Murphy partnered with Emil Fritz in running a saloon and sutler's store near Fort Stanton. They called their enterprise L. G. Murphy and Company. By 1868 they were running a large trading post near the fort. They later operated a store and hotel in the new town of Lincoln. Fritz and Murphy purchased cattle from both the local Apaches and Anglo ranchers, not really interested in where they came from. In turn, they sold these beeves to the army. For several years what became known as the House of Murphy controlled most of the mercantile and cattle trade in Lincoln County. Such control eventually led to the Lincoln County War and the rise of Billy the Kid. Another Sumner soldier who contracted with the army after he mustered out was Samuel Gorham. With James Patterson, who sold many cattle to Fort Bascom, Gorham supplied two ox-drawn trains of ten wagons each, full of forage, to Maj. Andrew W. Evans's 1868 expedition down the Canadian. [25]

The last ex-officer from Fort Sumner to find a home on the Pecos was Capt. William P. Calloway. Like Jennings, Vose, Wood, Murphy, and Fritz, he came to New Mexico with the California Column. Calloway was instrumental in creating the Bosque Redondo Indian Reservation. As thousands of Navajos filed into their new home, he helped organize the first camps. He supervised the planting of the first crops and also took the lead in the construction of their homes. General Carleton thought so much of Calloway's work that he requested that headquarters continue to utilize him in this capacity after he mustered out in 1864. Civilian Calloway remained superintendent of the Indian farm at Fort Sumner for another year.[26]

Before Captain Calloway mustered out and Apache agent Labadie was forced out, they were involved in an expedition up the Pecos in pursuit of about one hundred Navajos who had escaped with part of an Apache horse herd. A major battle took place about thirty-five miles north of the fort that involved a contingent of vengeful Apaches, two companies of infantry and one of cavalry, and Gallinas Crossing rancher and forage agent James Whittemore. Approximately sixty-five Navajos were killed or wounded in this battle. Many of the horses were eventually retrieved. While Calloway was not involved in the firefights that occurred along the Pecos, it is interesting to note that along with Whittemore and Labadie, he decided to settle along the Pecos River, about a day's ride north of the main battlefield.[27]

Like Labadie, Calloway found land to his liking north of Fort Sumner on José Leandro Perea's old land grant. Government documents also call this grant Rancho de los Esteros. He built his house near the junction of two old Comanchero routes. As noted above, Esteros Creek was a tributary that fed the Pecos. Despite its seemingly desolate location, Los Esteros was situated along a well-traveled route with good water, amidst some old ruins. While little is known of Calloway's activities, we do know he purchased hotel, retail, and liquor licenses for Los Esteros two months before he mustered out of the service, and he maintained those licenses while he was managing the Indian farm at Fort Sumner as a civilian. Calloway and Emil Fritz, captains in the California Column, served together at Forts Union and Sumner. Fritz, as a partner in L. G. Murphy and Company, could have been a business mentor of Calloway's. In December 1868 the Santa Fe *Daily New Mexican* informed its readers that Fritz and Calloway were visiting the town of Las Vegas together. Los Esteros, Gallinas Crossing, Anton Chico, and Hatch's Ranch were all within a day's ride of each other. According to the 1870 census, José Piedad Tafoya also lived nearby. Such information entices the historian to make a connection between the ex-army officers and the Comanchero. Unsubstantiated claims, described as "folk tales" by one historian, noted that Calloway might have been involved in a "horse stealing ring." Despite such rumors, no evidence links Tafoya's Comanchero activities to Calloway. The same could not be said for Charles Jennings. While certain business relationships, whether legal or not, did develop between Anglos and Hispanos along and between the Canadian and Pecos Rivers, there is also evidence that continued Anglo-American encroachment made relations between the two worse.[28]

If some of these veterans were not engaged in the liquor, cattle, or retail trades before they mustered out, they certainly were shortly thereafter. Tax records from the period indicate that some sought to elevate their income through legitimate, although perhaps questionable, sources. Lt. Col. Francisco P. Abreu commanded Fort Bascom for a part of 1864, the same year he purchased licenses to sell liquor and operate an express station, or mail-carrying business, from Chaperito. Similarly, Col. Oscar M. Brown, post commander of Fort Sumner, purchased the same type of licenses for the same year. His address on these licenses was Fort Sumner. The ever enterprising John Watts, politician, lawyer, would-be-sutler, and cattle rancher, maintained a liquor license in 1864 just outside of Fort Bascom, undoubtedly selling spirits through Stapp and Hopkins's establishment. Studying the records of the period reveals that several ex-military officials took out liquor licenses at seemingly every stop between Las Vegas and Fort Sumner. Such an infiltration into what had previously been the domain of an entrenched group of New Mexican merchants provided conditions conducive to conflict.[29]

William Calloway did not become a successful Los Esteros merchant because he was forced to leave the territory in early 1869. After two Anglo cowpunchers were found bashed in the head and dead south of Fort Sumner, a posse of sorts, led by Calloway, focused its suspicions on several Hispanos who lived around Anton Chico. According to a letter published in the *Santa Fe Daily New Mexican,* Calloway, Dick Fowler, H. M. Hillburn, ex–Texas Ranger Sam Gholsen, and others, most originally from Texas, rounded up several of these Hispanos, took them to the plaza at Los Esteros, and executed them. Shortly thereafter Calloway abandoned his business establishment on the Pecos and left New Mexico Territory for good. A committee of concerned San Miguel County citizens, including Lorenzo Labadie, Manuel Chávez, and José Silva, published a detailed letter in the same newspaper that named the vigilantes and described what they had done. It is at least possible that some of the victims were associated with the Comanchero trade. One of the members of the committee, Manuel Chávez, was a well-known Comanchero who did business with R. C. Vose at Hatch's

Ranch. Certainly such an event would have had a psychological impact
on people living up and down the Pecos River. There is no documen-
tation linking these deaths with an upsurge in the Comanchero trade,
yet such events had to negatively color relationships between the
soldiers still posted to the frontier and the traders they were charged
with apprehending.[30]

Throughout the late 1860s, Comancheros often made it clear that
they saw Fort Bascom not just as a hindrance to their livelihoods, but
also as a place of opportunity. After the garrison was "raided . . . by
some Mexicans" in August 1867, Capt. John V. D. Dubois sent Sgt.
Charles Brown of the Third Cavalry and seventeen troopers from Company E in pursuit. Sixty miles east of the fort, Brown apprehended
six Hispano Comancheros leading eleven donkeys loaded with goods
toward the Llano Estacado. Although not the perpetrators that Sergeant
Brown had been ordered to capture, they were clearly in violation of
the law. The traders informed Brown that another group, farther toward
Texas, had their passes. The eleven pack mules were carrying

> [a]bout 200 pounds of corn meal, 500 of Mex. hard bread, 35
> or 40 butcher knives, 9 files, Vermillion, a lot of shirts, some red
> and white flannel, one vest, some iron hoops, ticking, calico, Monte
> cans, and shelled corn, tea, sugar, flour, letter paper, candy, one
> regalia, one box of Army caps (100) about (400) percussion caps
> (small)—several pounds of lead, about 5 pounds of Powder and
> 16 Enongated [elongated] Balls Cav. Cal. 58.[31]

This itemized list illustrates the variety of goods Comancheros used
to trade for Texas cattle and horses. By the time Sergeant Brown returned
to the post, Captain Dubois had been reassigned. In his place, the
recently promoted Capt. George Letterman of the 125th Colored Infantry made the official report to headquarters. He stressed that the
Comanches were interested in more than weapons and whiskey, the
most common historical refrain concerning the Comanchero trade.
On the contrary, Indians living along the Canadian River were apparently
just as interested in purchasing dry goods, food staples, and hardware
as any American consumer in the nineteenth-century American West.
Comanches loved the hard "sweet bread" most traders packed on their

Figure 6. Capt. John V. D. Dubois, Third Cavalry. Dubois served as post commander at Fort Bascom for parts of both 1867 and 1868. *Image Courtesy Wilson's Creek National Battlefield.*

journeys east. Letterman also noted that his men were constantly stopping "several parties with trains on their way to the Comanche Country to trade."[32]

Patrick Healy and Charles Jennings thought their knowledge of the Comanchero trade would serve them well at Hatch's Ranch, yet they failed to appreciate the fact that their competitors were not easily dissuaded by law or regulations. Healy and Jennings's attempt to control the Southern Plains Indian trade remains the incident most scholars use when referencing Fort Bascom. Yet, as noted above, such shenanigans were not isolated to the men of this frontier post and remain inconsequential when viewed in context of a larger historical study. More important than the soldiers' involvement is their failure to make good on their plans to monopolize the trade, legal or illegal. Their collapse sheds light on the deeply engrained nature of Comanchero activities in the region. Healy, Jennings, Vose, and Wood were neither the first nor the last Canadian River Valley newcomers to underestimate the skill, tenacity, and power this black market economy engendered in Hispano traders.[33]

Another report from Captain Letterman reveals that Fort Bascom soldiers were still busy patrolling along the Fort Smith road during early September. Over a ten-day period, different patrols rounded up eight hundred cattle being herded into New Mexico. This stock was taken to Fort Bascom, where Letterman described a near impossible situation. He was unprepared to handle the care and feeding of so many animals that were not in the best of health. Angry Hispano herders lingered outside the fort, demanding their property be returned to them. The beleaguered captain also reported that there were many Comanches in Texas about to move north with more cattle. These same Indians were reported to have in their possession some white children and "one negro captive." Despite the frustration in his correspondence to headquarters, a month later, Letterman was ready to withdraw his pickets from the same area: "The Comanche trade has entirely ceased." He informed Getty that illegal activity on the Fort Smith road had also stopped.[34]

One possible reason for the cessation in traffic was that on 21 October 1867 the Medicine Lodge Treaties were signed in Kansas. The Indian Peace Commission, a select group of military and civilian leaders that included both General Sherman and Commissioner of Indian Affairs Nathanial Taylor, had recently concluded that the United States was to blame for most of the violence and that an equitable and fair solution to the problem should be devised. This included creating a reservation for the Comanches and Kiowas, to be located between the North Fork of the Red River and the ninety-eighth meridian. It is possible that word of this series of treaties had already spread to the Canadian River Valley, causing illegal exchanges to slow or come to a stop.[35]

Letterman's request to remove his pickets from the Fort Smith road occurred just three days after the treaty was signed. Distance had never been an impediment to Southern Plains Indians. By 24 October 1867 illegal traffic into New Mexico had ceased, at least in the Canadian River Valley, and it is possible that events in Kansas impacted such activities. Yet peace would remain fleeting because the treaty was flawed from the start. Comanche Chiefs Mowway and Tábba-quena were not present at Medicine Lodge, Kansas, indicating they were not ready to contemplate

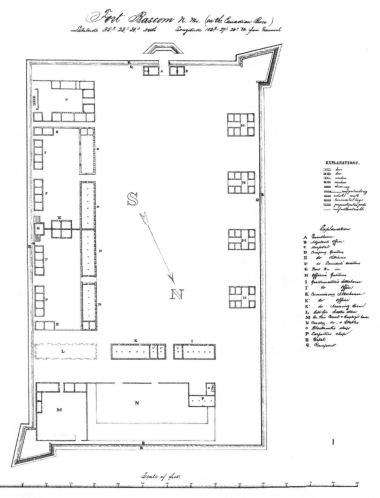

Figure 7. Fort Bascom ground plan, 1865. This plan's letter designations (looking south to north) are cross-correlated with figure 2. *Miscellaneous Fort File, Fort Bascom, sheet 1, Reservation File, Records of the Office of the Chief of Engineers, RG 77, DNM, NA, College Park, Md.*

moving to a reservation. After this agreement, approximately fifteen hundred Kotsoteka and Kwahadi Comanches still remained on the Llano Estacado. Of the agreement, Chief Mowway said, "When the Indians . . . [on the reservation] . . . are treated better than we are outside, it will be time enough to come in." Chief Tábba-quena's observation about the results of the Peace Commission's plan was even blunter. He preferred to "stay out on the prairie and eat dung" than be penned up on a reservation. Both of these men were very familiar with Fort Bascom. They had lived in the Canadian River Valley all their lives and did not plan on leaving any time soon. As a result, the year 1868 would prove to be critical in the history of this post.[36]

While officials in Washington, D.C., searched for a European-style, nineteenth-century solution to their problems with the Southern Plains Indians, such as sitting down at a table and coming to a verifiable agreement, the Indians continued to apply their own brand of negotiation, using survival skills that they had learned from their fathers and grandfathers. In late December 1867 seventeen Navajos raided Pedro Sandoval's New Mexico ranch of 150 sheep, 7 mules, and 225 sacks of flour. In early January, Comanches attacked several isolated ranches in North Texas, killing twenty-five settlers and kidnapping fourteen children. In February 1868 seven more Texas ranchers were killed, five more children were captured, and 50 horses and mules were stolen. During this period W. Fanning explained to Texas governor James W. Throckmorton that Montague County was being depopulated. Fanning cautioned Governor Throckmorton not to take any solace from statistics that indicated a drop in thefts, for there was not enough livestock in his county left to count. Even prior to 1868, the army, busy maintaining order in Reconstruction Texas, was unable or unwilling to protect the ex-Confederate ranchers who lived in Montague County. As a result, postwar Texas was devastated by raids in 1865 and 1866, when Comanches and Kiowas extracted 20,375 cattle, valued at $124,670. Of the Texans in Comanche County, H. Secrest wrote on 18 April 1867: "We cannot make a living. . . . I fear we will be compelled to give way." On 7 August of the same year, W. E. Jones of New Braunfels informed Governor E. M. Pease, "There is not safety for life or property . . . within forty or fifty miles . . . except immediately about the military posts or towns." Such ravages stretched from the heart of Texas to the farthest reaches of New Mexico, spanning approximately eight hundred miles in all directions. As the Texans were screaming for help, the army was in the process of scaling back its force. Such reductions were another reason why federal officials sought a nonviolent solution at the Medicine Lodge meetings. By mid-1867 the army was reduced to 56,815 officers and soldiers, with more cuts forthcoming. The forced reductions, when coupled with the Peace Commission's efforts, did not achieve the result distant Washington officials desired.[37]

General Sheridan became commander of the Department of the Missouri in the fall of 1867, but he did not arrive at his new headquarters until several months into 1868. Once situated at Fort Leavenworth, he began to put together a plan that would force Indians onto reservations if they refused to go on their own. As he formulated this strategy, four more Texas ranchers were killed along the Brazos River in July 1868, seeming to validate *his* decision to try a more forceful strategy. He believed that the Southern Plains Indians who remained on the Llano Estacado understood the language of violence much better than the language of peace. Sheridan was one of the Civil War's most articulate messengers of the former. In the waning days of the summer 1868, he put the final touches on the message he planned to send to Chiefs Mowway and Tábba-quena and their people. Once again, Fort Bascom would play a large role in the U.S. Army's effort to gain control of the region.[38]

Highlighting just how bold Indians who remained off the reservation could be, Capt. Louis Morris of the Thirty-Seventh U.S. Infantry and Bascom's post commander reported in early September that herders working for William Stapp and John Watts had been killed and their livestock stolen. Stapp had remained in the area after losing his sutler business. Along with partner Watts, he sold cattle to the army. Getty sent additional troops to Fort Bascom so Morris could mount a substantial operation in pursuit of the guilty parties. The reinforcements included a company of infantry and three cavalry companies. Wagons were allocated to carry supplies sufficient for two months in the field.[39]

Shortly thereafter, Sheridan formalized his plan to gain control of the southern plains. It was one that would have warmed General Carleton's heart. The commanding general's strategy called for three army columns to converge on a section of the Canadian River that was known to harbor recalcitrant Comanches and Kiowas. Such a convergence would trap them in an unbreakable vise. The operation was scheduled for the dead of winter, when a lack of forage would find the Indians' horses at their weakest. Such a plan found precedence in Carson's actions against the Navajos of Canyon de Chelly and the Comanches and Kiowas of the Canadian River Valley. Southern Plains Indians were less mobile from late November until the following spring, yet the timing of such an operation also posed significant hardships for the soldiers and animals charged with executing it. Sheridan knew this, but the tactical advantage he believed the army could gain was worth the hardships. Due to its location on the doorstep of Comanchería, Sheridan could not help but include Fort Bascom in his plans.[40]

Orders for Sheridan's 1868 winter campaign were distributed in October, not long after the raid on Stapp's ranch. Maj. Andrew W. Evans, stationed at Fort Stanton, was to lead one of the three columns from Fort Bascom. This prong of the attack would penetrate the Texas Panhandle and move toward the Antelope Hills. Comanches were known to winter in this location. A column led by Maj. Eugene A. Carr, also targeting the Antelope Hills, was to move down from Fort Lyon, Colorado Territory. These two groups were to drive any Comanches or Kiowas found in the area to the east, where they would be attacked by another column, this one first led by Lt. Col. Alfred Sully of the Third Infantry and later commanded by Col. George Armstrong Custer.[41]

Major Evans's specific mission included following the Canadian River to Adobe Walls, where Col. Kit Carson's troops had made their stand in 1864, and there to find the best location for a supply depot. Once this was established, he would conduct military operations in whichever direction he deemed prudent. The supply depot was an essential component of the mission, because just like the Indians' livestock, the army's horses would find little forage on the prairies in winter, and the soldiers could only carry so much food in their packs. Custer and Sully were also required to construct a depot and did so about one hundred miles south of Fort Dodge, Kansas. They called it Camp Supply.[42]

The second front in the U.S. Army's war against the Southern Plains Indians was opened from Fort Bascom. Evans arrived at the post on 5 November 1868. One of his first orders of business was to request that headquarters send him Colonel Carson's Canadian River Expedition report. There were several similarities between Evans's mission and Carsons's 1864 expedition. When Evans arrived at Fort Bascom, post commander Capt. Louis Morris was away on a prolonged scout with a portion of Company F, Thirty-Seventh Infantry, and three companies of the Third Cavalry. He was pursuing the Indians who had rustled Watts and Stapp's cattle. Like Carson before him, Col. Albert Hinrich Pfeiffer, stationed at Fort Garland in 1868, was ordered to Cimarron, New Mexico Territory, to convince the Utes to participate in another expedition. The army was also interested in convincing some Apaches to join the expedition. Pfeiffer's efforts were fruitful, for when Evans arrived at Fort Bascom the Utes were already at the post, outfitted, supplied, and ready to move east. That they were standing by so early became a problem. The army was far from ready and would not be for several more days. The Utes would soon become impatient. Captain Morris returned from his expedition on 9 November 1868. Evans decided that Morris and most of his troopers were too depleted to participate, just as Captain Bergmann and his men and mounts had been too worn to accompany Carson on his expedition. So, like Bergmann, Morris was charged with coordinating all supplies and logistics that would flow through Fort Bascom. Evans did select three officers from Morris's company to take part in the mission. Lieutenants Samuel Hildeburn, John K. Sullivan, and Adolph H. Luettwitz of the Thirty-Seventh Infantry were all given significant responsibilities during the expedition. By mid-November 1868 soldiers, civilians, and wagons were streaming into Fort Bascom from all directions.[43]

Fort Bascom was soon teeming with soldiers from all over the region, most of who had served at the post in some capacity in the past. Capt. James H. Gageby arrived with Company I, Thirty-Seventh Infantry, from Fort Stanton. Capt. Ezra P. Ewers led Company D of the Thirty-Seventh Infantry from Fort Sumner. Company F of the Third Cavalry, as well as some men from Company F, Thirty-Seventh Infantry, were already camped outside the post when Evans arrived. Capt. William Hawley and Company A of the Third Cavalry rode into Fort Union from Cimarron on 28 October and left the next day for Fort Bascom, accompanied by Maj. Elisha W. Tarleton and Company I of the Third Cavalry.[44]

From the beginning, Evans was concerned about having sufficient supplies. Getting quality food and forage delivered to the post on such short notice proved to be a daunting and frustrating task. Evans inspected the wagons as they rolled in from Fort Union, Fort Sumner, and local villages. At one point, he was forced to reject a wagon loaded with spoiled oats. Upon sending scouts to find out why a large delivery of bacon had not arrived, Evans found that the wagons carrying this load had broken down and the civilian teamster had off-loaded the goods on the side of the road. The major sent several army wagons to retrieve the supplies. As all manner of medical supplies, food, and forage began to arrive, Evans concluded that the thirty-one wagons he had were not going to be enough to haul the materials he needed to survive a Texas Panhandle winter. In the midst of this confusion, he got word that the Utes had disappeared. Having grown tired of waiting for the expedition to get started, they had left for their homes in the Sangre de Cristo Mountains.[45]

Evans dispatched a letter to Lucien Maxwell, whom Colonel Carson had visited when he was charged with convincing the same band of Southern Plains Indians to join his 1864 expedition. Evans told Maxwell to inform the Utes that if they wanted to partake of the huge stores of bison robes, animals, and foodstuffs that awaited them in Texas, there was still time. Despite this plea, Evans's main focus remained getting the column headed east. Assessing his situation, he determined that he needed more wagons, and he commandeered sixteen that had been hauling corn between Bascom and Fort Sumner. This brought the expedition's total to forty-seven wagons, which did not include three ambulances and a vehicle to haul the blacksmith's forge. The wayward bacon finally arrived on 17 November 1868. Evans immediately ordered everyone to prepare to move out.[46]

Fort Bascom's role in Sheridan's winter campaign began on 18 November 1868 when the column started toward Texas. Four miles to the south of Bascom, it passed Bergmann's ranch house, then, as Major Evans reported, it turned east after striking Carson's old trail. The size of the caravan, almost biblical in nature, included 442 enlisted men, 10 officers, 72 civilians, 9 scouts, 47 supply wagons, 3 ambulances, 329 horses, 27 mules, and 20 packers. Three hundred cattle were also a part of this caravan, ensuring the men a fresh supply of beef along the way. Evans's preoccupation with wagons continued. Even as he made his final plans to depart, he contracted with James Patterson for two ox trains. Obsessed with ensuring his animals would have enough to eat, these last-minute additions meant the expedition could carry a total of 93,000 pounds of corn and 64,600 pounds of oats into Comanchería. Despite the major's efforts, his planning could not account for the realities of taking hundreds of wagons, animals, men, and supplies down a nineteenth-century Indian trail in the middle of winter. Only one of Patterson's ten-wagon ox trains left with the expedition, and that one had a difficult time keeping up. The other, hauling an additional 60,000 pounds of corn, remained several days behind the main party.[47]

Evans's first goal was to establish the supply depot. Once this was accomplished, he could focus on the mission, which was to search out and destroy the Comanches' main winter haunts. Every fall, these Indians left the plains for the shelter afforded them by deep-walled canyons and secluded mountain valleys. The War Department knew this, yet it had failed to mount a major mission into Comanchería in four years. There were several good reasons why this was so. The Civil War required the Union army to remain focused on Confederates, not Comanches. After the war, there was a strong faction within the government that demanded a peaceful solution to its conflict with Southern Plains Indians. This resulted in the Peace Commission. Reduction in forces after the war also played a role. Some well-respected westerners argued that winter campaigns were just wrong-headed. When mountain man Jim Bridger heard what General Sheridan had planned, he openly voiced his objections. Bridger asked why Sheridan thought soldiers from New Jersey and Kentucky would be able to withstand the Llano Estacado winter better than its native people could. Sheridan was disturbed by this meeting but refused to change his plans. He believed his strategy was a good one, and he was determined carry it out despite the hardships he knew his men would have to endure during the campaign.[48]

Major Evans's obsession with wagons illustrates his own concerns regarding the mission. Each enlisted man carried twenty days of supplies on his person or his horse. The wagons carried an additional forty days of rations for each soldier. Fifty-five Fort Bascom troopers participated in this expedition. Most came from Company D of the Third Cavalry, but several officers from the Thirty-Seventh Infantry also took part. Lieutenant Sullivan of Bascom was put in charge of the column's four mountain howitzers and their twenty gunners. Both Lieutenants Hildeburn and Luettwitz also distinguished themselves during this mission. Many of the soldiers who came from other New Mexico posts had once served at Fort Bascom in some capacity.[49]

Four days after leaving the garrison, Bridger's warnings proved prescient. On 22 November 1868, only forty-seven miles from the post, a blizzard struck the column. The caravan had traveled through the Eroded Plains and was high atop the Llano when the storm hit. Evans kept the men moving. The only defense against the elements was a single tent for each company. Headquarters was also confined to one tent. On the morning of 26 November, Evans was informed that his animals were already running low on forage. That same day, 135 cattle and some oxen wandered off. One of the main arguments of this study is that while evolving military tactics played a crucial role in defeating the Comanches and Kiowas, it was moments of adversity such this, and how American soldiers fought through them, that best illustrate how the army finally defeated the Southern Plains Indians.[50]

Evans ordered a search party to find the cattle. He sent another to find Patterson and Gorham's second supply train, which was still somewhere behind them. The major also sent several empty wagons back to Fort Bascom for more forage. Such details delayed Evans from his objective another five days before he was able to lead the rest of the column deeper into Texas. They passed Adobe Walls, the farthest penetration Carson and his New Mexico volunteers had made in December 1864. At this point, the column angled off into the northeastern corner of the Texas Panhandle. Approximately thirty miles from the adobe ruins, they struck Wolf Creek, a Canadian tributary. The river and its creeks wound around low mountains and cut gaps in the high plains, leaving deep arroyos and canyons, a topography very familiar to Fort Bascom soldiers. It resembled the country north of the post near Corazon Mountain and Cañón Largo. Just northeast of present-day Borger, Texas, they entered a region where American Indians had been living for centuries. Here, the Ogallala Aquifer bubbled out of the ground through a broken country of canyons, small mountains, and lush valleys. Someone unfamiliar with the region might miss the spring-fed creeks entirely. The Antelope Creek focus people of the fifteenth century knew them, and four hundred years later both Comanches and Comancheros knew them, for this was a well-known rendezvous site. Somewhere in this vicinity, about twenty or so miles north of the Canadian, Major Evans ordered the construction of the supply depot. He called it Monument Creek. The expedition had only eight thousand pounds of forage left.[51]

While soldiers and civilians felled cottonwood trees and filled sandbags with dirt, he ordered his remaining wagons back to Fort Bascom for more supplies. It took about a week to build the depot. The logs were strategically placed between the sandbags to fashion an earthworks of sorts. Within these earthworks several tents were erected to house the supplies. Once this task was accomplished, Evans organized his departure with a majority of the soldiers to look for the Comanches. He left Fort Bascom's Lieutenant Luettwitz with twenty men of the Thirty-Seventh Infantry in charge of the depot.[52]

Evans and the balance of the expedition moved out on 15 December, having no idea where Carr or Custer were or what they were doing. The Fort Bascom column rode south. On 20 December it crossed the frozen North Fork of the Red River and crossed it again on Christmas Eve. Despite the bitter cold, campfires were restricted. Still moving east, the Wichita Mountains of the Indian Territory came into view. The temperatures kept dropping, at one point forcing the men to seek shelter behind a low bluff. On Christmas Day they rode through a recently abandoned campsite. At the same time, some of Evans's men alerted him that they were being followed. He ordered Major Tarleton to take Company I of the Third Cavalry and investigate. Tarleton pursued a small group of Indians into a nearby canyon.[53]

When these soldiers rode into the canyon, they carried more lethal firepower with them than had been available to Colonel Carson's volunteers. Carson's men carried muzzle-loading muskets when they squared off against the Southern Plains Indians that swarmed around them during the Battle of Abode Walls. By 1869 the army had replaced most muskets with breech-loading rifles that were easier to use and more accurate. The Sharps carbines from the Civil War were still in use, but many soldiers had replaced the rifle's larger .58 caliber barrels with more accurate .50 caliber tubes. Infantry and cavalry also carried Springfield breech loaders into battle. These rifles took center-primed metallic cartridges, which cut down on loading time and hit more targets. Despite such improvements, these frontier soldiers faced the same dangers the California and New Mexico volunteers had faced in 1864 when they traveled down the Canadian River in search of Kiowas and Comanches.[54]

Although he did not know it at the time, Major Evans and his men had just found a large Nokoni Comanche village. These Nokonis, led by Chief Horseback, were suspected of carrying out many of the attacks that had occurred in North Texas during the previous summer. Terheryaquahip (Horseback), was probably away when the army arrived. In his place, Chief Arrow Point led an attack on Tarleton and his men. Shortly thereafter, the captain sent a messenger back to the main

column for help. Evans ordered Capt. Deane Monahan and Fort
Bascom's Company G, Third Cavalry, to join the battle. A nearby band
of Kiowas led by Chief Woman's Heart also heard the shots and came
to the Comanches' aid. When Company G arrived, they found Company I heavily engaged with Indians in their front and overhead, as
many were hidden among the canyon wall's crevices. The two Third
Cavalry troops managed to inch their way forward, pushing the Comanches and Kiowas down the mouth of the North Fork of the Red River.
Evans remained on top, listening. It was clear that his men had kicked
a hornet's nest. He ordered Lieutenant Sullivan and his howitzer battery,
along with Captain Hawley and Company A, to join the battle.[55]

According to Evans's official report, about 134 soldiers, both cavalry
and infantry, were sent down into the canyon. The soldiers moved
forward, following a bend in the river around a canyon wall until the
Nokoni village came into view. Its inhabitants were in the midst of a
chaotic evacuation. Evans later estimated that this winter camp housed
approximately 500 Comanche men, women, and children. Of that
number, 150 were warriors. Evans made no mention of how many
Kiowas were also involved in this battle.[56]

After ordering Sullivan and Hawley to engage the Indians, Evans
started the rest of the column in a wide arc around the canyon, trying
to block the Indians' escape. Meanwhile, Tarleton, Hawley, and the rest
were pinned down by Comanche sharpshooters deep in the canyon
and fell back to await further orders. These officers expected Evans
to ride up and take control of the scene. By the time Tarleton's messenger rode out in search of their commander, he was already halfway
around the canyon. This pause in the battle as the soldiers awaited
help or new orders gave the Comanches just what they needed—time
to escape. Despite Evans's efforts, the women, children, and most of
the camp's horses escaped. Once that happened, the warriors silently
withdrew and melted into the Wichita Mountains.[57]

This Nokoni band was able to flee, but in the process they lost six
months of supplies, their homes, twenty of their best warriors, and
their leader, Chief Arrow Point. Evans's detailed inventory of what his
troopers found included 25,000 pounds of dried bison meat, 200 sacks
of cornmeal, 12,000 pounds of "killikinick tobacco," 150 bushels of
corn, copious amounts of sugar, numerous hatchets and axes, and

molds to form the 250 pounds of lead they found into innumerable bullets. His men ate some of the dried beef, fed the corn to their horses, and then set fire to the camp.[58]

Although the battle was over, the soldiers' war against the elements continued. They spent the next several days scouting up and down the Washita River in search of Southern Plains Indians who refused to live on the reservation. Another winter storm blew in, covering the men, their horses, and the ground with snow. On 30 December 1868, four of Sheridan's scouts found the Evans column on the Washita River. Evans had no idea that they were only twenty miles from their commander's headquarters at Fort Cobb, in what is now Caddo County, Oklahoma. He was informed that Custer had fought the Cheyennes on the same river in late November. Major Evans sent Lt. Edward Hunter back with these scouts to file his report and request an immediate resupply of food and forage. While they waited, a Private Von Cleve from Company F, Thirty-Seventh Infantry, died from wounds received in the battle. As it turned out, Fort Cobb would not be sending supplies. Hundreds of Southern Plains Indians were filing into this post to surrender. They were hungry. Sherman ordered Evans and his column to return to their depot on Monument Creek. They had been gone for two-and-a-half weeks. Sherman's decision not to resupply Evans hindered his ability to continue with his mission. On the way back, the horses began to starve. Soldiers fed them the bark from cottonwood trees during the ten days it took to get back to Monument Creek. During the month-long expedition away from the depot, 172 horses and 66 mules died from the elements, starvation, or both.[59]

During the main column's trek toward the Wichita Mountains and afterward, Lieutenant Luettwitz had remained at the depot, busily sending empty wagons back to Fort Bascom and off-loading fresh supplies at Monument Creek. Back at Fort Bascom, Captain Morris oversaw the expeditious exchange of draft animals when they returned from Texas and continued the resupply efforts from the post. He directed the proper packing of food and forage onto the empty wagons that were returned to the front. It was his responsibility to ensure that the army and its animals did not starve on the frozen prairies of Texas. The day after Evans and his men returned to Monument Creek, two wagon trains arrived from Fort Bascom with more food and forage.[60]

Evans's troops spent their last days in Texas hunkered down at the subdepot trying not to freeze to death while they awaited new orders. During this wait, the major received word that a large band of Comanches, hiding far into Texas, wanted to surrender. He had yet to get orders from Sheridan when he received this message. With each day, he had watched his men's rations dwindle away. After serious deliberation, Evans decided his column was in no shape to travel deeper into Texas to accept a surrender. Instead, he decided he could no longer wait for Sheridan and prepared move out. He later explained that his men were exhausted, his animals were dying, and his chances of getting back to New Mexico were uncertain. Like Carson in the winter of 1864, Evans could not remain on the winter plains of northwest Texas.[61]

Major Evans's immediate impression of his expedition was that it was a failure. He wrote that the blame could be placed on him. Yet he wrote these words without the luxury of hindsight. His report was also written in the afterglow of Custer's November victory along the Washita River. Unlike Carson or Custer, Evans did not have a champion at headquarters to hail his achievements. Carson had Carleton. Custer had several well-placed advocates, including Sherman and the American press. So despite the obvious significance of the elimination of a major Comanche winter camp by the Thirty-Seventh Infantry and the Third Cavalry, the operations of the Seventh Cavalry overshadowed those of Fort Bascom's men in Sheridan's overall mission.[62]

Custer had left Sheridan at Camp Supply during a snowstorm on 23 November, leading eleven companies of the Seventh Cavalry south toward the Antelope Hills. After striking a large trail in the snow, the column turned east, finding fifty Cheyenne lodges on the Washita River on the 26th. Custer divided his troops and attacked the village. In the battle that followed, Black Kettle and 103 warriors, as well as 53 women and children, were killed. Such was the great victory that Sheridan reported back to Sherman.[63]

Sheridan's original plan of using three converging columns to smash the enemy was largely a success, but not in the way he intended. For the Cheyennes, Arapahos, Kiowas, and Comanches who continued to live independently between the Arkansas and Red Rivers, the idea of becoming wards of the United States seemed a fate worse than death. After watching their families suffer through the winter campaign, most of their leaders were forced to reconsider, and by the spring of

1869 they agreed to move to the Indian Territory. Their surrender was not simply a reaction to Custer's assault on Black Kettle and the Cheyenne. The destruction of the Nokoni camp at Soldier Spring was just as important. A large contingent of Arapahos and Cheyennes remained on the defensive, unwilling to surrender even after Custer's victory. Only after Evans's column destroyed Chief Horseback's village did the majority of Southern Plains Indians from across the region begin to report to their designated reservations. This event did great psychological damage to Plains tribes from Kansas to the Texas Panhandle. The total war concept Sherman and Sheridan perfected in Georgia during the Civil War began to produce dividends on the southern plains. In late December 1868 and early January 1869, Cheyennes and Arapahos began to file into the reservation located next to Camp Supply. Many Comanche and Kiowa bands also ready to submit rode to Fort Cobb. This second group was eventually located on the east side of the Wichita Mountains after Fort Sill was established. Additionally, some of the Comanches who battled Evans's troopers showed up at Fort Bascom before the soldiers did, ready to surrender.[64]

Sheridan's winter strategy also forced two of the Comanches' most defiant bands, the Kwahadis and the Kotsotekas, to reconsider their options. They sent word to Santa Fe that while they were opposed to settling in the Indian Territory, they were willing to relocate to New Mexico. Colonel Getty, commander of the District of New Mexico, redirected them to Sheridan. Chief Mowway of the Kotsotekas ignored this directive and rode into Fort Bascom to plead his people's case. It should have come as no surprise that these Canadian River Valley Indians would lobby for a home in New Mexico, where they had both cultural and economic ties with the Hispano community. Major Morris sent Mowway with chiefs Wild Horse, Buffalo Robe, Quajipe, and Ventura to Getty in Santa Fe. After some negotiations with the district commander and Superintendent of Indian Affairs Norton, they decided coming to Santa Fe had been unwise and tried to slip away in the middle of the night. This led to their arrest and removal to Fort Union. Anglo and Hispano civilians were fearful that this turn of events would ruin any chance of a lasting peace. The five chiefs were later transferred to Fort Leavenworth, but they were eventually released.[65]

While attacks across the Texas frontier subsided for a while, they did not cease. Sheridan believed New Mexicans were to blame, as they continued to supply their trading partners with both food and weaponry. He believed the Comancheros were the main reason the Kwahadi were able to remain in the field after the winter campaign. Thus, eliminating this trade became paramount to forcing the Comanches and their Kiowa allies onto the reservation. Sheridan ordered Colonel Getty to burn any trade goods found on Hispanos heading onto the Llano Estacado and to shoot any cattle they led back into New Mexico. Such orders proved Sheridan was deadly serious about ending the trade. The U.S. Army soon came to appreciate what Carleton, Carson, and Bergmann had learned long ago: the Comancheros were more formidable than anyone in the War Department in distant Washington could fathom. The black market economy that tied Hispanos to Comanches was rooted in the region's culture, and the generational alliances that formed against common enemies could not easily be broken.[66]

In the summer of 1866, General Sherman replaced New Mexico's volunteers with regular army personnel. He had long believed this was the key to gaining control of the region, yet nine years would pass before the Southern Plains Indians were completely subdued. The failure of the volunteer army to contain the Indians and stop the black market trade was used by army regulars to denigrate the New Mexico soldiers. It is possible that their inability to gain control of the region, when taken with some officers' dealings with Comancheros, confirmed the division commander's own thoughts concerning the volunteer soldiers, yet such myopia was not useful to either Sheridan or to the historical record. In fact, the Comanchero trade grew more active after the regular army took over. Whether volunteer or regular, the soldiers of Fort Bascom contributed to the military's efforts to gain control of the region, which began in 1863 and did not end until 1874. Expanding upon the earlier efforts of the volunteers, regular army regiments such as the Third Cavalry, the Fifty-Seventh Colored Infantry, the Thirty-Seventh Infantry, and, finally, the Eighth Cavalry did yeoman service in the Canadian River Valley, just as the Colorado, New Mexico, and California volunteer regiments did before them. One weakness in Sheridan's 1868 strategy of converging columns was the omission of Texas troops. This allowed some of the Indians an escape from the general's vise. Thus the Comancheros and Comanches continued to do business. As long as that was the case, the U.S. Army used Fort Bascom as a base of operations.[67]

CHAPTER 7

Texas's Northernmost Frontier Fort

The Kwahadi and Kotsoteka Comanches and their Kiowa cohorts remained a viable and dangerous force on the Texas frontier even after Gen. Philip Sheridan's winter campaign ended in 1869. The Southern Plains Indians were able to maintain their way of life, in part because of the Comancheros, regardless of the army's determination to bring it to an end. Thus, despite Fort Bascom's official closure in the fall of 1870, for the next four years hundreds of Fort Union troopers spent their summers at Bascom. As map 4 indicates, these soldiers' operational range had always closely followed the Llano Estacado's geographic footprint. From 1871 until 1875 they regularly patrolled throughout the Eroded Plains and participated in major expeditions into Texas, leading further credence to the argument that Fort Bascom was Texas's northernmost frontier post.[1]

In early March 1869 four men were reported to have been killed in New Mexico Territory near the Texas border. Lt. William J. Cain of the Third Cavalry took ten troopers from Company C and rode east from Fort Bascom to investigate. Two days and sixty miles later, they found the dead men strewn about a dry lake bed. It was obvious that they had been loading salt when they were attacked. This same location is probably where Lt. Col. Silas Hunter and thirty members of the Fifty-Seventh Colored Infantry had extracted salt in 1866. Cain noted that a man by the name of Wright, the only Anglo-American, had been scalped. The lieutenant did not know, or did not report, the names of the three Hispano workers found with Wright. He did note that all four victims had been shot in the head, and they were riddled with additional

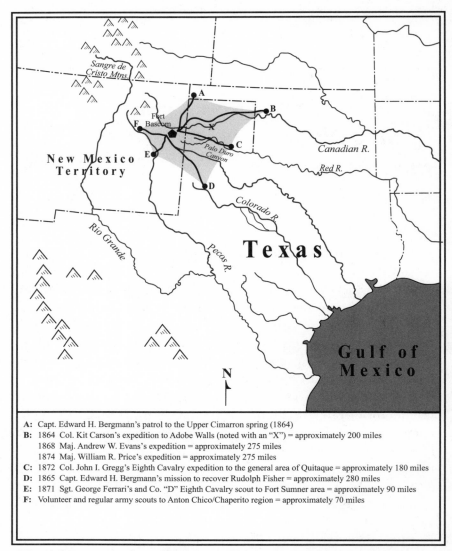

A: Capt. Edward H. Bergmann's patrol to the Upper Cimarron spring (1864)
B: 1864 Col. Kit Carson's expedition to Adobe Walls (noted with an "X") = approximately 200 miles
   1868 Maj. Andrew W. Evans's expedition = approximately 275 miles
   1874 Maj. William R. Price's expedition = approximately 275 miles
C: 1872 Col. John I. Gregg's Eighth Cavalry expedition to the general area of Quitaque = approximately 180 miles
D: 1865 Capt. Edward H. Bergmann's mission to recover Rudolph Fisher = approximately 280 miles
E: 1871 Sgt. George Ferrari's and Co. "D" Eighth Cavalry scout to Fort Sumner area = approximately 90 miles
F: Volunteer and regular army scouts to Anton Chico/Chaperito region = approximately 70 miles

Map 4. Scouts, patrols, and major expeditions that originated at Fort Bascom took both the volunteer and regular army across the Eroded Plains, into Indian Territory, and deep into Texas. Copyright © 2016 The University of Oklahoma Press, Publishing Division of the University. All rights reserved.

bullet holes. Cain also reported that the fingers and thumb of each man's right hand were missing. An empty wagon sat near the lake's bank. The lieutenant found some stray cattle that he assumed had belonged to the deceased party, hitched them to the wagon, and then loaded the bodies into its bed. Troopers found fresh horse tracks nearby that led toward the Sangre de Cristo Mountains. Cain admitted that he had no idea who had committed these crimes. The lieutenant and his men returned to Fort Bascom with their tragic cargo.[2]

The citizens of New Mexico were not surprised by Cain's discovery. They immediately correlated this atrocity with Col. George Getty's recent arrest of five Comanche chiefs in Santa Fe. Locals believed these murders were in reprisal for the chiefs' incarceration and feared it was only the beginning. The *Santa Fe Daily New Mexican* blamed the Navajos, even though Cain had been unable to identify the culprits. Despite the success of the winter campaign, the Canadian River Valley was still a dangerous place, and it would remain so for several years.[3]

For the Southern Plains Indians, 1869 was a transitional year as many of them began to settle on their designated reservations in Oklahoma. Even those who refused found it beneficial to make an occasional appearance so they could get government rations. Such was the case with Mowway's Kotsotekas and Satanta's Kiowas. But the Comanches and Kiowas who had resigned themselves to the reservation system continually expressed their displeasure with its operation. Indian agent Lawrie Tatum and several officials who served on the Board of Indian Commissioners reported these Indians' grievances to Washington. Despite a willingness on the part of some Indian leaders to cooperate with the government, such grievances convinced a certain contingent of Kiowas and Comanches that living on the Llano Estacado was far better than anything the U.S. government had to offer.[4]

The summer of 1869 saw a lull in Comanchero sightings. This was due, in part, to Colonel Getty publicizing Sheridan's order to burn trade goods and kill all animals seized by the army during its patrols. By the fall, the situation had changed. Fort Bascom's new commander, Capt. Horace Jewett of the Fifteenth U.S. Infantry, responded to a series of renewed Comanchero sightings by sending thirty men on a three-week patrol into Texas. The same Lt. Wilson Hartz of the Fifteenth Infantry who had overseen so much reconstruction at the post led his troopers on the scout to disrupt the trade "carried out by citizens of this territory and hostile Indians." After traveling 160 miles to the east, Hartz and his men were engulfed in a winter blizzard that forced them to return to the post prematurely.[5]

While this patrol did not apprehend any Comancheros, similar operations in 1870 yielded better results. Several Hispano traders were captured that spring. They were caught traveling east down the Fort Smith road to Texas. Afterwards, Jewett posted a picket between Fort Bascom and Fort Sumner to catch future caravans. He also informed his men to be on watch for a band of Cheyennes and Arapahos who had abandoned their reservation in the Indian Territory. Jewett's own patrols detained two Comancheros returning to New Mexico with stolen livestock. To make clear that army leaders meant what they said, Jewett had their cattle destroyed.[6]

Officers within the District of New Mexico knew their problems with the Southern Plains Indians were far from over. In 1870 William B. Stapp's ranch once again became a target. As noted in chapter 4, in the early morning hours of 15 June 1870, a woman employee who lived on Stapp's property near Fort Bascom found herself in harm's way when between forty or fifty Indians raided the ranch. The culprits posted sentinels between Stapp's property and Fort Bascom to prevent anyone from alerting the post, then stole several of his horses. They scalped the woman before brazenly moving on to the post, where they absconded with five of trader Hugh Masterson's mounts. Jewett noted, "These Indians were well-armed and mounted and had a change of animals and are supposed to be under the command of Eagle Tail." Getty ordered Jewett to "check any demonstration that may be made in this direction. . . . Keep a Cavalry scout constantly in the field and on the move and relieving it [sic] from time to time by fresh detail." While posted to the picket detail at Hubbell's Ranch, Lt. Robert Carrick of the Eighth Cavalry reported to Jewett that he had discovered a new Comanchero campsite on the Llano Estacado. The major sent Carrick nine additional troopers from the Eighth and three privates from the Fifteenth Infantry and ordered him to pursue the Comancheros into Texas. Jewett then recommended to headquarters that all pickets stationed along the old trade routes be abandoned. Instead of stationary camps, he wanted his troopers in the saddle, constantly moving throughout the Eroded Plains, camping at the same location for only a day or two. He believed such a plan made the army less predictable and thus more apt to catch Hispano traders as they tried to weave their way around his patrols.[7]

Illegal traders became more active during this period for two reasons. One was related to government inefficiency and the other to Fort Bascom's closing. Kiowas, Cheyennes, and Comanches who had agreed to move to the reservation grew tired of waiting on the federal government to make good on its promises. Many returned to the plains and began to steal cattle and horses from the settlements in northern and northwestern Texas. Afterward they exchanged stolen livestock for the goods they needed to sustain their old way of life. Despite this increased activity, in the fall of 1870 Brig. Gen. John Pope, the new commander of the Department of the Missouri, pushed forward his order to close several frontier posts, including Fort Bascom.[8]

On paper, General Pope's decision to close Fort Bascom might have made sense, but the new, interim commander of the District of New Mexico, Col. John I. Gregg of the Eighth U.S. Cavalry, was keenly aware that a strong military presence along the Fort Smith road was still needed. While Pope was confident that the army could handle any major outbreak of hostilities after his plan was implemented, Colonel Gregg was not so sure. In March 1871 Gregg sent sixty-year-old Frank de Lisle, Fort Bascom's longtime guide, on an undercover mission across the Llano Estacado to see what the Comanches and their Comanchero partners were doing. He ordered de Lisle to travel through the Eroded Plains, check known trails into Texas, talk with settlers, look for signs of Indians and Comancheros, and then report his findings to Maj. David R. Clendenin of the Eighth Cavalry. By the time de Lisle returned, Clendenin had been relieved of his command at Fort Union and ordered to Fort Bascom along with Companies D and F of the Eighth Cavalry. Gregg ordered Clendenin to prepare his men for "active service. . . . Each trooper will have two extra shoes fitted for his horse, and a quantity of nails pointed, to be carried in the saddle pouch." This directive makes clear the new commander's thoughts regarding a spring campaign and his concern for the 135 horses and 54 mules that were to participate. Private Eddie Matthews of Company L noted that they were kept busy in March, "making ration sacks [and] mending clothes," in preparation for a "six month scout."[9]

By April 1871 the "closed" Fort Bascom was teeming with Eighth Cavalry troopers. Initial operations consisted of two companies in the

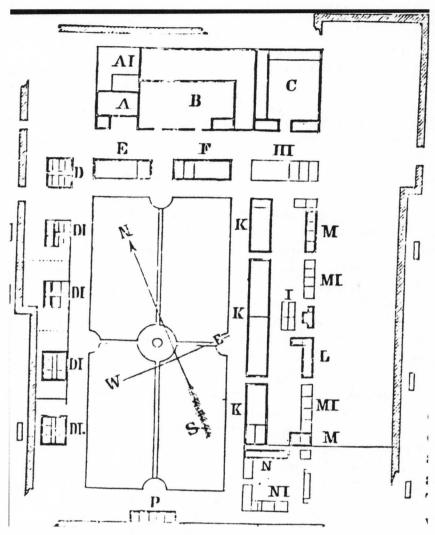

Figure 8. Fort Bascom ground plan, 1870. Five years after the first ground plan was drawn (figure 7), an updated version was produced. This more recent plan noted that several of the buildings were never completed according to the original design. Like the 1865 plan, this version identified the different buildings with a letter system and accompanying legend. The 1870 plan (looking north to south) identified the uncompleted structures with an "I"; thus "AI" stands for the uncompleted stables. Figures 2, 7 and 8, when coupled with military correspondence between headquarters and the post, indicate that most if not all of the exterior shells of the buildings had been completed in 1865, but some of the interiors had not, or if they had been, they were very substandard. *Records of the Office of the Chief of Engineers, RG 77, DNM, NA, in Arrott Collection, 49: 1.*

field at all times: one patrolling between Bascom and Fort Sumner and the other scouting up and down the Fort Smith road. Major Clendenin stressed that no "laundresses or camp followers" were to come near the post. He ordered his troopers to remain in the field as long as they had supplies. He also emphasized to his men that taking care of their horses was essential to the mission's success.[10]

Capt. James F. Randlett of the Eighth Cavalry soon found evidence to support historian Charles L. Kenner's claim that Fort Bascom's closure led to the "Indian Summer of the Comanchero." Randlett's troop captured twelve traders headed toward Texas with "powder, lead, cloth, Trinkets and Fancy Articles" loaded on twenty-three mules. Captain Randlett followed Sheridan's orders to the letter, setting fire to the trade goods. The average pack mule could carry 20 percent of its body weight, meaning the troopers set fire to approximately two-and-a-quarter tons of materials. The smoke from such a fire would have created an apocalyptic cloud that could be seen for miles in all directions. Also following orders, Randlett killed the mules. He informed Clendenin that these Comancheros, from Mora, San Miguel, and Santa Fe Counties, were led by a "Comanche squaw." The next day Randlett's company came across another group of traders herding five hundred cattle north into New Mexico. Clendenin sent a courier to Randlett in the field, ordering him to bring the cattle back to Bascom, where he personally counted them. The major wanted Colonel Gregg to make the final decision regarding destroying the cattle. Clendenin also informed Gregg of the rumor that more Comancheros would soon arrive in New Mexico with three thousand Texas cattle. He had been told that these traders were prepared to fight to keep their livestock. Of Randlett's exploits, the *Santa Fe Daily New Mexican* said, "The vigorous campaign opened by the military authorities upon the Comanche traders, is already showing its affect [*sic*]."[11]

In response to Clendenin's report, Gregg ordered the major to keep the most recent herd of confiscated cattle in Fort Bascom's corrals and "guard them until further orders." The commander of the Eighth Cavalry also sent Company L to join Companies D and F at the post. These three companies did duty in the Canadian River Valley throughout the summer of 1871, rotating back from extended scouts every thirty days. While at the post, some of the troops found sleeping arrangements inside the old commissary building. Others had to bunk in two-man tents pitched on the parade grounds.[12]

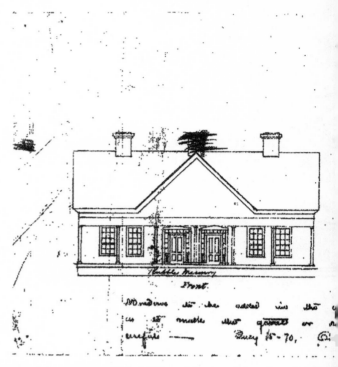

Figure 9. Fort Bascom's captain's quarters. This 1865 architectural drawing details w
the exterior of the captain's quarters looked like (identified with the letter "D" in fig
8). This building also appears in figure 2 in the far northwest corner of the post.
obvious from both this drawing and the one in figure 2 that this building was far m
elaborate than the other officers' quarters. Information shown in figure 8 and co
spondence between headquarters and the post indicate that not all the officers' quar
had been completed in 1865. Another discrepancy is found when we compare the n
ber of officers' quarters in figures 7 and 8. The 1865 ground plan does not show
captain's quarters, yet most documents indicate that this was the only officers' quarters

Colonel Gregg ordered these troopers to restrict their horses and
mules to half rations. In a letter to Gregg, Randlett complained that
his animals were suffering the effects of too little forage. Acting Asst. Adj.
John Lafferty of the Eighth responded that the twenty thousand pounds
of grain that had been delivered to Fort Bascom for the summer campaign should be sufficient for his animals, as long as the captain let his
horses stop and graze every fifteen or twenty miles when on patrol.[13]

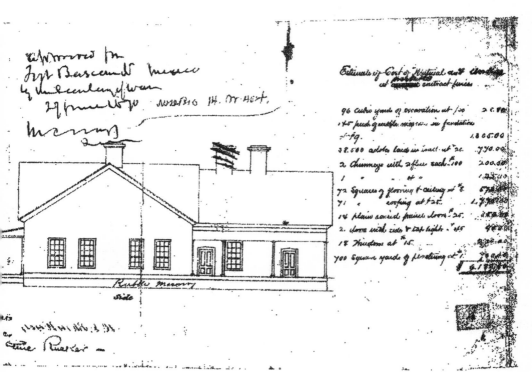

completed. The 1870 ground plan does show the captain's quarters. Perhaps a nota-
₁ on the 1865 architectural plans partially explains these inconsistencies: "Approved
Fort Bascom, New Mexico, by the Secretary of War 17 March 1870." The signature
₁der this statement appears to be that of Charles McClure, chief commissary of subsis-
₁ce for the Department of New Mexico. While this drawing raises many more ques-
₁s than it answers, the 1870 notation certainly fits the period when Fort Bascom was
₁dergoing several major construction projects. *Miscellaneous Fort File, Fort Bascom, sheet 3,
₁ervation File, Records of the Office of the Chief of Engineers, RG 77, DNM, NA, College Park, Md.*

Lafferty's terse response was quickly field-tested by Company D,
Eighth Cavalry, a few days later when it left Fort Bascom for an extended
scout that took it south of Fort Sumner. Sumner had been closed in
1869 and was purchased by Lucian Maxwell, who was converting the
fort into a working ranch. Unlike Bascom, soldiers were never stationed at Sumner after it closed. As a result, Bascom's troopers began
to range farther south to cover area once patrolled by troops from

Sumner. Led by Sgt. George Ferrari, this troop captured eight Hispano travelers with burros loaded with "buffalo meat" and other provisions between Hubbell's Ranch and Trout Springs. These traders were able to produce licenses that allowed them to trade with the Indians, so they were let go. After camping at old Fort Sumner, Company D struck several fresh trails of "cattle, horses, and mules," but "being very much fatigued, on half rations of grain, and grazing on the trail being very poor," Ferrari decided his animals were in no shape to pursue and returned to Fort Bascom. Randlett supplemented his subordinate's report with one of his own, explaining to Assistant Adjutant Lafferty that Lucian Maxwell's livestock had eaten up the grasses around the abandoned fort. Ferrari's troopers could find no place to graze their horses. Randlett wryly added that even restricted to half rations, Company D would have pursued the suspiciously fresh trails if there had been available forage in the area, but that was not the case.[14]

Fort Bascom soldiers had other issues to contend with regarding maintaining healthy mounts. A lack of blacksmiths forced cavalrymen to shoe their own horses. According to Lt. John K. Sullivan, "The inferior manner in which the great part of them have been shod . . . [makes them] incapable of enduring long, and fatiguing marches." In other words, the troopers were not good farriers. Sullivan requested that a blacksmith be sent to the post to take care of this important though neglected duty. He informed headquarters that as a result of his men shoeing their own mounts and pack animals, both horses and mules were "unfit to send on long journeys."[15]

In the latter part of 1871, Gregg's equivocation on Sheridan's order to slaughter all stolen livestock that his soldiers retrieved created additional problems. Some of the cattle taken to Fort Bascom wandered away or were stolen again. Captain Randlett was court-martialed over such losses. Major Clendenin came to his defense, explaining it was impossible to protect all the animals they had collected over the summer. In mid-September Clendenin informed Gregg that 340 cattle were still being cared for. As winter approached, he asked for further instructions on what to do with the animals and wondered how much longer his men needed to stay at Fort Bascom. Shortly thereafter the animals were turned over to local authorities, and all but a handful of troopers left for Fort Union.[16]

Clendenin understood the logistical difficulty of trying to patrol all the Comanchero trails in the region and recommended to Colonel Gregg that some troopers also be posted at "Maxwell's Ranch" (formerly Fort Sumner). In mid-summer 1871 Gregg was thinking along the same lines. Additionally, in a letter to Gen. Gordon Granger, who on May 1st replaced Gregg as the full-time district commander, Gregg recommended that a summer camp comprised of Eighth Cavalry troopers be posted "one hundred miles Eastward" in the Texas Panhandle. Gregg explained that any plan that did not include setting up a military camp where the Comanchero and Comanche trails crossed was doomed to fail. He also offered that such a mission, "could be readily assigned to this District." Such an endeavor meant the District of New Mexico would insert itself into Texas, something Majors Edward Bergmann and Andrew Alexander could have appreciated. Gregg closed his letter to Getty by noting that such a move "should have happened long ago." It would not be the last time the Eighth's commanding general would make such a suggestion.[17]

In 1872 and 1873, the total damages exacted upon Texans by Southern Plains Indians, as estimated by the claimants, topped $48 million. Almost all of that was lost in North and West Texas. Officials charged with determining the validity of these claims based such losses on current value alone. Although the amount officials verified was much lower, $11 million, this was still a significant amount of money. Nevertheless, such staggering amounts for a two-year period are just statistics. They cannot begin to describe the destruction and disruption visited upon Texans in the early 1870s. While a portion of these losses can be attributed to Mescalero Apaches and Kickapoos working with Mexicans operating out of Mexico, the records also reveal that widespread physical and economic destruction occurred in the northwestern half of Texas during this period, and much of this devastation was directly attributable to the Comanchero trade.[18]

The U.S. Army in Texas responded by pushing their patrols into New Mexico. In March 1872 Sgt. William H. Wilson and a company of Fourth Cavalry troopers from Fort Concho crossed from Texas into New Mexico Territory in search of Comancheros. They found fifty Hispano travelers loaded with trade goods along the Pecos River near Alamogordo. These men informed Sergeant Wilson that they were headed

to Muchaque to parlay with the Comanches. Gregorio Jaramillo of
Puerto de Luna, a village just to the north on the Pecos, and Juan
Gallegos of La Cuesta had led the caravan south down the Pecos to
Alamogordo where they met Wilson and his men. Most of the traders
lived in small Hispanic villages located between Puerto de Luna and
San Miguel, all situated along the Pecos. Maj. John P. Hatch, Wilson's
commander at Fort Concho, later reported to Gen. Christopher C.
Augur, commander of the Department of Texas, and District of New
Mexico commander Gen. Gordon Granger that the goods these men
were carrying came from "a store in La Cuesta, a branch of a Santa Fe
House." The term "house" was generically associated with a frontier
merchandising operation. With these letters, Major Hatch linked the
"illicit trade" to specific New Mexican individuals.[19]

According to Hatch, La Cuesta, about nine miles south of San Miguel
and fifteen north of Anton Chico, was where a majority of these traders
lived. One such resident, Polonio Ortiz, was arrested and forced to
return to Fort Concho with Wilson. Ortiz proved to be a valuable
source of information regarding the Comanchero trade. He gave
Fourth Cavalry officers details regarding trails, distances between water
sources, and rendezvous locations that they had previously only theor-
ized about. Lt. Gen. Philip Sheridan, in command of the Division of
the Missouri, received copies of Hatch's letters and distributed them
to military departments across the Southwest, emphasizing to his commanders that it was past time to destroy the Comanchero trade.[20]

During this period, reports generated within the U.S. House of
Representatives recorded 262 submitted claims to the federal government for losses due to "Indian Depredations." Many of these claims
came from northern, north central, and northwestern Texas. Detailing
some of these losses illuminates that such numbers are more than statistics and helps to explain why Sheridan began to focus on the Comancheros. In January 1871, 1,020 cattle and 55 horses were stolen from
William Beddo of Palo Pinto County. He claimed $36,100 in losses, yet
the government approved only $18,600 in reparations. On 1 October
1872 the Comanches swept into Llano County and took 48 of Daniel
Moore's horses from his ranch. His loss was assessed to be $3,000. In
August 1873 A. J. Henson lost 5 horses to Indians in Jack County and
then lost 5 more in November to raiders in Clay County. Federal officials

awarded him $1,250 for his trouble. The combined losses for these four instances came to $22,850, yet the numbers did not account for related damages. Related damages included future income not realized due to the inability to bring stolen livestock to market or grow the herd. Crop losses sustained from not having the draft animals required to work the fields were not included. According to W. Fanning, not a month passed in 1867 that did not include Indian raiders passing through Montague County. The $44,572,415.43 in claims for North and West Texas during 1872 and 1873 came from a total of 354 petitions detailing Indian raids. Lewis A. Dickson of Wise County claimed that he lost cattle and horses worth $159,750 in raids from 1868 to 1873. Direct evidence did not link the Comancheros to these specific claims, yet Sergeant Wilson's arrest of fifty Hispano traders provided the impetus Sheridan needed to focus on stopping the redistribution of Texas's wealth into New Mexico's shadow economy.[21]

In 1872, shortly after Major Hatch's letters reached Sheridan, he wrote a follow-up to headquarters, District of New Mexico, wherein he claimed that New Mexicans were working in conjunction with the Comanches to steal livestock and other moveable goods in Texas, seeming to lay the blame at the District of New Mexico's feet. Colonel Gregg responded by writing to his superiors, noting that all three of his companies, camped on the Canadian either at or near Fort Bascom, should be allowed to relocate into the Texas Panhandle. Gregg urged that he be allowed to "occupy where this illicit trade takes place"— Texas. "To attempt or expect to break up this famous illicit trade, the growth of years[,] by the desultory actions of small attachments of troops seem[s] absurd." In this same letter, he protested having to relocate all stolen cattle his troopers captured to Fort Bascom, where they had to be minded until their Texas owners could retrieve them. He complained that such duty was a detriment to the goal Sheridan was now charging his officers with. Half of his men were restricted to herding cows. Surely Gregg had been stung by recent correspondences between his peers and his commander concerning the Comanchero trade. Perhaps he was bit defensive about the sudden interest in this "illicit trade." Within his response he clearly pointed out that these transactions were being carried out in Texas, not New Mexico. Gregg had previously requested authorization for his Eighth Cavalry troopers to bivouac in Texas, but none was granted. A year after this first request, and after the Fourth Cavalry had traveled deep into New Mexico, he again made a similar request, somewhat defensively.[22]

From the outside looking in, such as the view from Sheridan's headquarters, the mission to end the Comanchero trade meant arresting a seemingly lawless group of mountain Hispanos who should have been no match for the U.S. Army. Yet a powerful economic network that stretched from Northern Mexico to Kansas City was also at work. Chihuahuan ranchers and midwestern cowboys operated on opposite ends of a Comanche conduit that funneled stolen horses and cattle through the Llano Estacado to eastern markets within the United States. As John Chisholm and Charles Goodnight could attest, the cattle business could be very profitable. Success for the Comanches meant acquiring a steady stream of goods they otherwise had no access to. These goods included food, weapons, and other materials needed to sustain their way of life. The Comanchero was situated between markets, and thus was able to take advantage of his position to improve his own lot. Urban New Mexican entrepreneurs had access to merchandise and used village Hispanos who lived along the Pecos River and other streams that ran out of the Sangre de Cristos to facilitate trading. Strong economic forces pulling from the east helped drive this trade and keep it alive for over a decade after the end of the Civil War. Despite the congressionally mandated military cutbacks that occurred after 1865, by 1872 more manpower was allocated to the Canadian River Valley in New Mexico and Texas. Colonel Gregg, commander of the Eighth Cavalry, was ordered to take the field and personally lead operations against the Comancheros and their partners, the Comanches and Kiowas. Col. Ranald S. Mackenzie of the Fourth Cavalry received similar orders in Texas.[23]

In May 1872, as Gregg made preparations to leave Fort Union, he requested both a packer and a guide be allocated to his command. He noted to headquarters that a guide was crucial because neither his officers nor his troopers were familiar with the region. A good packer was also essential. As Darlis A. Miller has explained, few regular soldiers could master the art of packing. This art, Maj. Andrew Alexander once opined, was only "acquired after years of practice." He added that a poorly packed scout was destined for disaster.[24]

Not long before Gregg and the Eighth Cavalry ventured east down the Canadian toward Texas, Capt. N. B. McLaughlin and ninety-three

Fourth Cavalry troopers left Fort Concho for Muchaque, the Comanchero rendezvous site located near present-day Gail, Texas. La Cuesta resident Polonio Ortiz, the captured Comanchero taken to Fort Concho by Sergeant Wilson in late March, had provided McLaughlin with detailed directions to the rendezvous site. The captain later reported that they arrived in early May to a freshly abandoned camp. It was just where Ortiz said it would be. McLaughlin estimated that between 150 and 200 lodges had recently been hauled away from Muchaque. The Comanches had realized the Comancheros, for whatever reason, were not coming. They did not know that Sergeant Wilson had arrested the New Mexican traders. While McLaughlin's troopers were a day or so late to Muchaque, they were still able to chart accurate distances to the site from Fort Concho and specify exactly where water could be found and what forage was in the area.[25]

Back at Fort Concho, Major Hatch continued to extract useful information from prisoner Ortiz. With exquisite detail Ortiz described another heavily traveled Comanchero route well to the north of the Muchaque trail. Mountain Hispanos followed this other route out of the Sangre de Cristos and down the Gallinas River to its junction with the Pecos. Here the traders turned east, passed south of Mesa Rica, continued beyond Tucumcari Peak, and then followed the Canadian River onto the Llano Estacado. They eventually angled southeast to reach the Quitaque Valley. Cold-running streams could be found at this rendezvous site, which Ortiz informed Hatch was about fourteen days, "with wagons," from the Gallinas River junction. He also told the major that Comanche chief Mowway often made this rendezvous site his home.[26]

Just as Colonel Gregg was ordered to march east along the Canadian, Colonel Mackenzie of the Fourth Cavalry was ordered to scout up the Brazos River and follow any trails he might come upon that led him to the Comanches. As soon as Sergeant Wilson brought Ortiz back to Fort Concho in March, Mackenzie began sending requests to the Department of Texas for horses. In early May he requested the army send him an additional three hundred horses for the upcoming summer. In June 1872 the colonel led five companies of Fourth Cavalry troopers and one company of infantry out of Fort Concho on a mission to find the Comanches.[27]

Mackenzie patrolled across Texas, first camping in Blanco Canyon (near the present-day town of Crosbyton), where he established a supply base. Supplies concerned him throughout the summer. The colonel sent letters to the assistant adjutant general of the Department of Texas urging that "it would be well to keep a considerable supply of forage and rations on hand at Camp Supply." Indeed, patrols that split away from the main expedition were often slowed or cancelled because of a perceived or actual lack of forage for the animals. This expedition across the Llano Estacado—like Carson's in 1864 and Evans's in 1868—was a logistical nightmare. Five companies of Fourth Cavalry and one company of the Twenty-Fourth Infantry were under Mackenzie's command, as well as 12 six-mule wagon teams and pack animals from Fort Richardson; 8 six-mule wagon teams and pack animals from Fort Griffin; and 5 six-mule wagon teams from Fort Concho. All of these wagons hauling forage, food, and equipment were driven by civilian teamsters. A herd of cattle, two butchers, and an ambulance made up the balance of the caravan. Every man and beast of burden had to eat rations of some sort and drink water every day. All animals were restricted to half rations. Once again, the mission of containing the Southern Plains Indians was complicated by the always changing logistics that all leaders of expeditions across the Llano Estacado had to grapple with.[28]

Throughout July and into August, Mackenzie patrolled across the Texas Panhandle, eventually moving into New Mexico and traveling up the Pecos to the village of La Cuesta. He noted that the Comancheros who made this village their home were not there. In this same report he informed General Augur that in early August some of his men had gone to Fort Bascom for supplies and that "Colonel Gregg left Fort Bascom on the seventh intending to scout the headwaters of the Red River." The army was trying to coordinate the different departments' efforts to apprehend the traders, but their attempts at this point were more wishful thinking than well-planned operations. After two months in the field, Mackenzie returned to Fort Concho. Although the colonel failed to encounter any Comancheros, he did report to both General Granger and General Augur that he had seen plenty of fresh cattle trails leading into New Mexico. General Augur hailed Mackenzie's patrol as "the first instance . . . where troops have been successfully taken across the Staked Plains." Augur's claim contributed significantly to the blank spot in the historical record regarding Fort Bascom. Historians took the general at his word, yet if given the opportunity, Fort Bascom's troopers could have pointed to numerous patrols they had participated in across this same region, all long before Colonel Mackenzie made his first venture into the Canadian River Valley.[29]

Army officers and Texas civilians alike were frustrated by the Comancheros' ability to avoid capture. Fort Bascom post commander Horace Jewett had recommended that local citizens be authorized to apprehend any neighbors who were participating in the trade. As their reward, they could keep any contraband the traders were carrying. One reason Captain Jewett suggested such a plan, which headquarters never approved, was because local authorities seldom prosecuted any New Mexicans they arrested. By August 1870 Jewett believed the only way to stop the exchanges was to focus less on the Comancheros and more on the persons who were purchasing the stolen livestock from them. After capturing two Hispanos moving north with a herd of cattle, Jewett dispatched them to Santa Fe with the recommendation that headquarters find a way to wring damaging information out of them. He declared, "My theory of this trade is that there are some wealthy and prominent Mexicans in the Territory who furnish means and supplies to the poorer chap[,] taking no risks themselves of apprehension, but the lion's share of the profit." Indian agent A. J. Curtis voiced a similar complaint to Superintendent of Indian of Affairs Col. Nathaniel Pope, noting that when soldiers did manage to make an arrest, the juries in the ensuing trials were "composed wholly or in part of Mexicans, [and] there is little hope of justice." Exasperated by the situation, Texas cattleman John Hittson led a contingent of his fellow ranchers into New Mexico to retrieve their herds. General Granger in Santa Fe sent word to Gregg to stay out of it. He ordered him to "take no part in the matter . . . unless to help avoid bloodshed." Yet there was bloodshed. After arriving in the territory, the Texans found many of their brands in the valleys that fronted the eastern slope of the Sangre de Cristo Mountains. One of the most powerful men in the territory, Eugenio Romero, kept a large ranch just outside of Las Vegas, New Mexico. Hittson found some Texas brands on Romero's land, yet considering the man's political connections, the Texans kept moving. They found more Texas cattle at Loma Parda, just outside of Fort Union, grazing on Edward Seaman's property. According to Charles Kenner, Seaman was the "police chief and post master" of the area. He ordered the Texans off his ranch. Seaman was shot and killed for his trouble. The cattle became part of a larger herd that was rounded up and taken back to Texas without any interference from the army. Hittson later claimed that he recovered between five and six thousand of his own cattle in New Mexico.[30]

Any investigation into the Comanchero trade is wrapped within a larger story that includes common purpose, greed, and the economic destruction of northwest Texas. The common purpose was often linked to an undercurrent of subtle resistance that did not originate from an ideological center. As noted, the Comancheros' role in extracting pastoral wealth out of the Lone Star State facilitated a transnational exchange that stretched from northern Mexico to the Kansas plains. Such wealth enticed well-to-do Hispanos like Romero, Anglo cattlemen like the unfortunate Seaman, and American soldiers like Charles T. Jennings to participate in this trade. The redistribution of stolen Texas livestock did considerable economic damage to all Americans living in the region, and it slowed expansion into the area for at least a decade. This is why Colonel Gregg and his Eighth Cavalry troopers were gone when some of Mackenzie's men arrived at Fort Bascom in early August 1872.[31]

Gregg and the Eighth's target was Quitaque Canyon, where Polonio Ortiz said Comanche chief Mowway could often be found. Private Eddie Matthews of Company L wrote several letters to his parents in the days leading up to the Eighth's departure. On 3 August Matthews noted that Companies C and D had joined M, L, and B at Fort Bascom to make preparations for their "move to the front." He anticipated that they would meet Colonel Mackenzie and the Fourth Cavalry along the way. By then Mackenzie had already left Blanco Canyon and was scouting toward New Mexico. These two regiments did not cross paths, but they covered much of the same ground in the coming weeks. Private Matthews complained of sunburn, the food, and the comforts that his commanding officer enjoyed during the expedition. Matthews found it particularly galling that Gregg sent troopers on a five-mile trek each morning to purchase fresh milk while they were still camped on the Canadian. On 7 August 1872, with the southwestern sun beating down, 214 Eighth Cavalry troopers, 11 officers, 38 supply wagons, and a large herd of cattle moved east. Matthews was not too concerned about finding any Indians, and that was fine with the private of Company L:

"The less [fighting] we have the better it will suit me." It is likely that Gregg led his men southeast down the Quitaque Trail before reaching Quitaque.[32]

Like all expeditions into the Texas Panhandle, the environment exhausted the soldiers and their animals. Uncertainty regarding water often forced the column to stop at midday if they came across a clear-running stream. The Canadian River could not be counted on to hold fresh water, especially during the summer season. Their direction would have led them across an area called Las Escarbadas, its name derived from the lack of water found along Agua Fría, the stream the Eighth followed to Quitaque. Soldiers, Comancheros, and Indians usually had dig (or scrape, from the Spanish *escarbar*) below the sandy surface of the streambed to find water. Additionally, New Mexico streams and rivers were often too alkaline or too stagnant to drink. Tributaries that flowed as a result of snowmelt, thunderstorms, and natural springs offered the most popular campsites along all the trails. On this expedition, companies rotated their positions in the column so that no one troop had to continually suffer from the choking dust that drifted into the faces of the trailing forces. On both 8 and 10 August, the cattle herd stampeded in the middle of the night. Major Evans's 1868 expedition experienced similar headaches with cattle. Gregg ordered one company to remain behind on each occasion to look for the lost herd. Continuing his negative commentary on his commander, Matthews opined that he did not "think he [Gregg] is much of a horseman, but like father, prefers lying off in an ambulance to horseback riding." By 11 August, the column was deep into the plains. Unable to find firewood, the soldiers were forced to collect buffalo chips. Matthews admitted that the dung served its purpose, but it did not smell "like new mown hay." Only the officers were allowed to bring tents, so each night the enlisted men pulled off their boots, rolled up in their blankets, and slept under the stars. On 14 August they woke to a driving rain. Soaked to the skin, the column rode for four hours before setting up camp tentless once again.[33]

On 15 August, near present-day Canyon, Texas, they were attacked by a band of Kiowas in the middle of the night. Matthews awoke to what "sounded to me like Devils incarnate." He thought that "all the Demons of hell had issued forth in that one lonely spot to make the night hideous with their orgies." Bootless, he fell in with Capt. William McCleave's

Company B and began to fire into the darkness. Before this encounter, the young private explained to his family that he had no doubts about the army's capabilities in a fight, but that knowledge did not let him sleep any easier: "The dread of the Savages, and their unearthly yells . . . puts the fear of God in the white man's heart." In the ensuing battle, one soldier was wounded and four Kiowas were killed. According to Gregg's official report, several more of these Indians were wounded.[34]

The column broke camp on 17 August. Moving southeast, they passed Palo Duro Canyon. On the 18th the troopers came across a large bison herd. They killed twenty, took the meat from three, and left the rest to rot on the Texas prairie. Over the next several days they continued to encounter such large herds that Matthews grew sick of looking at them. Gregg led his troops past the Prairie Dog Town Fork of the Red River and through the canyons along the Caprock, still moving toward the Quitaque Peaks. On 23 August, Matthews wrote: "For the last few days we have been traveling over some of the roughest country I have ever saw [sic]. Country that a Maryland farmer would not risk driving his cattle over."[35]

The environment's withering grind eventually proved fatal. Private Hannah of Company B, Eighth Cavalry, posted to guard duty on 24 August, was so exhausted that he tied himself to his horse so he could remain upright and give the appearance of doing his duty. Unfortunately, something spooked his horse in the middle of the night, causing it to bolt across the prairie. Unable to extricate himself, Private Hannah was killed. As the troops prepared to bury their friend, the ever verbose Private Matthews contemplated death on the Llano Estacado: "I am sick and tired of this kind of living, but believe to die and be buried in this God forsaken country, [I] would never rest easy in my grave, this thought is horrible to dwell upon."[36]

On 25 August, the troopers of the Eighth Cavalry could not help but dwell on death, for they buried Hannah that Sunday in the middle of nowhere. Matthews recorded:

At 10 A.M. the Command formed into a line. The remains placed in an ambulance. On each side walked four pall-bearers. In the rear of the Ambulance, his horse was led by one of the troop, following came the firing party. As the Ambulance came in front of the troops on the left of the line the troop presented Arms and soon as the remains passed the troop would wheel and march by the Company front to the grave. Arriving at the grave the body was lowered. When Lieutenant Boyd read the Episcopal burial service, this finished with three volleys over the grave, and [as] soon as it was filled up[,] one of the trumpeters sounded 'Taps' over the grave. . . . This death has cast a sadness over all the troop, and in fact over the Command.[37]

When the column broke camp the next morning, the entire command, including the wagons and the cattle, rode over the grave to ensure that all signs of Private Hannah's recent internment were obliterated.[38]

An aura of disaster hung over the column for the rest of the expedition. They searched for Comancheros along the Red River's tributaries, but like Mackenzie, Gregg found no success. As August came to a close, he ordered everyone on short rations. Turning back to the north, they ran short of water; many of the streams were dry or too salty to drink. As a result, their horses began to give out. The "half rations" of six pounds of forage per horse per day, which was the military norm in the 1870s, was reduced out of necessity to "two quarts of corn" and what little grass they could find growing on the Llano Estacado in the dead of summer. Many of the troopers were forced to shoot their starving mounts and walk. Deep within Comanchería, despite having a guide, the Eighth Cavalry realized they were lost. In desperate straits, the column finally crossed the Canadian River and turned west. On 14 September 1872 the caravan stumbled back into Fort Bascom, their condition similar to that of both Carson's and Evans's forces after their expeditions into the Llano Estacado. Instead of the blizzards and mind-bending cold snaps of winter, Gregg's men had suffered from the blistering heat waves and dried-up creek beds of summer. Neither Mackenzie nor Gregg accomplished their goals in 1872, yet the experience their men gained was not futile, for what they learned could be used in future operations. The following year, the army once again sent the Eighth Cavalry back to Fort Bascom for summer operations.[39]

The townsfolk of Liberty were glad to see Companies L and M, Eighth Cavalry, return in March 1873. Colonel Gregg placed Capt. Samuel Baldwin Marks Young in charge of the post, with orders to keep one scout in the field looking for illegal traders at all times. A few weeks before Captain Young and his troops arrived on the Canadian, Sgt. John Rowalt and a few of his Company L cavalrymen had engaged the Kiowas in a firefight. This action had sent a wave of fear through the valley. One citizen was so happy to see Company L return to the region that he promised to bring them a milk cow the following day.[40]

Almost immediately Captain Young requested more troops to patrol the region. General Pope, still commanding the Department of the Missouri, denied the request. He bluntly told Young that if he used his men properly, he had enough to carry out his orders. Young had originally requested help because Hispano traders were still slipping past his patrols. This meant a number of Southern Plains Indians were able to remain off the reservation. A newly promoted Sgt. Eddie Matthews explained the situation to his father: "These territories are infested with a lot of scoundrels who trade with Indians. And I have no doubt [that] for one gun, twenty head of cattle would be given in exchange." One such trader, Juan Lucero, was apprehended that summer with eighteen stolen horses and sent to Las Vegas, New Mexico, for prosecution. Judge J. G. Palen immediately let Lucero post bond. Young was infuriated. Judge Palen later determined that there was not enough evidence to prosecute Lucero and ordered his horses be returned to him.[41]

Such incidents led Matthews to comment, "It is a good thing for the Country when Indians kill Mexicans, for when they do this they shut off their supplies." Such comments were little more than wishful thinking, for while herders and traders did occasionally fall victim to attack, their losses were miniscule when compared to what was going on in Texas. Farmers in Montague County, Texas, were more concerned with protecting their families and livestock than trying to decipher Comanche motivations.[42]

Ongoing raids and rustling in 1873 and 1874 created tensions between the various departments and districts. The commander of Camp Supply, Indian Territory, Col. J. B. Brooks, blamed Gregg's inability to stop the Comanchero trade in New Mexico for the Cheyennes' access to alcohol in Indian Territory. Texas officials also blamed New Mexicans and the army for the rampant plundering of their resources. Gregg blamed any failings on his lack of manpower and resources, which reflected back on General Pope, who refused requests for more men. Officers in the territory were also not shy about charging a select group of Anglo-

and Hispano-Americans living in Santa Fe, San Miguel, and Mora Counties with funding Comanchero operations, yet few officials or ranchers outside the immediate zone of exchange were aware of the multiple layers of complicity that underlay the problem, or how difficult it was to stop.[43]

Orders issued from headquarters never quite squared with the situational reality soldiers faced in the Canadian River Valley. Despite this contradiction, Fort Bascom's officers, whether Maj. Edward H. Bergmann or Captain Young, continued to carry out their orders, which often led them to Texas. Between 28 August and 24 October 1873, Young took fifty troopers from the Eighth Cavalry on a thousand-mile scout that carried them past old Fort Sumner, to Blanco Canyon in Texas, and back into New Mexico Territory through the northeastern tributaries of the Canadian. Although they did not apprehend any Comancheros, they did determine that the traders had moved their main route north of this river. In his report to headquarters Young noted that he had seen vast herds of bison in the Texas Panhandle, generally a good indication that Southern Plains Indians could not be far away. In the summer of 1874, the Eighth Cavalry would make good on their captain's assessment.[44]

The history of Fort Bascom is inextricably linked to the history of the Canadian River, the history of the adobe fort, and the history of Indian attacks, kidnappings, and stock rustling in Texas. The Canadian River provided a habitat for bison and other animals and created an almost unbreakable bond between mountain and plains cultures. Charles Bent and Ceran St. Vrain were among the first Anglos to establish a permanent business relationship with the Comanches on the Canadian River. From what is now known as Bent's Old Fort (or Fort William) in southern Colorado, these two ex–mountain men sent wagons of goods across the South Canadian River into Texas in the early 1840s to establish a new business operation. Bent and St. Vrain purposely placed their new Texas post close to the Comanche settlements to gain their trade, yet its location proved to be a double-edged sword. These entrepreneurs certainly maintained easy access to the Southern Plains Indians who lived in the Canadian River Valley, yet this placement made them equally vulnerable to attack. The losses incurred in raids and threats of raids eventually exceeded profits, and the famous partners abandoned the Canadian River post in 1848. Afterward merchants, hunters, and military personnel continued to use the location as a way station of sorts when they traveled between Texas, New Mexico, and Kansas. During this period it came to be known as Fort Adobe, and later, Adobe Walls. Although never an official fort, it afforded Anglo travelers some sanctuary when traveling along the Canadian River. Colonel Carson, married to Charles Bent's sister-in-law, was no stranger to the site of old Fort Adobe when he led the first major U.S. Army expedition into the Llano Estacado in late 1864. In 1868 Maj. Andrew J. Evans carried Carson's Canadian River Expedition report with him as he prepared to battle the same Comanches and Kiowas. The roof was missing from the old trading station, but its adobe walls were still intact. Thus, when violence broke out along the Red and Canadian Rivers in 1874, the third major military expedition to leave Fort Bascom sought Adobe Walls as one of its only guideposts as it ventured into Texas.[45]

The fuse for further violence was lit in May 1874 when several bands of Comanches rendezvoused on Sweetwater Creek, not far from the North Fork of the Red River, to perform a Sun Dance. At the behest of Esatai, a Kwahadi medicine man, both reservation and nonreservation Comanches gathered there. Throughout the month Kotsoteka and Kwahadi Comanches, as well as various groups of Kiowas and Arapahos, made pilgrimages to this encampment. At these meetings the Indians engaged in spiritual cleansings and discussed their future as a people. No Southern Plains Indian was happy with the government's inability to make good on its promises, but few were able, or willing, to do anything about their circumstances. Additionally, the massive bison herds Captain Young had reported in 1873 had lured hundreds of buffalo hunters into the area the following spring. The Indians at Sweetwater Creek discussed how the hunters were destroying the large herds of bison in the region. The seemingly ageless Comanche chief Mowway remained discontented, belligerent, and still ready to defend his homeland in 1874. Some Indians wanted to raid the settlements and take their revenge against the Texans for taking the sacred lands. One contingent wanted to raid the Tonkawa Indians down in Central Texas because these people often worked for the army as scouts. Others wanted to focus on the buffalo hunters, who symbolized everything the Indians hated about U.S. citizens. Some wanted no part of such reprisals because they feared everyone would be punished for the acts of a few.[46]

Anticipating trouble, Maj. Andrew J. Alexander returned to Fort Bascom in May 1874 with Companies B, L, and M of the Eighth Cavalry. Capt. Louis Morris, another Fort Bascom veteran, led Company L. As was the case during every summer season since Bascom's official closing, these soldiers were prepared to remain in the field until late fall. The *Chicago Tribune* noted, "The command will carry with it all subsistence and quartermaster stores" required to carry out operations in the region.[47]

In the meantime, after weeks of debate, Esatai, the Kwahadi medicine man, and Quanah, a Comanche war chief, persuaded enough of their compatriots on Sweetwater Creek that they should attack the buffalo hunters who were camped at Adobe Walls. One reason the majority decided to follow Esatai was that he had convinced them that his powers made him invulnerable to bullets. He promised this medicine would help them eradicate the hunters and lead to the elimination of the Texans from their homeland. On 27 June 1874 Esatai and Quanah led several hundred Kotsoteka and Kwahadi Comanches on an attack against the buffalo hunters. An hour or so before the Indians were about to attack, some kind of noise woke the hunters up. Some claimed the ridge pole cracked that supported the roof they were sleeping under. Others were unsure what the noise was, but as fate would have it, most of the men were stirring about when the Indians attacked. The hunters were able to fend off the first wave of warriors. As these Indians began to fall, they realized that Esatai's medicine did not make them invulnerable to a .50 caliber Sharps rifle cartridge. Crack shots like buffalo hunter Billy Dixon quickly found their range and began to take down the attackers. As a result, Esatai's raid on Adobe Walls was a failure. While disappointed and rebuffed, Quanah and his followers were not ready to surrender and retreated to the refuge of the nearby canyons that cut through the Llano Estacado. From deep in the Texas Panhandle they occasionally raided isolated ranchers on the Texas frontier. Cheyennes and Comanches not affiliated with Quanah rode north and raided merchant trains along the Santa Fe Trail. Small bands also ventured farther into Colorado and Kansas. General Sherman ordered Department of the Missouri commander Gen. Philip Sheridan to get control of the region. This directive led to the last major battles between the U.S. Army and the Southern Plains Indians.[48]

The 1874 military operation, the largest yet conceived for the region, has collectively become known as the Red River War. Sheridan's strategy involved the use of converging columns, with a general rendezvous within the Antelope Hills of the Canadian River Valley, located in Indian Territory. This time troopers from Texas would take part in the mission. The military District of Texas had recently been placed under Sheridan's control to better manage operations in the region. One of the failures of the 1868 winter campaign had been the lack of such a Texas column, which allowed many Indians to escape down the Red and Brazos Rivers. Once again, Sheridan incorporated Fort Bascom into his plans.[49]

Maj. William Redwood Price of the Eighth Cavalry at Fort Union was ordered to relocate to Fort Bascom and lead this portion of the mission into Texas. On 20 August his adjutant telegraphed headquarters to request Col. Kit Carson's report of his 1864 "scout" down the Canadian. He wanted it forwarded to Fort Bascom. Major Price left Fort Union with 119 troopers and traveled to Las Vegas, New Mexico, where he picked up an additional 46 men. It so happened that Sgt. Eddie Matthews was also spending the night in Las Vegas. Matthews was on his way back to Fort Union to muster out of the service, having fulfilled his obligations to the U.S. Army. Of Price's mission, the always verbose Matthews noted, "The Indians seem to have made a great out break all over the country. I would not be surprised if the boys found plenty of work to do before the Summer was over." The next morning Matthews bid goodbye and continued on his journey north. Major Price and a large contingent of Eighth Cavalry rode to the southeast, the Sangre de Cristo Mountains at their backs as they made their way across the Las Vegas Plateau and down into the Canadian River Valley.[50]

Like Evans in 1868, Price wanted Carson's report in his hands before he ventured into Comanchería, once again highlighting the significance of Fort Bascom's location. The cumulative knowledge that was gained by soldiers of all stripes who served there was assimilated and redistributed throughout the District of New Mexico, the Department of the Missouri, and headquarters in Washington, D.C. Price's request supports the argument that operations that originated from Fort Bascom helped shape the government's strategies and policies regarding wresting control of the Texas Panhandle from Southern Plains Indians.

When Major Evans had arrived at Fort Bascom in 1868, Captain Morris, the post commander, was absent on a major scout like his predecessor, Captain Bergmann. A few days later, after three hard weeks in the field, Morris and his troopers had returned to Bascom. In 1864 Carson had determined that Bergmann would remain at the post, coordinating activities there. In 1868 Evans did the same with Morris and most of his men. If nothing else, these incidents highlight that Fort Bascom's commanders were often away from the post, leading patrols and scouts. Yet when Price's column rode out of the post on 28 August 1874, he took Captain Morris and 66 men from Company L, Eighth Cavalry, already at Fort Bascom, with him. This military caravan included 20 mule-drawn wagons provided by the army, an additional 24 mule-drawn wagons provided by contractors, and 30 pack mules. They hauled 20 days of rations, munitions, and forage for the 225 Eighth Cavalry troopers, civilians, and the various horses and beasts of burden taking part in the mission. Led by five Navajo and three New Mexican guides, the column moved east down the Fort Smith road toward Texas. Meanwhile, Maj. Gen. Nelson Miles started another column south from Camp Supply in Indian Territory. Two columns of the Fourth Cavalry, one led by Colonel Mackenzie out of Fort Concho, the other commanded by Lt. Col. George P. Buell of Fort Richardson, also moved toward the Antelope Hills. Rounding out this five-pronged assault, Lt. Col. John W. Davidson, commanding the Tenth Cavalry out of Fort Sill, Indian Territory, led the last contingent of troops toward the Comanches' homeland.[51]

On 4 September Major Price ordered Lt. Henry J. Farnsworth and Company H to the northeast with all the wagons to set up a supply base near Adobe Walls. Price kept the pack mules and the rest of the troopers with him and turned to the southeast, where they soon struck a fresh Comanchero trail. This old path led Price and Companies C, K, and L on a course between McClellan Creek and Mulberry Canyon. Two days later they traversed "White Sandy Creek," finding evidence that Major General Miles's column had already been in the area. Price followed these tracks down the Salt Fork of the Red River. On 7 September they rode through a driving rain, finding Miles's camp during the late afternoon. Price's report makes clear that Miles was not in a good mood. Amidst miserable conditions, the general informed Price that there were plenty of signs that Indians were "out," but he could not find them. Miles related that he was low on forage and food and was preparing to leave the area and find his supply train. Cavalry often left their wagon trains far behind on major expeditions. To do otherwise defeated the purpose of inserting mobile troops into the field. By 10 September Price found himself in a similar situation. By then Miles and his men were gone. Camped on McClellan Creek, Price ordered his men to shoot flares into the night sky to alert his own train as to his location. It continued to rain. The next day the column moved north until they reached Sweetwater Creek, near where the Comanches had gathered in May. On 12 September they broke camp and continued toward Antelope Hills. Between Sweetwater Creek and the Dry Fork of the Washita, they came face-to-face with a group of Kiowa warriors and their chief, Lone Wolf.[52]

The Eighth Cavalry was soon engaged in their portion of the Red River War. The Kiowa warriors were positioned on a "steep ridge" between the troops and the Kiowa village, which was in the process of evacuating. One of the Indians perched on this ridge was another war chief, Set-maunte (Bear Paw). Price sent skirmishers in that direction. These troopers were immediately met by about fifty warriors, and shots were fired by both parties. Like previous expeditions, Price's column had hauled along Fort Bascom's howitzers. Several days of rain made them less effective, yet such weaponry was still a plus in any fight on the plains. Over the next hour and a half the Kiowas unsuccessfully tried to break through Price's lines. The major ordered three companies, including Captain Morris and Company L, to move around the enemy's flank, which had the desired effect. The Kiowas disengaged and retreated down Sweetwater Creek. With the warriors keeping themselves between the soldiers and the villagers, a running gun battle ensued, which covered seven or eight miles. The Kiowas were eventually able to escape across the rain-swollen creek. Price did not follow.[53]

Much like his predecessors' expeditions, the rest of Price's expedition turned into a struggle to survive. After the battle, the column camped on Sweetwater Creek. One reason Price did not continue the pursuit was because he had yet to link up with his supply train. By 13 September he was more interested in finding those wagons than Indians. While searching for his supplies, he stumbled across Billy Dixon, one of Miles's scouts, wandering across the prairie. This is the same Dixon who was involved in the buffalo hunters' battle at Adobe Walls. Acting as messengers for Miles, Dixon and several other scouts had been ambushed on their way to Camp Supply by a large band of Comanches and Kiowas near Gageby Creek. Dixon led Price back to his compatriots, one of whom had died from wounds suffered in the attack.[54]

Price left his surgeon and an ambulance with these men but kept moving, still focused on finding his supply train. At one point, his troopers heard a cannon shot. Price sent scouts in the direction of the boom, but could not find anyone. It turned out that they had heard a distress signal from Capt. Wyllus Lyman, who was in charge of Miles's wagon train. At the time of the cannon fire, Lyman and his men were being attacked by another group of angry and defiant Southern Plains Indians. Miles later charged Price with failing to come to the aid of his men, yet in light of the desperate circumstances the Fort Bascom column found itself in, it is hard to corroborate such charges. Ironically, Miles had recently commandeered a civilian supply train en route to Price and his men. Possibly Miles's actions contributed to the Eighth Cavalry's critical situation. Clearly the challenges the U.S. Army faced in its endeavor to gain control of the region were considerable.[55]

The most famous and successful piece of the mission occurred on 28 September 1874. On that morning, Colonel Mackenzie led the Fourth Cavalry into Palo Duro Canyon, surprising Comanche leader Quanah and the most defiant group of Indians left on the Llano Estacado. While few Comanches were killed in this attack, the Fourth Cavalry captured more than one thousand of their horses. Mackenzie ordered his men to shoot each one. This action well illustrates how Sheridan's concept of total warfare was implemented during the southwestern Indian wars. The destruction of the Comanches' horses made them far less powerful. The psychological impact of this slaughter was just as damaging. No longer the masters of the Llano Estacado, both the Comanches and Kiowas eventually accepted defeat and moved onto their reservations. To do otherwise would have forced them to watch their families freeze or starve to death.[56]

Mackenzie was able to locate Quanah and the Kwahadis as a direct result of the converging columns strategy. Despite the blind-leading-the-blind aspect of the larger mission, Sheridan's plan worked because of the combined efforts of all the commands. After their battle on

Sweetwater Creek, Price and his men were finally resupplied and were later placed under Miles's command. These soldiers remained in the field until the end of the year, crisscrossing the region, forcing the Indians to constantly flee from one refuge to the next. By the time Mackenzie's cavalrymen approached Palo Duro Canyon on 27 September, Price's and Miles's patrols had eliminated the space in which Quanah could operate, effectively funneling him toward the Fourth Cavalry.[57]

Although the destruction of the Comanches' horses on 28 September 1874 led to their subjugation, small bands of Southern Plains Indians, particularly the Cheyennes, remained off their reservations until the spring of 1875. The last battle of any significance that Fort Bascom soldiers participated in occurred, appropriately enough, just south of Adobe Walls. As a part of Miles's cleanup operations, on 6 November Lt. Henry Farnsworth and twenty-eight men from Company H, Eighth Cavalry, attacked about one hundred Cheyennes along McClellan Creek. A very hot firefight ensued, in which one trooper was killed and ten were wounded. Six cavalry horses were also killed. Lieutenant Farnsworth estimated that his men dispatched four to seven warriors in the engagement and wounded four others. The remaining Cheyennes escaped toward Indian Territory. During this period Price's troopers also constructed a supply base for the rest of Miles's command. This mission continued through deep winter in the Texas Panhandle. On 28 December 1874, just a few weeks after Mackenzie and the Fourth Cavalry returned to Fort Concho, Price led his soldiers back to Fort Bascom for the last time. Miles remained in the field through the spring, chasing down the few remaining Cheyennes who refused to submit to the will of the U.S. government.[58]

After the army gained control of the Southern Plains Indians, there was little need to continue summer operations along the Canadian River. The military continued to store grain and hay at Fort Bascom for the occasional patrols that ventured there from Fort Union. In May 1875 Maj. Andrew Alexander, again serving as the post commander at Fort Union, reported that the forage stored at Bascom was missing. He accused Wilson Waddingham, now owner of most of the land around the fort, of taking it. From beginning to end, forage and supplies were always points of contention in the Canadian River Valley[59]

Isolated from its historical context, this remote outpost does not appear to warrant much attention, yet the hundreds of cavalry and infantry who served at Fort Bascom from 1863 to 1874 would beg to differ. What these soldiers did and how they did it shaped the Southwest, regardless of how little has been written about them. Long before Col. Ranald Mackenzie received his well-deserved acclaim, Fort Bascom's "horse marines" served in the heart of Comanchería. The soldiers engaged in a gritty, slow process that seldom involved any grand or glorious bugle-led charges. Mackenzie's electrically quick victory at Palo Duro Canyon may obscure the importance of the work performed by Fort Bascom soldiers, yet their contribution to the effort to contain the Southern Plains Indians and the Comancheros was, in the long run, just as significant. The early ventures into the Texas Panhandle by Colonel Mackenzie and the Fourth Cavalry failed to strike a blow against the Comanches or the Comancheros, yet the commander of the Department of Texas, General Augur, hailed them as a boon to the army because of the knowledge gained in the effort. If Augur was correct, then surely the journeys of Private Matthews and Company L across this same "God-forsaken country" were just as useful. Mackenzie's first expedition originated from Fort Richardson, which has often been called Texas's northernmost frontier fort. Yet this study has demonstrated that that title could easily belong to Fort Bascom. Perched on the edge of Comanchería, facing the Llano Estacado, located between the Comancheros and the Comanches, it played a significant role in gaining control of the Southern Plains Indians.[60]

CHAPTER 8

More Than a Sign

In the late 1860s and early 1870s, many New Mexicans and Southern Plains Indians profited from the well-developed shadow economy known as the Comanchero Trade. The Comanches transported plunder taken from south of the Rio Grande, the Edwards Plateau, and North Texas to rendezvous sites located between the Texas Panhandle and eastern New Mexico. Within well-concealed canyons, Comanchero middlemen exchanged calico, bread, sugar, whiskey, and rifles for stolen livestock. They then redistributed these animals throughout the Sangre de Cristo Mountains. Although both Hispano and Anglo merchants were involved in this traffic, the Comancheros facilitated much of the exchange. Men such as José Piedad Tafoya, Julian Baca, José Medina, and Manuel González sold cattle and horses throughout the mountains, and they also herded them to markets in Colorado and Kansas. New Mexican mountain men played key roles in meeting the market's growing demand for horses and cattle, while Texas cattlemen were economically ravaged by this activity. Santa Fe Trail merchants, New Mexican entrepreneurs, and midwestern ranchers were happy to purchase this influx of livestock, regardless of its origin. Buyers were less interested in the odd brands seared into the animals' hides than they were the cost per head. Thus, during and long after the Civil War, the U.S. Army had to remain on duty in the Canadian River Valley.[1]

Indian attacks and raids increased in Texas after Fort Bascom closed in 1870. This upsurge verified that Maj. Edward H. Bergmann's instincts were correct when he placed the post eleven miles north of Tucumcari Peak. It proved to be a good jumping-off point for soldiers ordered into Comanchería, where their challenges remained formidable for the next decade. Only after the Department of Texas came under the control of the Department of the Missouri, which coupled it with the military District of New Mexico, did Texas's northwestern frontier become a safe place for settlers. Placing New Mexico and Texas under Lt. Gen. Philip Sheridan's command facilitated better communication and cross-referencing of experiences between the two districts.

This move toward better coordination was significant, yet the key to military success in Comanchería remained the daily grind, the mere act of doing. Monotonous Fort Bascom patrols that never made the papers eventually blocked avenues of escape, reduced access to weapons, and funneled the remaining holdouts to their last refuge, Palo Duro Canyon. William H. Goetzmann, in his study of the army's topographical engineers, wrote about the "importance of viewing exploration as activity rather than sequence."[2] Bascom is a good example of what he was talking about. Daily patrols on tired horses, in cold camps, and on wild goose chases were essential actions that disrupted the economic lifeline that existed between Comancheros and Southern Plains Indians. Seen from such a perspective, Bascom becomes more significant, as do all the soldiers whose names never appeared in the newspapers. After Maj. Gen. John Pope closed Fort Bascom, the Comanchero trade exploded, a fact 301 New Mexicans predicted would happen in the letter that accompanied their petition to the secretary of war protesting this action. More concerned with San Miguel County, they could not have predicted the new wave of violence and the resulting economic ruin that swept across North Texas, but it surely did not surprise them. Pope's cost-cutting measures cost the state of Texas dearly, something he surely did not anticipate when he first began to ponder such a closure.

In 1875 the Eighth U.S. Cavalry left the Canadian River Valley for South Texas. Stationed at Fort Brown (near present-day Brownsville) and also operating out of Ringgold Barracks (where Rio Grande City stands today), Maj. Andrew Alexander, Capt. James Randlett, and Maj. David Clendenin used strategies honed on the Llano Estacado to track Mescalero Apaches, Kickapoos, and Mexicans in the Rio Grande Valley. Skills gained in the Eroded Plains of New Mexico proved just as effective along the southern Mexican border. The same troopers who patrolled the Fort Smith road scoured the Valley. While some were posted to picket details, others remained in the saddle, occasionally rotating these duties so troopers were always in the field. Such was the life of a U.S. cavalryman in the American Southwest in latter part of the nineteenth-century.[3]

After the Eighth Cavalry left Fort Bascom for good in 1875, the military reservation reverted to private ownership. John Watts had sold the land surrounding the fort to Wilson Waddingham in 1870, not long after its official closure. Waddingham was affiliated with the Maxwell Land Grant and raised cattle. He continued to purchase land in the Canadian River Valley over the next several years. When the army finally left the area, he did acquire the buildings that once comprised the fort. By 1875 he owned approximately 430,000 acres in northeastern New Mexico. His cowboys used the fort as their bunkhouse. Waddingham extracted the sandstone bricks from the officers' quarters and used them to build his ranch house. Ten years later, he owned the largest cattle operation in the country, running 25,000 longhorns on what would become the Bell Ranch. This ranch still functions as one of the largest cattle operations in the country, but the site on which Bascom stood is no longer within its boundaries.[4]

In September 1870 the news that Fort Bascom, in the midst of a major renovation, was about to close had spread quickly throughout the territory. As noted, several prominent New Mexicans made their feelings known in Washington, D.C. Brigadier General Pope had expected such an outcry from local citizens, but was perhaps a little surprised, or at least aggravated, that so many of them were able to make personal contact with the quartermaster general of the army, the adjutant general of the army, and the secretary of war. In the end, it was General-in-Chief Sherman who best explained why Fort Bascom ceased to be a fulltime post. Pope had already clarified that its closure was related to economic realities, but Sherman came closer giving the explanation that any "horse marine" would have understood: Fort Bascom had to close because its "animal maintenance [was] exceeding the aggregate value of the property—it is a disappointing prospect." A cavalryman was only as good as his horse. Ultimately, the post was closed because of the terrible logistics involved with keeping it open. "Animal maintenance" was all about procuring and storing enough forage and grains. Continuing to allocate such resources, in a land

Figure 10. Turn-of-the-twentieth-century Fort Bascom ruins. After the army abandoned the post, it eventually became part of the Bell Ranch, one of the largest cattle ranches in the United States. Based on information found on the 1865 ground plan (figure 7) and sketch (figure 2) of the post, this building was one of the officers' quarters. Note the brick or "sandstone" exteriors, the pitched eaves, and chimney at the end. Photographer: P. Clinton Borell. Title: Ruins of Fort Bascom, Bell Ranch, New Mexico. *Courtesy Palace of the Governors Photo Archives (NMHM/DCA), no. 055343.*

of little water, had become cost-prohibitive. So the army scaled back. Both New Mexican and Texan pioneers paid the price.[5]

The town of Liberty, which had developed near Fort Bascom, tried to remain a viable place to live after the troops left, yet unlike many other military communities in the Southwest, it was unable to do so. In the first decade of the twentieth century, six enterprising ranchers read that the Chicago, Rock Island and Pacific Railroad's westward line would soon pass through Dalhart, Texas, before continuing southwest across New Mexico. Gambling that the tracks would run near Tucumcari Peak, they began to purchase tracts of nearby land and in 1901 incorporated as the Tucumcari Townsite and Investment Company. Their gamble paid off, as the railroad did run its tracks by their property. As a result, they were soon busy selling lots. The railroad town of Tucumcari sucked the remaining life out of Liberty. Once the railroad did come, the success of the Bell Ranch influenced the construction of a spur to old Fort Bascom, which maintained a second life as a cowboy barracks, shipping point, and post office for years to come.[6]

Tucumcari also profited from its location along the old Fort Smith road. U.S. Route 66 followed this old Comanchero trail out of Texas in the late 1930s. Once the highway was completed, Tucumcari became the first town of any consequence for travelers driving west from Amarillo or east from Albuquerque. The postwar automobile boom saw the town become a popular rest stop for southwestern travelers. Yet when Interstate 40 was constructed a few decades later, engineers were more interested in developing a road system that could get travelers from point A to point B without many stops along the way. The new freeway bypassed Tucumcari, which meant fewer travelers would spend their money there. In 1975 the looming national bicentennial celebration prompted one last official attempt to give Fort Bascom the recognition it deserves. In the lead-up to the nation's birthday, the federal government started allocating large amounts of money to each state so citizens could have proper commemorations.

This gave Alan Morris, the Tucumcari city manager, an idea. Morris had long heard stories about the fort that had once existed just a few miles northeast of town. He devised a plan to build a replica of Fort Bascom, believing that such a site would generate income for the city.

Figure 11. Early-twentieth-century photo of Fort Bascom ruins. Based on details found in the 1865 ground plan (figure 7), these buildings were probably the barracks. Photographer: Nowell. Title: Ruins of Fort Bascom, Quay County near Tucumcari, N.Mex. Date: 1912. *Courtesy Palace of the Governors Photo Archives (NMHM/DCA), no. 014502.*

People who were currently bypassing the town might stop if they knew there was a replica frontier post nearby. Morris submitted his request to the New Mexico American Revolution Bicentennial Commission in Santa Fe to highlight the region's local history. It declared, in part, that "today the importance of Fort Bascom cannot be overestimated, particularly when all the old Forts within New Mexico are either destroyed, in great disrepair, or designated as National or State Monuments." Morris requested $30,565 from the state, which he planned to match with city funds. Yet Chris Krahling, the director of the commission, denied Morris's request. Perhaps it would have been more appropriate if Morris had asked the Texas Bicentennial Commission for the funds, for the men posted to this garrison were often on patrol in Texas.[7] From 1863 to 1874 they were the point of the spear in the U.S. Army's efforts to penetrate and destroy Comanchería, "an awful country," of eroded mountains, endless prairies, bad-tasting water, and powerful adversaries. Troopers continued to return to Fort Bascom until the Southern Plains Indians were defeated. Only then did the fort's crumbling adobes finally erode and melt away, as did its historical significance. All that remains is a sign along Highway 104, about eleven miles north of Tucumcari. It deserves better.

Regimental and Company Histories

The legend below identifies regiments and companies by letter for both tables. The bolded letters in the legend correspond with the letters at the top of each table.

A = 7th U.S. Inf. Co. "F"; **B** =1st NM Vol. Cav. Co. "I"; **C** = Co. "M"; **D** = Co. "C"; **E** = Co. "E"; **F** = Co. "D"; **G** = 5th U.S. Inf. Co. "E"; **H** = 1st NM Vol. Inf. Co. "D"; **I** = 1st NM Vol. Cav. Co. L; **K** = 1st NM Vol. Inf. Co. "E"; **L** = 3d U.S. Cav. Co. "A"; **M** = Co. "C"; **N** = Co. "D"; **O** = Co. "E"; **P** = Co. "G"; **Q** = 57th USC Inf. Co. "E"; **R** = 57th USC Inf. Co. "E"; **S** = Co. "G"; **T** = 125th USC Inf. Co. "K"; **U** = 37th U.S. Inf. Co. "F"; **V** = Co. "C"; **W** = 37th U.S. Inf. Co. "K"; **X** = 15th U.S. Inf. Co. "D"; **Y** = 8th U.S. Cav. Co. "B"; **Z** = Co. C; **AA** = Co. D; **BB** = 8th U.S. Cav. Co. "F"; **CC** = Co. "L"; **DD** = Co. "M"; **EE** = Co. "K"; **FF** = Co. "H"

TABLE 1.

Fort Bascom regimental and company history, part 1.

		A	B	C	D	E	F	G	H	I	J	K	L	M	N	O	P	Q	R	S	T	I	V	W	X	Y	Z	AA	BB	CC	DD	EE	FF
Aug	1863		■																															
Sept	1863		■																															
Oct	1863		■																															
Nov	1863		■																															
Dec	1863		■																															
Jan	1864	■	■																															
Feb	1864		■																															
March	1864		■																															
April	1864		■	■																														
May	1864		■																															
June	1864		■																															
July	1864		■																															
Aug	1864		■																															
Sept	1864		■																															
Oct	1864		■																															
Nov	1864		■																															
Dec	1864		■																															
Jan	1865		■		■																													
Feb	1865		■		■																													
March	1865		■		■		■																											
April	1865		■		■																													
May	1865		■		■		■																											
June	1865		■		■		■																											
July	1865		■		■																													
Aug	1865		■		■																													
Sept	1865		■		■																													
Oct	1865		■						■																									
Nov	1865		■						■																									
Dec	1865		■																															
Jan	1866		■																															
Feb	1866		■																															
March	1866		■																															
April	1866		■																															
May	1866		■								■																							
June	1866		■								■																							
July	1866		■								■																							
Aug	1866		■								■																							
Sept	1866															■			■														
Oct	1866															■																	
Nov	1866															■					■												
Dec	1866															■					■												
Jan	1867															■					■												
Feb	1867															■																	
March	1867															■	■																
April	1867															■																	
May	1867															■																	
June	1867															■																	
July	1867															■																	
Aug	1867															■					■												
Sept	1867															■					■												

NOTE: tables 1 and 2 do not include companies that were temporarily attached to Fort Bascom due to major expeditions, patrols, or training assignments. The main source for these tables was Returns from Military Posts, Fort Bascom, August 1863–June 1874, RG 94, NA, Washington, D.C. (Microfilm 617A, Roll 81). Also used were Letters Sent and Received, District of New Mexico, RG 393, NA, Washington, D.C., and Arrott Collection; Letters Sent and Received, Department of New Mexico, RG 393, NA, Washington, D.C.; and Eddie Matthews, "Letters from Home and Journal of His Military Years," transcribed by Ora Matthews Bublitz," Fort Union National Monument, N.Mex.

TABLE 2.
Fort Bascom regimental and company history, part. 2.

		A	B	C	D	E	F	G	H	I	J	K	L	M	N	O	P	Q	R	S	T	I	V	W	X	Y	Z	AA	BB	CC	DD	EE	FF
Oct	1867															■					■												
Nov	1867															■																	
Dec	1867														■																		
Jan	1868														■									■									
Feb	1868														■																		
March	1868														■																		
April	1868														■						■												
May	1868														■																		
June	1868														■																		
July	1868														■																		
Aug	1868														■																		
Sept	1868														■																		
Oct	1868														■																		
Nov	1868														■							■											
Dec	1868														■						■												
Jan	1869														■								■										
Feb	1869													■																			
March	1869													■																			
April	1869													■																			
May	1869													■							■												
June	1869													■							■												
July	1869													■							■												
Aug	1869													■																			
Sept	1869														■																		
Oct	1869														■									■									
Nov	1869														■									■									
Dec	1869														■									■									
Jan	1870														■																		
Feb	1870													■																			
March	1870																																
April	1870																							■									
May	1870																							■				■					
June	1870																							■									
July	1870																							■				■					
Aug	1870																							■				■					
Sept	1870																							■									
Oct	1870																							■				■					
Nov	1870																											■					
Dec	1870																																
May	1871																											■					
June-Nov	1871																											■	■				
May-Nov	1872																													■		■	■
May-Nov	1873																													■		■	■
June-Nov	1874																					■									■		■	■

SOURCES: see table 1.

Notes

CHAPTER 1

1. On repairs, see Jewett to Kobbe, 14 May 1870, Letters Sent, Department of New Mexico, Record Group 98 (now 393), National Archives and Records Administration, Washington, D.C., in James W. Arrott Collection, Donnelly Library, New Mexico Highlands University, Las Vegas, vol. 49: 227–28 (hereafter LS, DNM, RG 393, NA, in Arrott Collection, followed by volume and page numbers); U.S. Congress, *Report to the Secretary of War*, 35, 36.

2. Romero to Belknap, 28 September 1870, Records of the Adjutant General's Office, Reservation File, Record Group 94, National Archives and Records Administration, Washington, D.C. (hereafter AGO, RF, RG 94, NA); Romero to Pile, 25 June 1870, Letters Received (LR), DNM, RG 393, NA, in Arrott Collection.

3. Watts to Meigs, 31 October 1870, AGO, RF, RG 94, NA.

4. Watts to Belknap, 1 November 1870; Belknap to Watts, 22 November 1870, both in AGO, RF, RG 94, NA.

5. Pope to Townsend, 9 November 1870, Headquarters, Department of the Missouri, AGO, RF, RG 94, NA; Getty, Special Orders No. 105, 20 October 1870, LS, DNM, RG 393, NA, in Arrott Collection; Returns from Military Posts, Fort Bascom, November 1870, Record Group 94, National Archives, Washington, D.C. (microfilm 617A, Roll 81) (hereafter Returns, Fort Bascom, followed by month and year).

6. Sherman to Belknap, 17 November 1870, AGO, RF, RG 94, NA.

7. See Cutler, General Orders No. 20, Headquarters, Department of New Mexico (hereafter DNM), 11 August 1863, RG 393, NA, in Arrott Collection, 49: 1–3; Kobbe, Special Orders No. 105, Headquarters, DNM, 20 October 1870, RG 393, NA, in Arrott Collection, 24: 91.

8. Wallace, *Ranald Mackenzie on the Texas Frontier*, 56; Rathjen, *Texas Panhandle Frontier*, 202.

9. Stanley, *Fort Bascom*; Foster, "History of Fort Bascom, New Mexico." Foster's work, while more scholarly in nature than Stanley's, incorporates the triumphalist theme of most 1950s and 1960s historians of the American West.

10. Kenner initiated renewed scholarly interest in the region in 1969: see *New Mexican–Plains Indian Relations*, 155. Weber followed Kenner, creating a historiography all his own. For the purposes of this study, one should begin with *Mexican Frontier, 1821–1846*. Also see deBuys, *Enchantment and Exploitation*; Flores, *Horizontal Yellow*; Brooks, *Captives and Cousins*, 271, 317; Merlan and Levine, "Comanchero," 43; Hämäläinen, *Comanche Empire*; and DeLay, *War of a Thousand Deserts*. The relationships between kinship, violence, and a Southwestern indigenous economy are expanded upon in Anderson, *Indian Southwest*; and Smith, *From Dominance to Disappearance*. On Fort Bascom's place within Comanchería, see the map on page 316 in Hämäläinen, *Comanche Empire*. The term "cultural shatter zone" comes from Nathans's "ethnic shatter zone" discussed in *Beyond the Pale*, 380. In a recent environmental history of the Canadian River, Margaret Bickers illustrates the Comancheros' close ties to this stream but does not address the larger implications of this transnational black market economy: see "Three Cultures, Four Hooves, and One River." For early descriptions of the Canadian River Valley, see Hammond and Rey, *Don Juan de Oñate*, 401, 402; and Gregg, *Commerce of the Prairies*, 349, 363, 379.

11. For details on several of the volunteer soldiers who served in New Mexico, see Pettis, "The California Column." For more on the fluidity of the borderlands, see Hämäläinen, "Emergence of New Texas Indian History," in Buenger and de León, eds., *Beyond Texas through Time*, 52.

12. Kenner, *Comanchero Frontier*, 206. Information on the importance of cattle during the war and afterward can be found in Ely, *Where the West Begins*, 45–49.

13. Details of those major expeditions can be found in a variety of documents. For Col. Kit Carson's 1864 mission, see Carson to Carleton in Scott et al., *War of the Rebellion*, ser. 1, vol. 41, pt. 1: 940–42 (hereafter *OR* followed by series, volume, and page numbers). For the major expeditions of 1868 and 1874, see Peters, *Indian Battles and Skirmishes*, 14, 15, 44, 45; and Price to Headquarters, Santa Fe, 20 August 1874, Telegrams Sent and Received, DNM, RG 393, NA, in Arrott Collection, 29: 141. Information on routine scouts and patrols that originated out of Bascom can be found in LS, DNM, RG 393, NA, in Arrott Collection; and in *OR*.

14. Webb, *The Great Plains*, 507; to understand the arc of Webb's influence, see Malin, "Ecology and History"; Worster, "New West True West," 146; Malone, *Historians and the American West*, 2; "In an unforgiving environment . . . ," deBuys, *Enchantment and Exploitation,* ix. Two other works that have influenced my thinking on this region are Morris, *El Llano Estacado* and Flores, *Horizontal Yellow.*

15. Miller has illustrated the significant impact on the area of soldiers who mustered out of the service and remained: see *California Column in New*

Mexico; and *Soldiers and Settlers.* Miller's books were in response to Prucha's "Commentary," in *American Military on the Frontier,* 177.

16. The reference to "horse marines" is found in "Camp on the Canadian River, N.M.," *Freeport* (Ill.) *Journal,* 16 October 1872.

CHAPTER 2

1. Wozniak, *Across the Caprock,* 29.

2. Deep history involves a study of a region's geologic history, an overview of its flora and fauna, and how humans have interacted within the same environment over the centuries. Environmental historians such as Dan Flores term this type of history "bioregionalism." See Flores, "Argument for Bioregional Review," 2.

3. Turner, "Significance of the Frontier in American History," in *Does the Frontier Experience Make American Exceptional?,* 27–28.

4. Gassett, "List of Elevations," 99; Hughes and Wiley, *Archeology at Mackenzie Reservoir,* 10–13.

5. Gassett, "List of Elevations," 99.

6. Hammack, *Archaeology of the Ute Dam,* 4.

7. Ibid.

8. Darnton, *"Red Beds,"* 298.

9. Lucas and Hunt, "Stratigraphy of the Anton Chico and Santa Rosa Formations," 27.

10. The description of the various layers found within Mesa Rica comes from Darnton, *"Red Beds,"* 302. An outlier, as described by geologists, is an eroded, pyramidlike rocky formation left standing in an ancient river valley; some examples rise several hundred feet above the valley floor.

11. Darnton, *"Red Beds,"* 297.

12. Wozniak, *Across the Caprock,* 143.

13. Williams and McAllister, *New Mexico in Maps,* 65; Hilley et al., *Soil Survey of San Miguel County Area, New Mexico,* 53; MacCameron, "Environmental Change in Colonial New Mexico," 51. One such example of the government becoming aware of the difficulties with the soil can be found in Eaton to Secretary of War, 10 April 1868, "Unsuitableness of the Bosque Redondo Reservation for Navajo Indians," U.S. Congress, 40th Cong., 2nd sess., Ex. Doc. 248.

14. On springs, see Hammack, *Archaeology of the Ute Dam,* 6.

15. Ibid.

16. Hughes and Wiley, *Archeology at Mackenzie Reservoir,* 10–13. Also see Hammack, *Archaeology of the Ute Dam,* 6. On antelopes, see Gregg, *Commerce of the Prairies,* 363, 379.

17. Gregg, *Commerce of the Prairies,* 2.

18. One of the first historians to write about the challenges found in the arid West was Webb in *The Great Plains,* 507. Three works that best describe these environments and the people who made them home are deBuys, *Enchantment and Exploitation;* Flores, *Horizontal Yellow;* and Morris, *El Llano Estacado.*

19. Hammack, *Archaeology of the Ute Dam*, 4; Flores, *Caprock Canyonlands*, 2. Both Hammack and Flores hypothesize that these early people migrated west from the Mississippian woodland cultures. Most of the archeological evidence concerning their existence is found near present-day Amarillo, Texas. Alex Krieger believes some of the people who moved to the Caprock area in the fifteenth century could have been displaced Puebloans: see "Eastward Extension of Puebloan Datings," 143. On grama grasses, see Hughes and Wiley, *Archeology at Mackenzie Reservoir*, 10.

20. Kessell, *Spain in the Southwest*, 40; Kenner, *Comanchero Frontier*, 13.

21. Hammond and Rey, *Don Juan de Oñate*, 398. Oñate established Spain's first permanent settlements in New Mexico. During the Pueblo Revolt of 1680 the Spanish were forced out of this province, only to return twelve years later. A broad look at the region and these events can be found in Kessell, *Kiva, Cross, and Crown*; and Simmons, *Last Conquistador*, 124–25.

22. Hammond noted that Zaldívar saw these bison north of Tucumcari and about six leagues from the Canadian River. Fort Bascom was eleven miles north of Tucumcari and a league is approximately 2.6 miles. Hammond and Rey, *Don Juan de Oñate*, 398, 399, 401, 402.

23. Ibid., 400.

24. Krieger, "Eastward Extension of Puebloan Datings," 143.

25. Flores, "Bison Ecology and Bison Diplomacy," 465–85.

26. Brooks, *Captives and Cousins*, 117, 161; Hämäläinen, *Comanche Empire*, 330; Bailey, *Indian Slave Trade in the Southwest*, 24.

27. Kenner, *Comanchero Frontier*, 25. This work was originally published in 1969 as *A New Mexican–Plains Indian Relations*.

28. Tiller, *Jicarilla Apache Tribe*, 2, 3.

29. Brooks, *Captives and Cousins*, 117, 161; Kavanagh, *Comanches*, 92, 121; Kenner, *Comanchero Frontier*, 7. See also Weber, *Taos Trappers*, 28, 29; and Hämäläinen, *Comanche Empire*, 250–53.

30. For a good examination of the impact of American markets on New Mexico, see Reséndez, *Changing National Identities at the Frontier*, 96. Guns flowed along a transatlantic pipeline that included British firearms entering through Canada, which were funneled to the Skiri Pawnees, who traded them to Comanches for horses. After acquiring French weapons in Louisiana, Caddo and Wichita tradesmen did the same thing, bartering them for Comanche horses, usually stolen from Mexico and Texas. See DeLay, *War of a Thousand Deserts*, 104, 105. The Skiri Pawnees were a part of the Skidi Federation.

31. Gregg, *Commerce of the Prairies*, passim.

32. Ibid., xxi.

33. This is just south of the Tucumcari outliers. See Gregg, *Diary and Letters*, 46.

34. Gregg, *Commerce of the Prairies*, 260, 349.

35. Ibid., 363, 379.

36. Ibid., 67.

37. Ibid., 233. Chief Tábba-quena was an important Comanche chief affiliated with the Tenewas.

38. Hämäläinen, *Comanche Empire*, 56, 79, 180–81, 273, 315–20; Kavanagh, *Comanches*, 70; DeLay, *War of a Thousand Deserts*, 58, 59; Morris, *El Llano Estacado*, 185, 187, 190; Kenner, *Comanchero Frontier*, 36; Weber, *Mexican Frontier*, 98.

39. Kavanagh, *Comanches*, 179, 368. Puebloans and New Mexicans who lived in the region that surrounded the southern Rockies made annual journeys to the Llano Estacado to trade manufactured goods, homemade products, and agricultural produce to the Comanches for mules, horses, and cattle, most of which had been stolen in Mexico and Texas. For an in-depth (if dated) analysis of this trade, see Haley, "Comanchero Trade," 157–76. For one of the most recent interpretations, see DeLay, *War of a Thousand Deserts*, 91, 100, 110–11.

40. Hammond and Rey, *Don Juan de Oñate*, 400. Kavanagh, *Comanches*, 179. The Canadian was usually followed southeast to La Tecovas, which, as stated above, is northeast of Amarillo. Most Comancheros following the Pecos River traveled to Cañón de Rescate, located near Lubbock. Kavanagh states both of these locations were established camps where the Comancheros met up with the Comanches to trade. Quitaque is southwest of Amarillo and Muchaque is southwest of Lubbock.

41. Morris, *El Llano Estacado*, 280.

42. Whipple, *Pathfinder in the Southwest*, 86. This site was La Tecovas: see above and Kavanagh, *Comanches*, 179.

43. Whipple, *Pathfinder in the Southwest*, 89, 93, 94.

44. Ibid., 93, 94, 99.

45. Hämäläinen, *Comanche Empire*, 1–10; Kenner, *Comanchero Frontier*, 15–19; still of use is Haley, "Comanchero Trade." The new historiography on Comanches includes Delay, *War of a Thousand Deserts;* Brooks, *Captives and Cousins;* Flores, "Bison Ecology and Bison Diplomacy," 465–85; and Flores, *Horizontal Yellow*, iv.

46. Examples of records that note where much of the Comanchero trade originated include Surveyor Gen. William Pelham's 1857 interviews with Francisco Montoya, found in the Spanish Archives of New Mexico, Series I, Surveyor General Records, Reel 12, Preston Beck Grant, 12, 26, located in Special Collections, Donnelly Library, New Mexico Highlands University, Las Vegas (hereafter noted as Preston Beck Grant, followed by page number); also Mackenzie to Assistant Adjutant General, Department of Texas, "Camp on Las Canaditas, New Mexico," 7 August 1872, in Wallace, *Ranald S. Mackenzie's Official Correspondence*, 127, 128 (hereafter noted as Wallace, *Mackenzie's Official Correspondence*, followed by page number); Mackenzie to Granger, District of New Mexico, 15 August 1872, in Wallace, *Mackenzie's Official Correspondence*, 127, 128, 131.

47. Preston Beck Grant, 12, 26; Spanish Archives of New Mexico, Series I, Land Grant Documents, Reel 14, José L. Perea Grant, 499–503, found in Special

Collections, Donnelly Library, New Mexico Highlands University, Las Vegas (hereafter noted as José L. Perea Grant, followed by page number).

48. Preston Beck Grant, 12.

49. Preston Beck Grant, 12, 28; Baxter, *Las Carneradas*, 93.

50. Preston Beck Grant, 26; José L. Perea Grant, 515, 516.

51. Esteros Creek was a known crossing for "prehistoric" Indians and Apaches, as well as a campground and possible old Comanchero trading station: see Julyan, *Place Names of New Mexico*, 127. I am aware of the controversy that has swirled around this site for decades. Esteros Creek was eight miles north of present-day Santa Rosa and is now a part of Santa Rosa Lake: José L. Perea Grant, 515, 516. Lt. Charles C. Morrison of the Sixth Cavalry, a topographical engineer and member of Lt. George W. Wheeler's western surveys in 1875, drew a detailed map of roads throughout New Mexico Territory. His road away from the "Gallinas Crossing, just above Whittemore's Ranch," notes a "fork" at what he designates as "Hurrah Creek," another name for Esteros Creek. In his official report, he describes this area as the "deserted plaza of Esteros." For Lt. Morrison's report, see Annual Report of Secretary of War, 1876, 44th Cong. 2nd sess., Ex. Doc. 1, pt. 2, 365 [Serial Set 1745]. On the map that accompanied this report Lt. Morrison identified the Gallinas Crossing as Gallinas Spring. This map can be found in Records of the Office of the Chief Engineer, 1875, DNM, RG 77, NA, in Special Collections, Donnelly Library, New Mexico Highlands University, Las Vegas.

52. Preston Beck Grant, 26; Morris, *El Llano Estacado*, 188.

53. For a map of the Comanchero heartland, see Hämäläinen, *Comanche Empire*, 176; Kavanagh, *Comanches*, 205, 206; Haley, *Charles Goodnight*, 190.

54. On Captain Beck's service at Fort Union and transition to ranching, see Oliva, *Fort Union and the Frontier Army in the Southwest*, 118, 137; Wilhelm, *History of the 8th United States Infantry*, vol. 2, 254; Ruff to Maury, "Near Hatch's Ranch," 26 June 1860, *Report to the Secretary of War*, 36th Cong., 2nd sess., Ex. Doc. 1, pt. 1, 57, 58, in Arrott Collection, 6: 102. These ex-officers' involvement will be detailed in chapter six.

55. Gregg, *Commerce of the Prairies*, 67; Morris, *Llano Estacado*, 186–88; for more on American perceptions of Hispanos, see Weber, "'Scarce More Than Apes,'" 299; see Carlson, *Buffalo Soldier Tragedy of 1877*, 36, 75. New Mexican José Piedad Tafoya probably knew the trails that connected New Mexico to Texas as well as or better than any other individual: quote from Merlan and Levine, "Comanchero," 40.

56. Ruxton, *Life in the Far West*, 87, 88, 99; Monroy, *Thrown among Strangers*, 131. An example of a "blood and thunder" is Averill, *Prince of the Gold Hunters*. Jacobs's quote is from Swagerty, "Marriage and Settlement Patterns," 159.

57. Augur to Fry, 28 September 1872, in Rister, "Early Accounting of Indian Depredations," 54–60; Swagerty, "Marriage Settlement and Patterns," 164–67; Merlan and Levine, "Comanchero," 43; Kenner, "Great New Mexico Cattle Raid," 245.

58. The best discussion of this blending of southwestern cultures remains Brooks, *Captives and Cousins*. On Mexican nationals participating in this trade, see Sánchez et al., *Fort Union National Monument*, 35, 36. The term transnational comes from Hämäläinen, *Comanche Empire*, 317.

59. Brooks, "Served Well by Plunder," 24.

60. Hyslop, *Bound for Santa Fe*, 26, 178; Gregg, *Commerce of the Prairies*, 363, 379.

61. Morris, *Llano Estacado*, 184–86.

62. Morris, *Llano Estacado*, 182; Office of the New Mexico State Historian, "Santo Domingo Traders-Comancheros 1880."

63. Bergmann to De Forrest, 11 August 1866, LS, DNM, RG 393, NA, in Arrott Collection, 49: 72; des Montaignes, *The Plains*, 119, 120; Letterman to De Forrest, 7 September 1867, LS, DNM, RG 393, NA, in Arrott Collection, 49: 135; Dubois to De Forrest, 24 May 1867, LS, DNM, RG 393, NA, in Arrott Collection, 49: 116; map concept from Morris, *Llano Estacado*, 185. As noted above, African Americans sometimes apparently preferred life on the plains to one lived as a slave or citizen of the United States: see Quintard Taylor, *In Search of the Racial Frontier*, 75. On not being able to distinguish between Navajos and Comanches, see Alexander to Hubbell, 4 January 1867, LS, DNM, RG 393, NA, in Arrott Collection, 49: 97.

64. Bergmann to De Forrest, 12 May 1867, LS, DNM, RG 393, NA, in Arrott Collection, 49: 42–43.

65. Williams and McAllister, *New Mexico in Maps*, 56.

66. Gregg, *Commerce of the Prairies*, 2.

67. Lane to Headquarters, Fort Union, 24 October 1866, LS, DNM, RG 393, NA, in Arrott Collection, 19: 150; Kenner, "Great New Mexico Cattle Raid," 254.

CHAPTER 3

1. Hämäläinen, *Comanche Empire*, 292; DeLay, *War of a Thousand Deserts*, xiii.

2. See Ball, "Fort Craig, New Mexico," 153–73; Leckie, *Military Conquest of the Southern Plains*; Rosenbaum, *Mexicano Resistance in the Southwest*.

3. McKarney to Price, 25 January 1847, "List of Killed and Wounded at Pueblo de Taos on 4 February 1847," in "Message from the President of the United States, Part I of IV," U.S. Congress, 30th Cong., 1st sess., Ex. Doc. 8, 532–33; Crutchfield, *Tragedy at Taos*, 123, 126; Reséndez, *Changing National Identities on the Frontier*, 254–55.

4. Brooks, *Captives and Cousins*, 161; Mares, "Signifying Spain, Becoming Comanche," 268, 269.

5. Sánchez et al., *Fort Union National Monument*, 4; for the New Mexico defense system, see Ball, *Army Regulars in the Western Frontier*, 30–36.

6. Frazier, *Blood and Treasure*, 5–11; Morris, *El Llano Estacado*, 228–41; Stegmaier, *Texas, New Mexico, and the Compromise of 1850*, 27.

7. Ball, "Fort Craig, New Mexico," 154–57.

8. Leckie, *Military Conquest of the Southern Plains,* 15, 18.

9. Ball, *Army Regulars in the Western Frontier,* 191–92; Frazier, *Blood and Treasure,* 13.

10. Frazier, *Blood and Treasure,* 35–36.

11. Frazier, *Blood and Treasure,* 47–50; Thompson, *Henry Hopkins Sibley,* 216.

12. Thompson, *New Mexico Territory during the Civil War,* 34; Frazier, *Blood and Treasure,* 50, 144; Muster Rolls, Archives Box 10822, Folder 09: 05, New Mexico State Records Center and Archives, Santa Fe.

13. Frazier, *Blood and Treasure,* 117–19.

14. Taylor, *Bloody Valverde,* 80–83; Alberts, *Battle of Glorieta,* 134–35; Simmons, *Little Lion of the Southwest,* 184; Thompson, *New Mexico Territory during the Civil War,* 155–58, 224–30; Miller, *Soldiers and Settlers,* 224.

15. Meketa and Meketa, *One Blanket and Ten Days Rations,* vi; Canby to Headquarters, 22 February 1862, *OR,* ser. 1, vol. 9: 487–91. Martin Hall's work is peppered with references to the "competency" of the New Mexico volunteers: see *Sibley's New Mexico Campaign,* 50, 68, 70, 72. For a Hispano participant's perspective, one that attacks Canby's report, see Albuquerque *Evening Citizen,* 16 June 1893. For additional context on relations between the regular army and volunteers, see Ball, "Fort Craig, New Mexico," 153, 157; and Smith, *View from Officers' Row,* 3, 126. The reference to negative "histories" comes from Dunlay, *Wolves for Blue Soldiers,* 25, 26–28.

16. Cutler, General Orders No. 20, 11 August 1863, LS, DNM, RG 393, NA, in Arrott Collection, 49: 1.

17. Cullum, *Biographical Register of Graduates,* 341; U.S. Bureau of the Census, Tenth Census, 1880, New Mexico, Colfax County, Springer, Precinct 12, Enumerated District 7, 3 June 1880, Record Group 29, NA; Santa Fe *Daily New Mexican,* 4 December 1895, 4; Thompson, *New Mexico Territory during the Civil War,* 247. The First New Mexico Infantry later merged into the First New Mexico Cavalry.

18. Cullum, *Biographical Register of Graduates,* 341; Returns, Fort McLane, March, May, July 1861; Frazier, *Blood and Treasure,* 60.

19. Thompson, *New Mexico Territory during the Civil War,* 247; Cullum, *Biographical Register of Graduates,* 341; Returns, Fort Craig, November and December 1861 and January 1862; U.S. Department of War, Compiled Service Records of Union Soldiers Who Served in the Organization for the Territory of New Mexico, Record Group 94, NA.

20. Hall, *Sibley's New Mexico Campaign,* 64, 66.

21. Hall, *Sibley's New Mexico Campaign,* 60; Taylor, *Bloody Valverde,* 80–83; Col. Canby to Headquarters, "Engagement at Valverde, N. Mexico," 22 February 1862, *OR,* ser. 1, vol. 9: 487–91; Plympton to Selden, 24 February 1862, in Wilson, *When the Texans Came,* 242–43.

22. Canby to Headquarters, 22 February 1862, *OR,* ser. 1, vol. 9: 487–91; Plympton to Selden, 24 February 1862, Fort Craig "Union and Confederate

Correspondence," in Wilson, *When the Texans Came*, 243. On Plympton's report, also see Meketa, *Legacy of Honor*, 177, 178. While it is true the some Hispanos dropped their guns and ran during the battle, so did many of their Anglo counterparts. Much has been written about Union officers criticizing New Mexican actions in this campaign. Although there is an occasional aside that relates to isolated incidents where New Mexican Volunteers stood fast and fought bravely, the most publicized histories characterize the majority of these volunteers as undependable. Yet if Hispanos were so undependable, why were so many killed or wounded during these campaigns? Although Company B of the Fifth New Mexico Volunteers suffered a 53 percent casualty rate defending Capt. Alexander McRae's battery at the Battle of Valverde, this fact seldom came out in the weeks that followed the battle.

23. Plympton to Selden, 24 February 1862, in Wilson, *When the Texans Came*, 243; Office of the New Mexico State Historian, "Fort Wingate"; "Fort Wingate," DNM, RG 393, NA, in Arrott Collection, 55: 2; "Fort McRae," DNM, RG 393, NA, in Arrott Collection, 56: 249; Wilson, *When the Texans Came*, 242, 243. For more information on the battle, Wingate's injury, who ran, who stood firm, and Hispano casualty rates, see Frazier, *Blood and Treasure*, 176, 177. In the Albuquerque *Evening Citizen* (16 June 1893), a Hispano veteran took issue with the regular army's report. While Captain Bascom had recently been promoted to the Sixteenth U.S. Infantry, he was commanding a company of his old regiment, the Seventh, during the battle.

24. Plympton to Selden, 24 February 1862, in Wilson, *When the Texans Came*, 243. Over the years, historians have disagreed on who was responsible for starting the war that became known as the "Bascom Affair." For a negative view of Bascom's role, see Hafen and Rister, *Western America*, 500; and Foster, "History of Fort Bascom, New Mexico," 11, 12. For an opposing view see Utley, *Frontiersmen in Blue*, 161–63; and Thrapp, *Conquest of Apacheria*, 16–19. Although Bernard Irwin performed his heroic actions on 13 and 14 February 1861, he did not receive the Medal of Honor until 24 January 1894. For more on Irwin's Medal of Honor, see U.S. Army Medical Department, "Medal of Honor Awardees: Bernard J. D. Irwin." In General Orders No. 20, Cutler noted the fort was named for Bascom "to perpetuate the memory of the gallant Captain George N. Bascom . . . who fell in the defense of our colors," LS, DNM, RG 393, NA, in Arrott Collection, 49: 1.

25. Alberts, *Battle of Glorieta*, 134–42; U.S. Department of War, Compiled Service Records of Union Soldiers Who Served in Organization from the Territory of New Mexico, Record Group 94, NA. For the specifics on Carson's request for Bergmann, see Carson to Cutler, 23 November 1863, DNM, RG 393, NA, in Arrott Collection, 12: 316. Bergmann spent about twelve hundred dollars of his own money to purchase two pair of socks, one pair of shoes, two suits of cotton flannel underclothes, hickory shirts, overalls, cotton-made blouses, and straw hats for every man in his company. Bergmann also claimed that he paid his men out of his own pocket for several months and was never reimbursed

by the army. See Bergmann to Laughlin, 22 April 1902, Court of Claims (Civil War), Edward H. Bergmann vs. United States, New Mexico State Records Center and Archives, Santa Fe, folder 30, no. 2.

26. Returns, Fort Bascom, December 1863, May 1864, August 1866.

27. Meketa and Meketa, *One Blanket and Ten Days Rations*, vi.

28. Watts to Halleck, 23 March 1862, *OR*, ser. 1, vol. 15: 650, 651.

29. Walker and Teal, "Soldier in the California Column," 34; Canby to Carleton, 11 August 1862, *OR*, ser. 1, vol. 9: 574–75.

30. Thompson, *New Mexico Territory during the Civil War*, 9, 25.

31. Carleton to Backus, 12 October 1862, LS, DNM, RG 393, NA, in Arrott Collection, 10: 264–265.

32. Thompson, *New Mexico Territory during the Civil War*, 10; Frazier, *Blood and Treasure*, 208–30. For specifics on John R. Baylor, see Carleton to Plympton, 16 November 1862, LS, DNM, RG 393, NA, in Arrott Collection, 10: 351; Cutler to Updegraff, 15 November 1862, LS, DNM, RG 393, NA, in Arrott Collection, 10: 348. The numerous communiqués between headquarters and field officers regarding a second invasion might seem a bit paranoid when looking back 150 years later, yet the men charged with maintaining the integrity of the Union in New Mexico had to face that reality. Captain Backus and his Colorado volunteers, as well as Captain Plympton and the Seventh U.S. Infantry, had already drawn and shed blood against the Confederates at Fort Craig and at the battles of Valverde and Glorieta Pass. The war was tangible, the Texans were deadly, and Carleton knew that to have a chance he must be forewarned of another assault.

33. Backus to Carleton, 1 December 1862, *OR*, ser. 1, vol. 15: 153–58. "Chief Mowa" was more than likely Chief Mowway of the Kotsoteka Comanches. See Kavanagh, *Comanches*, 5, 383; Thompson, *New Mexico Territory during the Civil War*, 223.

34. Such reports include Davis to Headquarters, 30 October 1864, *OR*, ser. 1, vol. 15: 212. Davis led Company B, First New Mexico Volunteer Infantry. See also Pettis, "California Column," 8; Henderson to Headquarters, Fort Bascom, LS, DNM, RG 393, NA, in Arrott Collection, 49: 33; and Letterman to De Forrest, 31 August 1867, LS, DNM, RG 393, NA, in Arrott Collection, 49: 31. Letterman was captain of the 125th U.S. Colored Infantry. During this period he was also Fort Bascom's post commander. Company K of the 125th Colored Infantry was stationed at Fort Bascom during portions of 1866 and 1867. See U.S. Department of War, Compiled Records Showing Service of Military Units in Volunteer Union Organizations, Kentucky, 125th Regiment, Record Group 94, NA. Originally a member of the First Colorado Volunteers, De Forrest served as Carleton's aide-de-camp and assistant adjutant general. See Pettis, "California Column," 35.

35. Carleton to Camp Easton, 21 June 1863, LS, DNM, RG 393, NA, in Arrott Collection, 11: 291.

36. See Fort Butler, Records of the War Department, Office of the Adj. Gen., LS, DNM, RG 393, NA, in Arrott Collection, 56: 408; and Frazer, "The Fort That almost Was," 258–63.

37. Bailey, *Bosque Redondo*, 27, 47; Kelly, *Navajo Roundup*, 12; Dunlay, *Kit Carson and the Indians*, 247; Williams and McAllister, *New Mexico in Maps*, 65.

38. Dunlay, *Kit Carson and the Indians*, 309, 317; Williams and McAllister, *New Mexico in Maps*, 65; Kelly, *Kit Carson's Expedition against the Navajo*, 134, 135.

39. Carleton to Camp Easton, 21 June 1863, LS, DNM, RG 393, NA, in Arrott Collection, 11: 291; Hoagland, "Village Constructions," 224.

40. "Synopsis of Operations in the Department of New Mexico, 16 May–28 December 1863," in *OR*, ser. 1, vol. 26, pt. 1: 23, 26.

41. Cutler, General Orders No. 20, 11 August 1863, LS, DNM, RG 393, NA, in Arrott Collection, 49: 1. In November and December 1863, thirty officers and soldiers of the Seventh Infantry called this post home. At the same time, seventy-five men of Company I of the First New Mexico Volunteer Cavalry were stationed there. See Brown to Headquarters, Fort Bascom, 21 December 1863, LS, DNM, RG 393, NA, in Arrott Collection, 49: 1. On Captain Bergmann selecting the site, see Thompson, *New Mexico Territory during the Civil War*, 247.

42. Watts acquired the land after serving as the "Attorney for the Petitioner." Watts was an attorney for the heirs of the previous owner, Pablo Montoya. This land was later developed into the Bell Ranch, one of the largest cattle enterprises in the United States: see Reports of the Committee on Private Land Claims, Senate Miscellaneous Document 81/3, U.S. Congress, 44th Cong., 1st sess.; "Descriptions of U.S. Military Posts and Stations," Reservation File, Department of New Mexico, Record Group 393, Entry 464, Box 8, Folder 38, National Archives, Washington, D.C. (hereafter Descriptions, RF, DNM, RG 393, NA.) Lt. Adolph Luettwitz received correspondence from headquarters that John Lambert, a surveyor for New Mexico Territory, would soon arrive and begin mapping out the military reservation: see Ludington to Lt. Luettwitz, 11 April 1868, LR, DNM, RG 393, NA.

43. Cutler, General Orders No. 20, 11 August 1863, LS, DNM, RG 393, NA, in Arrott Collection, 49: 1.

44. Miller, *Soldiers and Settlers*, 224, 225. There is no identification within this letter as to who these civilians were, yet since they would be working with adobe, they were probably local New Mexicans.

45. Quotes are taken from Description of Military Posts, LS, DNM, RG 393, NA, in Arrott Collection, 49: 1–3.

46. Carleton to Plympton, 14 November 1863, LS, DNM, RG 393, NA, in Arrott Collection, 12: 293.

47. Descriptions, RF, DNM, RG 393, NA; Carleton to Camp Easton, 21 June 1863, LS, DNM, RG 393, NA, in Arrott Collection, 11: 291; Carleton to Plympton, 14 November 1863, LS, DNM, RG 393, NA, in Arrott Collection, 12: 293; Gregg, *Commerce of the Prairies*, 349; Alexander, *Cavalry Wife*, 114.

48. Jewett to assistant acting adjutant general, 14 February 1870, LS, DNM, RG 393, NA.

49. Description of Military Posts, Fort Bascom, 11 August 1863, Circular 4, Surgeon General's Office, 1870, LS, DNM, RG 393, NA, in Arrott Collection, 49: 1–3; Alexander to Headquarters, 1 February 1867, LS, DNM, RG 393, NA, in Arrott Collection, 49: 107–108; Alexander, *Cavalry Wife*, 114.

50. Dubois to mother, 5 April 1867, LS, DNM, RG 393, NA, in Arrott Collection, 62: 209–10. Dubois was in the Third U.S. Cavalry, and he was brevetted to lieutenant colonel while commanding at Fort Bascom for portions of 1867. Details specifying the windows can be found in Miscellaneous Fort File, Fort Bascom N. Mex., Sheet 1, Ground Plan, Office of the Chief of Engineers, Record Group 77, National Archives, College Park, Md.

51. Plympton to Headquarters, 29 August, 16 November, and 9 December 1863, and 12 January 1864, LS, DNM, RG 393, NA, in Arrott Collection, 49: 8–10, 13.

CHAPTER 4

1. Alexander, *Cavalry Wife*, 114.

2. Carleton to Bergmann, 12 January and 28 February 1864, LS, DNM, RG 393, NA, in Arrott Collection, 13: 30, 129.

3. Returns, Fort Bascom, March 1864; Brown to Enos, 26 August 1865, LS, DNM, RG 393, NA, in Arrott Collection, 13: 129.

4. Miller, *Soldiers and Settlers*, 225.

5. For a general description of river topography, see General Orders No. 20, 11 August 1863, LS, DNM, RG 393, NA, in Arrott Collection, 49: 1–3; Brown to Enos, 26 August 1865, LS, DNM, RG 393, NA, in Arrott Collection, 13: 29; De Forrest to Dubois, 10 August 1867, LS, DNM, RG 94, Entry 464, box 8, folder 38, NA; Dubois to mother, 5 April 1867, LS, DNM, RG 393, NA, in Arrott Collection, 62: 209, 210.

6. Description of Military Posts, Fort Bascom, 11 August 1863, Circular 4, Surgeon General's Office, 1870, LS, DNM, RG 393, NA, in Arrott Collection, 49: 1–4; Oliva, *Soldiers on the Santa Fe Trail*, 195, 196; Returns, Fort Bascom, July 1867.

7. Clary, *These Relics of Barbarism*, 275, 282, 338; Private Eddie Matthews, "Letters from Home and Journal of His Military Years" (hereafter Matthews, Letters [or Journal], followed by title and date). See the bibliography for a complete list of the Matthews letters used in this volume: in this instance, "Camp Near Fort Bascom," 1 July 1872. Rickey, *Forty Miles a Day*, 79.

8. Clary, *These Relics of Barbarism*, 283, 339; Returns, Fort Bascom, June 1868.

9. Records note at least two soldiers drowned in the Canadian River as a result of these monsoons. Private John Hendricks of the Third Cavalry drowned while herding cattle on 18 August 1868. See Returns, Fort Bascom, August 1868. Private Matthews of the Eighth Cavalry noted in 1870 that "one man of 'M'

Troop drowned and one horse of our Troop shared a similar fate," in Matthews, Letters, "Camp at Fort Bascom," 3 August 1872. The reference to the Canadian's quick rise out of its banks comes from Description of Military Posts, Fort Bascom, 11 August 1863, Circular 4, Surgeon General's Office, 1870, LS, DNM, RG 393, NA, in Arrott Collection, 49: 1–4.

10. Smith to commissary of subsistence, 11 January 1866; Alexander to De Forrest, 2 January 1867, LS, DNM, RG 393, NA, in Arrott Collection, 49: 38, 93; Eaton to Garrison, Headquarters, 24 February 1864, LS, DNM, RG 393, NA, in Arrott Collection, 55: 94. Prior to moving into San Miguel County, James and Tom Patterson were government agents at the Bosque Grande in 1864: see Caldwell, *John Simpson Chisum*, 189n.143. James Patterson continued to pursuing military contracts after moving north, assuring himself a place within Fort Bascom's history.

11. Alexander to De Forrest, 26 January 1867, LS, DNM, RG 393, NA, in Arrott Collection, 49: 93; Matthews, Letters, "Camp at Fort Bascom," 3 August 1872.

12. Miller, *California Column*, 24. Private Matthews described the bread and the worms in Letters, "Camp at Fort Bascom," 26 August 1872. The "bean bellied army" quote comes from Matthews, Letters, "Fort Bascom, N.M.," 17 July 1874.

13. Miller, *Soldiers and Settlers*, 42; Dubois to Eaton, 5 July 1867, LS, DNM, RG 393, NA, in Arrott Collection, 49: 119; Returns, Fort Bascom, March 1866.

14. Information on the location of the sutlers' store is taken from Leonard Slesick's hand-drawn map, found in Slesick, Personal files, Panhandle-Plains Historical Museum Research Center. Frazer, *Forts and Supplies*, 55; Rickey, *Forty Miles a Day*, 36.

15. For Bergmann's lawsuit see, *Edward H. Bergman [sic] v. William V. B. Wardwell*, Records of the U.S. Territorial and New Mexico District Courts for Socorro County, Civil Case #00168, Folder 168, New Mexico State Records Center and Archives, Santa Fe. For specifics on Wardwell, see Parish, *Charles Ilfeld Company*, 72; and http://wc.rootsweb.ancestry.com/cgi-bin/igm.cgi?op=GET&db=ryder10&id=I73205 (accessed 24 August 2014). Bergmann's connection with Thomas B. Catron and Stephen B. Elkins is only one of many such associations he shared with New Mexico Territory's leading historical figures. For more on Catron and Elkins, see Caffey, *Chasing the Santa Fe Ring*, 84–103. On Watts's and Patterson's involvement in the cattle trade, see Luettwitz to McClure, 17 March 1868, LR, DNM, RG 393, NA. On the Watts contracts to sell hay, see Ludington to Watts, 6 December 1867, LS, DNM, RG 393, NA. Watts's son, also named John, was also involved in this trade (set up no doubt by his father) and did business with Fort Bascom. For more on the son's ties see Remley, *Bell Ranch*, 49.

16. Rickey, *Forty Miles a Day*, 116, 121.

17. Ibid., 82.

18. Miller, *Soldiers and Settlers*, 99; Sullivan to Ludington, 3 July 1869, LS, DNM, RG 393, NA, in Arrott Collection, 49: 210. The names Gallinas Spring and Gallinas Crossing are almost interchangeable. Lt. Charles C. Morrison

of the Sixth Cavalry, a topographical engineer and member of Lt. George W. Wheeler's western surveys in 1875, drew a detailed map of the roads, trails, and topography throughout New Mexico Territory. When Morrison made his report, he called it Gallinas Crossing, but on his accompanying map he noted this area as Gallinas Spring: see Annual Report of Secretary of War, 1876, 44th Cong. 2nd sess., Ex. Doc. 1, pt. 2: 365, [Serial Set 1745]; and Map by Lt. Charles C. Morrison, Sixth Cavalry, 1875, Office of the Chief Engineer, DNM, RG 77, NA, in Special Collections, Donnelly Library, New Mexico Highlands University, Las Vegas. Another map that designates this area as Gallinas Spring can be found in an investigation into the "Star-Route Cases," found in *Testimony Taken by the Committee on Expenditures,* U.S. Congress, 48th Cong., 1st sess., House Misc. Doc. 38, pt. 1, vol. 2.

19. McClure to Luettwitz, 29 October 1868, LR, DNM, RG 393, NA.

20. Bergmann to Enos, 26 February 1864, LS, DNM, RG 393, NA; Letterman to Enos, 23 January 1867, LS, DNM, RG 393, NA; Letterman to Enos, 1 March 1867, LS, DNM, RG 393, NA; Ludington to Hildeburn, 2 January 1868, LR, DNM, RG 393, NA; Luettwitz to Romero, 15 February 1868, LS, DNM, RG 393, NA; Luettwitz to Ludington, 6 March 1869, LS, DNM, RG 393, NA.

21. Sullivan to Ludington, 3 July 1869, LS, DNM, RG 393, NA, in Arrott Collection, 49: 210; Miller, *Soldiers and Sutlers,* 98.

22. Armistead, *Horses and Mules in the Civil War,* 49, 50; McGowen, *Horse Sweat and Powder Smoke,* 83; see Evans, "Canadian River Expedition," 287.

23. Dubois to Hunter, Headquarters, 17 December 1867, LS, DNM, RG 393, NA, in Arrott Collection, 49: 146.

24. Frazer, *Forts and Supplies,* 55; Abreu to Headquarters, Fort Bascom, General Orders No. 51, 5 November 1864, LS, DNM, RG 393, NA, in Arrott Collection; Morris to Stapp and Hopkins, 7 March 1869, LS, DNM, RG 393, NA, in Arrott Collection, 49: 16, 199; Jewett to Florsheim, 19 May 1870, LS, DNM, RG 393, NA.

25. Smith to Hopkins, 8 June 1866, LS, DNM, RG 393, NA, in Arrott Collection, 49: 63–65.

26. Morris to acting assistant quartermaster, Fort Bascom, 19 December 1869, LS, DNM, RG 393, NA, in Arrott Collection, 49: 190; Matthews, Letters, "Fort Bascom, N.M.," 30 March 1873; and "Fort Union, N.M.," 16 December 1873. Henry Strong's recollections are found in Rickey, *Forty Miles a Day,* 34.

27. Kobbe to Morris, 24 June 1869, LR, DNM, RG 393, NA; Morris to Kobbe, 3 July 1869, LS, DNM, RG 393, NA; Kobbe to Morris, 9 July 1869, LR, DNM, RG 393, NA.

28. Clark, *History of New Mexico,* 6–8.

29. Description of Military Posts, Fort Bascom, 11 August 1863, Circular 4, Surgeon General's Office, 1870, LS, DNM, RG 393, NA, in Arrott Collection, 49: 3; Matthews, Letters, "Fort Bascom, N.M.," 26 March 1873; Dubois to mother, 5 April 1867, LS, DNM, RG 393, NA, in Arrott Collection, 62: 209–10.

30. Miller, *California Column*, 26. References to Company L, Eighth Cavalry, and baseball can be found in Matthews, Letters, "Fort Bascom, N.M.," 26 March 1873 and "Summer Camp on the Canadian River, N.M.," 5 September 1873.

31. Miller, *California Column*, 25; Rickey, *Forty Miles a Day*, 35.

32. Miller, *California Column*, 25. Details on providing rations to women who worked at this post are found in Bergmann to Bell, Headquarters, Santa Fe, 17 August 1865, LS, DNM, RG 393, NA, in Arrott Collection, 49: 25; Miscellaneous Fort File, Fort Bascom, Sheet 1, Ground Plan, Office of the Chief of Engineers, RG 77, NA, College Park, Md.

33. Miller, *California Column*, 24–26; Thompson, Special Orders No. 4, Headquarters, Fort Bascom, 22 January 1865; Bergmann to Bell, Headquarters, Santa Fe, 17 August 1865; Brown to Bell, 31 August 1865, all in LS, DNM, RG 393, NA, in Arrott Collection, 49: 18, 25, 28; Returns, Fort Bascom, August, September, October, November 1865.

34. Alexander, *Cavalry Wife*, 111, 114.

35. Returns, Fort Bascom, May 1866; Alexander, *Cavalry Wife*, 71.

36. Russell, *Land of Enchantment*, 116, 119.

37. "Indian Scouts and Their Results for the Year 1863—Headquarters Department of New Mexico, Santa Fe, February 24, 1864," in Moore and Everett, *From the Rebellion Record*, 746; Returns, Fort Bascom, February 1866; Jewett to Kobbe, 15 June 1870, Headquarters, Santa Fe, LS, DNM, RG 393, NA, in Arrott Collection, 49: 232–33. Special Orders No. 41, 17 June 1870, Headquarters, Fort Bascom, LR, DNM, RG 393, NA. After losing his position as sutler, Stapp had remained in the area and raised cattle.

38. U.S. Bureau of the Census, Ninth Census, 1870, New Mexico, San Miguel County, Division: Fort Bascom Military Reserve (hereafter cited as 1870 Census, NM, San Miguel Co.).

39. U.S. Bureau of the Census, Tenth Census, 1880, New Mexico, Colfax County; Returns, Fort Bascom, November 1864; Bergmann to Bell, 17 August 1865, LS, DNM, RG 393, NA, in Arrott Collection, 49: 25. Baca was a man of some significance in the territory. He settled down in Lincoln County after the war and became a part of the Billy the Kid saga. Several veterans of Fort Bascom were involved in the Lincoln County Wars: see Nolan, *West of Billy Kid*, 39. Other persons who served at Fort Bascom who were later involved in Lincoln County events include Sheriff William Brady, killed by Billy the Kid; merchant Lawrence. G. Murphy; the aforesaid Baca; and Capt. James F. Randlett of the Eighth Cavalry. For details concerning their roles in Lincoln County, see Utley, *High Noon in Lincoln*, 11, 30, 53, 60, 82. For the specific battle that led to Lucero's and Ortiz's deaths, see "Synopsis of Operations in the Department of New Mexico, May 16–December 28, 1863," *OR*, ser. 1, vol. 26, pt. 1: 26; Meketa and Meketa, *One Blanket and Ten Days Rations*, vi.

40. Cutler, General Orders No. 25, Headquarters, Santa Fe, 22 September 1863, LS, DNM, RG 393, NA, in Arrott Collection, 12: 195–97; Muster Rolls,

8 March 1864, Fort Bascom, Box 10822, folder 03, Item 01, New Mexico State
Records Center and Archives, Santa Fe.

41. Returns, Fort Bascom, April, May, June, July 1866.

42. "Dear Mother," Dubois Journal, 15 April 1867, LS, DNM, RG 393, NA,
in Arrott Collection, 62: 109; Alexander, *Cavalry Wife*, 73; Dubois to De Forrest,
24 May 1867, LS, DNM, RG 393, NA, in Arrott Collection, 49: 116.

43. Returns, Fort Bascom, August 1863, January 1864, April 1866; 1870
Census, NM, San Miguel Co.; Emmons, *Beyond the American Pale*, 213.

44. Millett and Maslowski, *For the Common Defense*, 277.

45. Returns, Fort Bascom, July, August, September, October, December 1867;
Matthews, Letters, "Summer Camp on the Canadian River," 20 August 1873.

46. Returns, Fort Bascom, August, September 1868. On Hendricks's death
also see John Hendricks, Final Statements 1862-899, AGO, RG 94, NA. Compilation of ailments in 1868 supplied by "Information furnished by Assistant
Surgeons George S. Rose and W. H. H. Michler, and Acting Assistant Surgeon H. Duane, United States Army," LS, DNM, RG 393, NA, in Arrott
Collection, 49: 1–3; Matthews, Letters, "Summer Camp on the Canadian River,"
23 September 1873.

47. Miller, *California Column*, 26; Hartz to Ludington, 18 November 1869,
Headquarters, Fort Bascom Endorsement Book, LS, DNM, RG 393, NA, in
Arrott Collection, 49: 217.

48. The list is a compilation of the following sources: Devita, "Civil War Burial
Records in New Mexico" (noted with the letter D); Returns, Fort Bascom, June
1867, August 1868 (noted with the letter R); and Post Adj. W. D. Lang, Special
Orders No. 87, Fort Bascom Headquarters, 26 August 1870, LS, DNM, RG
393, NA, in Arrott Collection, 49: 250 (noted with the letter A).

49. For Bergmann's positive report, Alexander's quote, and the contractors'
orders, see Miller, *Soldiers and Settlers*, 225. (I have changed Miller's Gorman
to Gorham.) Ludington to Luettwitz, 9 April 1868, LR, DNM, RG 393, NA;
Ludington to Luettwitz, 14 April 1868, LR, DNM, RG 393, NA. Regarding
Ayres's failure to complete his contract, see Ludington to Luettwitz, 14 June
1868, LR, DNM, RG 393, NA. Alexander had submitted a detailed list of repairs
needed at the post the previous year that generated some of the work mentioned above. Alexander to De Forrest, 1 February 1867, LS, DNM, RG 393,
NA, in Arrott Collection, 49: 107, 108.

50. Hartz to De Forrest, 14 May 1870, LS, DNM, RG 393, NA; Hartz to Robinson, 19 May 1870, LS, DNM, RG 393, NA.

51. Jewett to De Forrest, 31 May 1870, LS, DNM, RG 393, NA.

52. Hartz to Clark, Santa Fe, 1 June 1870, LS, DNM, RG 393, NA; Hartz to
Leroux, Las Vegas, N. Mex., 14 July 1870, LS, DNM, RG 393, NA.

53. Hartz to Jewett, 20 July 1870, LS, DNM, RG 393, NA; Hartz to Jewett,
28 July 1870, LS, DNM, RG 393, NA.

54. Jewett to De Forrest, 4 September 1870, LS, DNM, RG 393, NA.

CHAPTER 5

1. Carleton to Plympton, 29 August 1863, LS, DNM, RG 393, NA, in Arrott Collection, 49: 8. See Holmes, *Fort Selden, 1865–1891*, 6; Morris, *El Llano Estacado*, 190.

2. Plympton to Carleton, 29 August 1863, LS, DNM, RG 393, NA, in Arrott Collection, 49: 8.

3. Returns, Fort Bascom, December 1863.

4. Bergmann to Headquarters, 12 January 1864, LS, DNM, RG 393, NA, in Arrott Collection, 49: 12.

5. Returns, Fort Bascom, May 1864.

6. Hyslop, *Bound for Santa Fe*, 124–25; Kavanagh, *Comanches*, 397. Travelers using the Mountain Route remained on a more westerly course after crossing the Arkansas River until they reached the location where Bent's Fort was established in Colorado Territory. From that location the Mountain Route turned southwest and climbed Raton Pass before reconnecting with the Cimarron Route on the eastern edge of the Sangre de Cristo Mountains about forty miles north of Las Vegas, New Mexico. De Forrest to Bergmann, 4 June 1864, LR, DNM, RG 393, NA.

7. Connelly to Carleton, 22 June 1864, LR, DNM, RG 393, NA.

8. Davis to Headquarters, 30 October 1864, *OR*, ser. 1, vol. 15: 212.

9. Cutler to Bergmann, 22 August 1864, *OR*, ser. 1, vol. 41, pt. 2: 812; the reference to de Lisle's experience is derived from Miller, *Soldiers and Settlers*, 266; on de Lisle's affiliation with St. Vrain and Bent, see Dunham, "Ceran St. Vrain," 153n.21.

10. Bergmann to Deus, 29 August 1864, LS, DNM, RG 393, NA; Cutler to Bergmann, 22 August 1864, *OR*, ser. 1, vol. 41, pt. 2: 812.

11. Cutler to Davis, 22 August 1864, *OR*, ser. 1, vol. 41, pt. 2: 811. Returns, Fort Bascom, August 1864. The two other forces were led by Capt. Nicholas S. Davis and Maj. Joseph Updegraff: see Oliva, *Soldiers on the Santa Fe Trail*, 155; Hunt, *Army of the Pacific*, 161. Rabbit Ears is near the present-day town of Clayton, New Mexico. On Carson and Camp Nichols see Dunlay, *Kit Carson and the Indians*, 340–41; and Russell, *Land of Enchantment, Memoirs*, 103. It is important to note that Mrs. Hal Russell, her daughter-in-law, changed her subject's name to Marian for publication purposes.

12. Carleton to Carson, 24 September 1864, *OR*, ser. 1, vol. 41, pt. 3: 243, 244.

13. For the formulation of this plan, see Carleton to De Forrest, 24 September 1864, *OR*, ser. 1, vol. 41, pt. 3: 353.

14. This visit is noted in both Kavanagh, *Comanches*, 398, and Kenner, *New Mexican–Plains Indian Relations*, 146. De Forrest to Deus, 24 September 1864, *OR*, ser. 1, vol. 41, pt. 3: 423. The order for Major Cháves to take command of Fort Bascom can be found in Carleton to De Forrest, 26 September 1864, *OR*, ser. 1, vol. 41, pt. 3: 399.

15. Carleton to Major (he was addressed with his brevet rank of lieutenant colonel) Cháves, 1 October 1864, and Carleton to Abreu, 1 October 1864, both in *OR*, ser. 1, vol. 41, pt. 3: 550. Cháves was a significant political figure in post-war New Mexico, often affiliated with the so-called "Santa Fe Ring." For more on Cháves, see Caffey, *Chasing the Santa Fe Ring*, 190, 191.

16. Carson to Carleton, 7 October 1864; Abreu to Cutler, 10 Oct 1864; Carson to Carleton, 10 October 1864; Carleton to Abreu, 24 October 1864, all in *OR*, ser. 1, vol. 41, pt. 3: 696, 771.

17. Carson to Carleton, 10 October 1864; Carleton to Carson, 14 October 1864, both in *OR*, ser. 1, vol. 41, pt. 3: 771, 877. Carleton to Carson, 20 October 1864; Carleton to Blunt, 22 October 1864, both in *OR*, ser. 1, vol. 41, pt. 4: 151, 197–98.

18. Carleton to Carson, 14 October 1864, *OR*, ser. 1, vol. 41, pt. 3: 877; Carleton to Blunt, 22 October 1864, *OR*, ser. 1, vol. 41, pt. 4: 197–99. On the Navajos' refusal, see Crocker to Cutler, 30 September 1864, *OR*, ser. 1. vol. 41, pt. 3: 525.

19. Carleton to Curtis, 23 October 1864, *OR*, ser. 1, vol. 41, pt. 4: 213.

20. Carleton to Steck, 29 October 1864, *OR*, ser. 1, vol. 41, pt. 4: 320–22.

21. Carson to Carleton, 3 November 1864, *OR*, ser. 1, vol. 41, pt. 4: 422.

22. Pettis, "Kit Carson's Fight with the Comanches," 8; Carson to Carleton, 4 December 1864, *OR*, ser. 1, vol. 41, pt. 1: 940; reference to Company D, First New Mexico Cavalry, in Returns, Fort Bascom, November 1864. The discrepancy in the number of Indians is due to the various reports. Carson was originally going to leave Cimarron with seventy-two auxiliaries, but his 3 November 1864 letter indicated that he had picked up eight more before he left. Later documents, including Pettis's, puts the number back at seventy-two. Other references in Pettis's account indicate a few Ute women also accompanied the expedition, which could also account for the discrepancy: Courtright, *Expedition against the Indians*, 63–182. Volunteers from California made up the regiments collectively known as the California Column. These soldiers helped New Mexican volunteers fill the vacuum left after the regular army moved east of the Mississippi River. They made a significant contribution in the army's efforts to protect the citizens of New Mexico Territory during the war. Many remained in the Southwest after the conflict, as this history will detail: see Masich, *Civil War in Arizona*, 10, 11; Miller, *California Column in New Mexico*, xiii.

23. In Carleton's reply, he referred to a 5 November letter he had received from Michael Steck: see Carleton to Steck, 8 November 1864, *OR*, ser. 1, vol. 41, pt. 4: 496, 497.

24. Curtis to Carleton, 28 November 1864, *OR*, ser. 1, vol. 41, pt. 4: 709.

25. Leckie, *Military Conquest of the Southern Plains*, 21–26; Utley and Washburn, *Indian Wars*, 226–27.

26. Carleton to Carson, 22 October 1864, *OR*, ser. 1, vol. 41, pt. 4: 198, 199.

27. Pettis, "Kit Carson's Fight with the Comanches," 9, 10. Alvin Lynn has meticulously tracked the expedition's movements in his excellent history, *Kit Carson and the First Battle of Adobe Walls*, 11, 14, 18, 23.

28. Pettis, "Kit Carson's Fight with the Comanches," 11-14; Carson to Carleton, 4 December 1864, *OR*, ser. 1, vol. 41, pt. 1: 940.

29. Pettis, "Kit Carson's Fight with the Comanches," 14, 15; Courtright, *Expedition against the Indians*, 63-184.

30. Pettis, "Kit Carson's Fight with the Comanches," 17, 18; quote from Courtright, *Expedition against the Indians*, 63-184; "Prairie carriage" is from Lynn, *Kit Carson and the First Battle of Adobe Walls*, 7.

31. Pettis, "Kit Carson's Fight with the Comanches," 20; Courtright, *Expedition against the Indians*, 63-184; Lynn, *Kit Carson and the First Battle of Adobe Walls*, 62.

32. Pettis estimated that the second village contained 500 lodges: see "Kit Carson's Fight with the Comanches," 24. Carson estimated 350 lodges: see Carson to Carleton, 4 December 1864, *OR*, ser. 1, vol. 41, pt. 1: 941.

33. Carson to Carleton, 4 December 1864, *OR*, ser. 1, vol. 41, pt. 1: 941; Pettis, "Kit Carson's Fight with the Comanches," 33.

34. Carson to Carleton, 16 December 1864, *OR*, ser. 1, vol. 41, pt. 1: 943; Pettis, "Kit Carson's Fight with the Comanches," 33; Lynn, *Kit Carson and the First Battle of Adobe Walls*, 86, 198, 199.

35. Carson to Carleton, 16 December 1864, *OR*, ser. 1, vol. 41, pt. 1: 943.

36. Cutler to Bergmann, 30 November 1864, LS, DNM, RG 393, NA, in Arrott Collection, 15: 191.

37. McFerran to Bergmann, 1 December 1864, LS, DNM, RG 393, NA, in Arrott Collection, 15: 192; McFerran to Mssrs. Martínez and Hornberger, Anton Chico, N. Mex., 1 December 1864, LS, DNM, RG 393, NA, in Arrott Collection, 15: 193.

38. Carson to Carleton, 16 and 26 December 1864, *OR*, ser. 1, vol. 41, pt. 1: 939, 943. More on Carleton and Steck's differences can be found in Kenner, *New Mexican–Plains Indian Relations*, 149.

39. The Comanche raid on Elm Creek in Texas illustrates this point. This was a battle between Anglo women and children and Comanche warriors led by Little Buffalo: see D. Smith, *Frontier Defense in the Civil War*, 132. Carleton gave Carson credit in Carleton to Carson, 30 January 1865, U.S. Congress, 34th Cong., 1st sess., Doc. 369, pt. 2, 689.

40. Carleton to Bergmann, 21 February 1865; Bergmann to Carleton, 9 March 1865, both in LS, DNM, RG 393, NA, in Arrott Collection, 16: 106, 122. The four companies of First New Mexico Cavalry were Company D, led by Lt. Charles Haberkorn; Company E, led by Capt. Saturnino Baca; Company I, led by Lt. Michael Cronin; and Company M, led by Capt. Charles Deus: see "Abstract for 1865," *OR*, ser. 1, vol. 48, pt. 2: 278. For the recap on Morrison's journey into Comanchería, see Morrison to Carleton, 10 May 1865, *OR*, ser. 1, vol. 48, pt. 1: 310.

41. Wood to Bergmann, 6 January 1865, in U.S. Congress, 34th Cong., 1st sess., House Doc. 369, pt. 2, 437.

42. See the report from Armstrong, Second United States Volunteer Infantry, 9 June 1865, Fort Dodge, Kansas, *OR*, ser. 1, vol. 48, pt. 1: 311. For raids near Fort Bascom, see Morris to Hunter, 2 October 1868, LR, RG 393, NA; and Jewett to Kobbe, 15 June 1870, LS, DNM, RG 393, NA, in Arrott Collection, 49: 232–33.

43. D. Smith, *Frontier Defense in the Civil War*, 141–43.

44. Smith to Bergmann, 15 November 1865, LS, DNM, RG 393, NA, in Arrott Collection, 49: 33; Carleton to Bergmann, 28 April 1866, LS, DNM, RG 393, NA, in Arrott Collection, 18: 74.

45. "May 10–19, 1865, Scout from Fort Sumner, N. Mexico," U.S. Congress, 34th Cong., 1st sess., House Doc. 369, pt. 1, 174.

46. Headquarters, Fort Bascom, 5 May 1865, LS, DNM, RG 393, NA, in Arrott Collection, 49: 19.

47. Cutler to Bergmann, 19 June 1865, LR, DNM, RG 393, NA.

48. Bergmann to De Forrest, 12 May 1866, LS, DNM, RG 393, NA, in Arrott Collection, 49: 42–43.

49. Hubbell to De Hague, Post Adj, Fort Bascom, 25 August 1865, LS, DNM, RG 393, NA.

50. Bergmann to Hubbell, 24 May 1866; Bergmann to Farnsworth, 27 May 1866; Bergmann to Carleton, 29 May 1866, all in LS, DNM, RG 393, NA, in Arrott Collection, 49: 50, 53, 54.

51. Bergmann to Headquarters, Santa Fe, 11 August 1866, LS, DNM, RG 393, NA, in Arrott Collection, 49: 70–73; Kavanagh, *Comanches*, 406, 407, 470.

52. Michno and Michno, *Fate Worse Than Death*, 279, 289; Kavanagh, *Comanches*, 406, 407. Goldbaum supplied beef to the army that Kavanagh reveals came from transactions with Comanches: see Kavanagh, *Comanches*, 470. Quotes are from Bergmann to Headquarters, Santa Fe, 11 August 1866, LS, DNM, RG 393, NA, in Arrott Collection, 49: 70–73.

53. For the streams and Comanchero trails Bergmann crossed, see Morris, *El Llano Estacado*, 185–90.

54. Morris, *El Llano Estacado*, 188; Bergmann to Carleton, 11 August 1866, LS, DNM, RG 393, NA, in Arrott Collection, 49: 70–73.

55. Bergmann to Carleton, 11 August 1866, LS, DNM, RG 393, NA, in Arrott Collection, 49: 70–73; Bergmann reported that he traveled 250 miles southeast. I derived my average per day by taking the distance and dividing by the days it took him to reach his destination.

56. Bergmann to Carleton, 11 August 1866, LS, DNM, RG 393, NA, in Arrott Collection, 49: 70–73. On Comanchero locations, see Morris, *El Llano Estacado*, 184–86; Hämäläinen, *Comanche Empire*, 317; Kenner, *New Mexican–Plains Indian Relations*, 163, 191; and Rathjen, *Texas Panhandle Frontier*, 200, 201.

57. Bergmann to Carleton, 11 August 1866, LS, DNM, RG 393, NA, in Arrott Collection, 49: 70–73.

58. Ibid.

59. Carleton to Carson, 30 January 1865, U. S. Congress, H. Doc. 369, pt. 1, 34th Cong., 1st sess. [Serial Set 3436], 689. For the identification of these chiefs, I relied on Kavanagh, *Comanches*, 407, and *Comanche Political History*, 399.

60. Bergmann to Carleton, 11 August 1866, LS, DNM, RG 393, NA, in Arrott Collection, 49: 70–73.

61. Ibid.

CHAPTER 6

1. Returns, Fort Bascom, August–November 1866; Billington, *New Mexico's Buffalo Soldiers*, 33.

2. Hawley to De Forrest, 15 November 1866, LS, DNM, RG 393, NA, in Arrott Collection, 49: 86.

3. Ibid. Carleton's reply came back as an endorsement attached to another Hawley correspondence: Hawley to De Forrest, 22 November 1866, LS, DNM, RG 393, NA, in Arrott Collection, 49: 88.

4. Alexander was promoted to major in the Ninth U.S. Colored Cavalry in early December 1866. He was to report to New Orleans to take command, but after Gen. Ulysses S. Grant read his report on Fort Bascom's structural deficiencies, he ordered him to inspect every fort in New Mexico Territory. This delay circumvented his transfer to the Ninth. He never served in this regiment. He was later transferred to the Eighth U.S. Cavalry: see Alexander, *Cavalry Wife*, 162. Returns, Fort Bascom, November 1866. On Tenth Cavalry recruits being trained at Bascom, see Special Orders No. 49, Headquarters, 20 December 1866, LR, DNM, RG 393, NA; Special Orders No. 20, Headquarters, 20 February 1867, LR, DNM, RG 393, NA; and Returns, Fort Bascom, February, March, April 1867.

5. Alexander to Sykes, 3 January 1867; Alexander to Hubbell, 4 January 1867, both in LS, DNM, RG 393, NA, in Arrott Collection, 49: 96, 97; Alexander, *Cavalry Wife*, 114, 115. For Hubbell's new role as a beef contractor, see Kenner, *New Mexican–Plains Indian Relations*, 178. Hubble's employment as a "guide and spy" is found in Letterman to Enos, 31 January 1867, LS, DNM, RG 393, NA.

6. Alexander to De Forrest, 12 January 1867, LS, DNM, RG 393, NA, in Arrott Collection, 49: 103–105; also see Morris, *El Llano Estacado*, 185, and Kenner, *New Mexican–Plains Indian Relations*, 125, 181. Guides were always in high demand. Headquarters sent several Utes and Jicarillas to serve the post as guides in the summer of 1867: see De Forrest to Dubois, 16 August 1867. Manuelito was a significant Navajo chief who was of an advanced age by the time Alexander ran across him near the Texas border. Over the years he had been involved in many conflicts with both the U.S. Army and the Utes, who often served as army auxiliaries: see McNitt, *Navajo Wars*, 380.

7. Alexander to De Forrest, 12 January 1867, LS, DNM, RG 393, NA, in Arrott Collection, 49: 103–105; Alexander, *Cavalry Wife*, 132.

8. Alexander to De Forrest, 26 January 1867, LS, DNM, RG 393, NA, in Arrott Collection, 49: 106. This agent's name is mentioned in Kenner, *New Mexican–Plains Indian Relations*, 176.

9. The context for this paragraph comes from Kenner, *New Mexican–Plains Indian Relations*, 176, 177.

10. Several scholars have written about the link between borderlands and black market economies: see Weber, *Mexican Frontier*, 284; deBuys, *Enchantment and Exploitation*, 114–19; Brooks, *Captives and Cousins*, 117, 337, 338; Hämäläinen, *Comanche Empire*, 317; Kenner, *New Mexican–Plains Indian Relations*, 97, 155; Rosenbaum, *Mexicano Resistance in the Southwest*, 26, 27. Similar shadow economies crop up in borderland regions throughout the world: see Nathans, *Beyond the Pale*, 380.

11. Letterman to De Forrest, 27 April 1867; and Dubois to De Forrest, 23 August 1867, both in LS, DNM, RG 393, NA, in Arrott Collection, 49: 112, 130.

12. Alexander to De Forrest, 26 January 1867, LS, DNM, RG 393, NA, in Arrott Collection, 49: 106; Hämäläinen, *Comanche Empire*; Kenner, *New Mexican–Plains Indian Relations*, 158, 177.

13. On General Carleton's defense of his actions, see Simon, *Papers of Ulysses S. Grant*, 74.

14. Letterman to De Forrest, 7 September 1867, LS, DNM, RG 98 393, NA, in Arrott Collection, 49: 13.

15. Letterman to De Forrest, 7 September 1867, LS, DNM, RG 393, NA, in Arrott Collection, 49: 13.

16. Kenner, *New Mexican–Plains Indian Relations*, 177.

17. Deposition of José Pieda Tafoya, 26 June 1893, Indian Depredation Case No. 9133, Records of the U.S. Court of Claims, RG 123, NA, found in Kenner, *New Mexican–Plains Indian Relations*, 157n.11; *Edward H. Bergman [sic] v. William V. B. Wardwell*, Records of the U.S. Territorial and New Mexico District Courts for Socorro County, Civil Case #00168, Folder 168, New Mexico State Records Center and Archives, Santa Fe.

18. Bristol to Cutler, 23 September 1864, Union Provost Marshal's File of Paper Relating to Individual Civilians, Publication No. M345, RG 287, NA, www.fold3.com/image/" \l "292132587 (accessed 9 January 2015). For brief example of other historical references, see Merlan and Levine, "Comanchero," 43; Carlson, *Buffalo Soldier Tragedy*, 36, 75.

19. Bergmann to De Forrest, 13 May 1866, Fort Bascom N. Mex. Collection, Panhandle Plains Historical Museum Research Center, Canyon, Tex.

20. Healy [Recorder], 28 January 1866, Council of Administration, RG 393, NA, in Arrott Collection, 49: 67; Kenner, *New Mexican–Plains Indian Relations*, 159. The quote about Jennings's job at the Bosque Redondo can be found in Returns from Military Posts, Fort Sumner, RG 94, NA, M617A, Roll 81, September 1864 (hereafter Returns, Fort Sumner, followed by month and year). Staples such as flour, bacon, ham, and coffee were shipped to Bascom from Fort Union: see 5 July 1868, Special Orders No. 102, LR, DNM, RG 373, NA.

21. While others have referred to this matter, all sources go back to Kenner, *New Mexican–Plains Indian Relations*, 159–60.

22. Ibid.

23. On Jennings's involvement in the Comanchero trade, see Jewett to De Forrest, 14 May 1870, LS, DNM, RG 393, NA, in Arrott Collection, 49: 151, 152; Letterman to De Forrest, 31 August 1867, LS, RG 393, NA, in Arrott Collection, 49: 132; Getty to Dubois, 12 September 1867, LS, DNM, RG 393, NA, in Arrott Collection, 21: 115; Kenner, *New Mexican–Plains Indian Relations*, 159–60. José Piedad Tafoya is noted in the 1870 Census, NM, San Miguel Co., Division: Ranch at Gallinas Crossing.

24. On Labadie's firing, during which he claimed to be innocent of the charges, see Wood to McCleave, Fort Sumner, 22 October 1864, "Condition of the Indian Tribes," 294; 1870 Census, NM, San Miguel Co., Division: Agua Negra.

25. Nolan, *West of Billy Kid*, 31–39; Nolan, *Lincoln County War*, 38, 39; Returns, Fort Sumner, September 1864. On Samuel Gorham's participation in Major Evans's expedition, see Evans, "Canadian River Expedition," 288.

26. Carleton to Crocker, 10 November 1864, *OR*, ser. 1, vol. 41, pt. 1: 357–59; Davis to Cutler, 25 March 1865, *OR*, ser. 1, vol. 48, pt. 1: 463–64; Returns, Fort Sumner, September 1864.

27. Wallen to Cutler, 6 January 1864, *OR*, ser. 1, vol. 34, pt. 1: 69–70.

28. José L. Perea Grant (also noted as Rancho de los Esteros), 499–503; 1870 Census, NM, San Miguel Co., Division: Ranch at Gallinas Crossing. William P. Calloway paid for his Los Esteros hotel, retail, and liquor licenses on 8 July 1864 but did not muster out of the service until September. Even after leaving the military he continued to play a major role on the Bosque Redondo Indian Reservation. He continued to pay taxes on his Los Esteros business enterprises through 1868. On Calloway's licenses, see "Internal Revenue Assessment Lists for the Territory of New Mexico": Calloway's records for 1868 can be found in "Record of Personal Taxes Assessed in New Mexico, 1868, Division 3, W. P. Calloway, Los Esteros," http://search.ancestry.com (accessed 14 December 2014). On when he mustered out, see U.S. Department of War, Compiled Service Records of Union Soldiers Who Served in Organizations from the State of California, William P. Calloway, RG 94, NA. On the "horse-stealing ring" see F. Levine, "Unified Anthropological Approach to Historical Archaeology," 100; Kenner, *New Mexican–Plains Indian Relations*, 159–60. On bloodshed between Anglo and Hispanic New Mexicans, see Nolan, *Lincoln County War*, 128; and Johnson, *Horrell Wars*, 71–81.

29. Records on all individuals acquiring licenses in 1864 can be found in "Internal Revenue Assessment Lists for the Territory of New Mexico."

30. Santa Fe *Daily New Mexican*, 6 and 7 January 1869. Without noting Calloway's participation, the execution of these Hispanos is also detailed in Haley, *Charles Goodnight*, 217–19.

31. Letterman to De Forrest, 31 August 1867, LS, RG 393, NA, in Arrott Collection, 49: 132. While this report has been used by several scholars to

highlight goods being traded, no one has really paused to consider how many loaves of hard bread it takes to make five hundred pounds. It takes about an hour to bake two to four one-pound loaves. The apprehension of these particular Comancheros, when taken in isolation, seems to be a minor event, yet when multiplied by the hundreds of traders doing exactly the same thing, sometimes twice per year for decades, the logistics become more interesting. For one scholar's use of Letterman's correspondence, see Kavanagh, *Comanches*, 470. On some of the basics of the bread ovens (*hornos*) both Hispanos and Puebloan peoples used to make this hard bread see, National Park Service, "Hornos."

32. Letterman to De Forrest, 31 August 1867; and Letterman to De Forrest, 7 September 1867, both in LS, DNM, RG 393, NA, in Arrott Collection, 49: 132, 135; Hämäläinen, *Comanche Empire*, 318; quote from Simmons, "Comancheros had a Colorful History in New Mexico."

33. Getty to DuBois, 12 September 1867, LS, DNM, RG 393, NA, in Arrott Collection, 21: 115.

34. Letterman to De Forrest, 7 September 1867, and Letterman to Hunter, 24 October 1867, both in LS, DNM, RG 393, NA, in Arrott Collection, 49: 135, 144.

35. Utley, *Frontier Regular*, 133, 134; Kenner, *New Mexican–Plains Indian Relations*, 182.

36. Both quotes come from Wallace, "Historic Indians of the Llano Estacado," 8.

37. The raid on Pedro Sandoval comes from Dubois to Hunter, 7 January 1868, LS, DNM, RG 393, NA, in Arrott Collection, 49: 150; Winfrey and Day, *Indian Papers of Texas and the Southwest*, 4: 182, 183, 237; Peters, *Indian Battles and Skirmishes*, 13, 14.

38. Peters, *Indian Battles and Skirmishes*, 13, 14.

39. Morris to Hunter, 2 October 1868, LR, RG 393, NA.

40. Utley, *Frontier Regulars*, 145, 149, 154; Hutton, *Phil Sheridan and His Army*, 42; Leckie, *Military Conquest of the Southern Plains*, 114.

41. Hutton, *Phil Sheridan and His Army*, 52, 53.

42. Hunter to Evans, Special Orders No. 160, 20 October 1868, LS, DNM, RG 393, NA, in Arrott Collection, 22: 335; Evans, "Canadian River Expedition," 279–82.

43. The idea that Fort Bascom opened up the "second front" on the Southern Plains Indians comes from a discussion with Durwood Ball on 9 May 2012. For Evans's request of Carson's report, see Leckie, *Military Conquest of the Southern Plains*, 117. Captain Pfeiffer was a veteran of Fort Bascom: see Returns, Fort Bascom, February 1866; Evans, "Canadian River Expedition," 282; Hunter to Pfeiffer, Fort Garland, 20 October 1868, LS, DNM, RG 393, NA, in Arrott Collection, 22: 360.

44. Captain Gageby and Company I, Thirty-Seventh Infantry, were familiar with Fort Bascom, having served there in July 1868. He was killed during the

NOTES TO PAGES 150–55 225

1868 campaign. See Returns, Fort Bascom, November 1868. Captain Hawley and Company A, Third Cavalry, were also veterans of the post, having first been stationed there in September 1866. See Returns, Fort Bascom, September 1866; Evans, "Canadian River Expedition," 282.

45. Evans, "Canadian River Expedition," 283.

46. Ibid.

47. Ibid., 284. The total forage number comes from combining the original tonnage in corn and oats with the amount acquired from James Patterson, as noted on pages 284–85.

48. Evans, "Canadian River Expedition," 286. For Sheridan's discussion with Bridger, see Rister's comments on page 289. Note: James Patterson contracted with Samuel Gorham to deliver these teams of oxen. Gorham served as a captain in the army at Fort Sumner: see Returns, Fort Sumner, September 1865.

49. Evans, "Canadian River Expedition," 282, 286. Two of the howitzers Evans hauled into battle were left at Bascom by Carson in 1864. Major Jewett alludes to this in Jewett to Shoemaker, Fort Union, 21 September 1870, LS, DNM, RG 393, NA.

50. Evans, "Canadian River Expedition," 282, 286, 287. Unknown to Evans, at about the same time his column was hit by the snowstorm, Sully, Custer, eleven companies of the Seventh Cavalry, and five companies of Nineteenth Kansas Cavalry were engaged in a battle with Black Kettle's Cheyenne in the Wichita Mountains: see Rathjen, *Texas Panhandle Frontier*, 188–89; and Leckie, *Military Conquest of the Southern Plains*, 95–97. By 1868 military horses were on half rations. Calculating horses' and mules' (numbering 429, not counting civilian mule trains) forage at six pounds per day for nine days meant that by 26 November Price's animals had eaten at least 23,166 pounds of their subsistence.

51. On early Native Americans in this region, see Hammack, *Archaeology of the Ute Dam*, 4; Flores, *Caprock Canyonlands*, 2; Krieger, "Eastward Extension of Puebloan Datings," 143; Evans, "Canadian River Expedition," 287.

52. Evans, "Canadian River Expedition," 287–89.

53. Ibid., 290–93. The location of this canyon is in present-day Greer County, Oklahoma, known at the time as Soldier Spring. Both the current location and information concerning "Woman's Heart," comes from H. A. Anderson.

54. In early January 1869, Captain Morris ordered 22,000 rounds of "Centre primed metallic cartridges and an additional 6,000 rounds of Sharps rifle cartridges": see Morris to Kobbe, 16 January 1869, LS, DNM, RG 393, NA; also see Utley, *Frontier Regulars*, 70.

55. Evans, "Canadian River Expedition," 293; Rathjen, *Texas Panhandle Frontier*, 191; Leckie, *Military Conquest of the Southern Plains*, 114–18.

56. Evans, "Canadian River Expedition," 294.

57. Ibid., 294–97.

58. Ibid., 298.

59. Evans, "Canadian River Expedition," 298; Rathjen, *Texas Panhandle Frontier,* 191. The expedition left the depot on 15 December 1868 and returned on 13 January 1869. The death count for animals on this expedition is from Evans, "Canadian River Expedition," 300.

60. Evans, "Canadian River Expedition," 299. Captain Morris was busy funneling supplies provided by local contractors and merchants east down the Canadian River to Evans's men. The Rosenwald Brothers' Las Vegas establishment supplied corn. William Stapp moved back and forth along the river throughout the expedition hauling material to the front in seventeen of his wagons. Samuel Gorham supplied grains for the horses: see Morris to Luettwitz, 17 December 1868, LS, DNM, RG 393, NA; Morris to Rosenwald and Co., 24 December 1868, LS, DNM, RG 393, NA; Morris to McClure, 29 December 1868, LS, DNM, RG 393, NA; Morris to Ludington, 31 January 1869, LS, DNM, RG 393, NA; Sullivan to Ludington, 12 June 1869, LS, DNM, RG 393, NA.

61. Evans, "Canadian River Expedition," 301.

62. Ibid., 300.

63. Hutton, *Phil Sheridan and His Army,* 62–68.

64. One of Kansas's foremost frontier historians argues that Evans's attack had a major impact on the Cheyennes' and Arapahos' decision to move to the reservation: see Garfield, "Defense of the Kansas Frontier," 467. Some scholars note that Chief Horseback (Terheryaquahip) was at the Soldier Spring battle. Kavanagh states he was at Fort Cobb when the fight took place (*Comanches,* 422). Major Evans reported that "Chief Arrow Point" was in command of the Indians during the battle. Rathjen simply stated that the attack was against Horseback's "village" (*Texas Panhandle Frontier,* 191). Nye declared that Horseback was there (*Carbine and Lance,* 79).

65. Kenner notes that the chiefs were moved from Fort Union to Fort Cobb (*New Mexican–Plains Indian Relations,* 182–83). Kavanagh states it was Fort Leavenworth (*Comanches,* 423).

66. Kenner, *New Mexican–Plains Indian Relations,* 184.

67. Such myopia can be found in Kenner's otherwise excellent work. He suggests the soldiers of Fort Bascom were "intimidated by the forbidding wastes which surrounded it [and] paid little attention to the trade." He also characterizes their patrols as "feeble attempts" to stop the trade, while in the same sentence he notes that they did halt some of the Comanchero exchanges. All other scholars use Kenner as the most important source on the Comancheros, and rightly so; however, this book counters his disdain for, or lack of respect for, Fort Bascom's soldiers by illustrating that their attempts to stop the trade were far from feeble: see Kenner, *New Mexican–Plains Indian Relations,* 177.

CHAPTER 7

1. On Fort Bascom's closing, see Getty, Special Orders No. 105, 20 October 1870, LS, DNM, RG 393, NA, in Arrott Collection, 24: 191.

2. Cain to Hunter, LS, DNM, RG 393, NA, in Arrott Collection, 49: 200–201; Billington, *New Mexico's Buffalo Soldiers*, 33.

3. Santa Fe *Daily New Mexican*, 16 March 1869, in Kenner, *New Mexican–Plains Indian Relations*, 183. For the five chiefs' incarceration, see Kavanagh, *Comanches*, 423.

4. Kavanagh, *Comanches*, 423–25.

5. Kenner, *New Mexican–Plains Indian Relations*, 184; Returns, Fort Bascom, December 1869.

6. Kenner, *New Mexican–Plains Indian Relations*, 184; Jewett to Kobbe, 2 July 1870, LS, DNM, RG 98, NA, in Arrott Collection, 24: 105.

7. Jewett to Kobbe, 15 June 1870, LS, DNM, RG 393, NA, in Arrott Collection, 49: 232–33; Kobbe to Jewett, 2 July 1870, LS, DNM, RG 393, NA, in Arrott Collection, 24: 105; Jewett to Kobbe, 26 August 1870, LS, DNM, RG 393, NA. Fifty-eight troopers from the Eighth U.S. Cavalry joined twenty-four Fifteenth U.S. Infantry soldiers at the post in May 1870. More Eighth Cavalry troopers arrived throughout the summer, indicating the army's concern with the illicit traffic. See Returns, Fort Bascom, May, July, August 1870. Research could not identify Jewett's "Eagle Tail," although Nye's report on Major Price's expedition references a Kiowa named Eadle-tau-hain, who was also called Botalye: see Price, Official Report, File 2815, Old Files, AGO, Files for 1874–75; Price, "Excitement on the Sweetwater," 245, 246.

8. On unhappy Comanches beginning to leave the reservations in the summer of 1870, see Kavanagh, *Comanches*, 427. On the uptick in raids as a direct result of Fort Bascom's closure, see Kenner, *New Mexican–Plains Indian Relations*, 185.

9. Gregg to Clendenin, 25 February 1871, LS, DNM, RG 393, NA, in Arrott Collection, 25: 48; animal count is from Chief Quartermaster to Lafferty, 25 February 1871, LS, DNM, RG 393, NA, in Arrott Collection, 25: 124, 125; Matthews, Letters, "Fort Union, N.M.," 3 March 1871.

10. Clendenin to Troops in the Field, Fort Bascom, 30 April 1871, LS, DNM, RG 393, NA, in Arrott Collection, 25: 161.

11. Kenner, *New Mexican–Plains Indian Relations*, 185; Clendenin to Kobbe, 31 May 1871, LS, DNM, RG 393, NA, in Arrott Collection, 25: 210. The second quote is from the Santa Fe *Daily New Mexican*, 6 June 1871. I derived my estimate of the goods Randlett captured by using a couple of sources regarding how much weight a mule could carry, of which a general rule of thumb is 20 percent of its body weight. The average pack mule weighed twelve hundred pounds. Col. Henry Inman estimated the load weight to be closer to three hundred pounds: see U.S. Forest Service, Dept. of Agriculture, "Pike and San Isabel National Forests"; Inman, *Old Santa Fe Trail*, 57.

12. Lafferty to Clendenin, 3 June 1871, LS, DNM, RG 393, NA, in Arrott Collection, 26: 12; Kenner, *New Mexican–Plains Indian Relations*, 188.

13. Randlett to Lafferty, 18 April 1871, LS, DNM, RG 393, NA, in Arrott Collection, 25: 141.

14. Bailey, *Bosque Redondo*, 27; Fort Sumner Closure, General Orders No. 19, AGO, 1871, in Arrott Collection, 54: 64; Ferrari to Randlett, "In the Field," 3 May 1871, LS, DNM, RG 393, NA, in Arrott Collection, 25: 166; Randlett to Lafferty, 3 May 1871, LS, DNM, RG 393, NA, in Arrott Collection, 25: 167.

15. Sullivan to Ludington, 21 April 1870, LS, DNM, RG 393, NA.

16. Clendenin to Lafferty, 17 September 1871, LS, DNM, RG 393, NA, in Arrott Collection, 26: 147.

17. Clendenin to Gregg, Fort Union, 28 June 1871, LS, RG 393, NA, in Arrott Collection, 26: 48–49; Gregg to Assistant Adjutant General, Headquarters, 3 July 1871, LS, DNM, RG 393, NA, in Arrott Collection, 26: 60.

18. Winfrey and Day, *Indian Papers of Texas and the Southwest*, 4: 182, 183, 237; U.S. Congress, 43rd Cong., 1st sess., Ex. Doc. 257, 3; also see Ely, "Gone to Texas and Trading with the Enemy," 446.

19. Hatch to Granger, Santa Fe, 31 March 1872, and Hatch to Assistant Adjutant General, Dept. of Texas, 15 April 1872, both in Wallace, *Mackenzie's Official Correspondence*, 45–47.

20. Sheridan to Augur, 20 April 1872, in Wallace, *Mackenzie's Official Correspondence*, 55.

21. U.S. Congress, 50th Cong., 2nd sess., Ex. Doc. 103; U.S. Congress, 48th Cong., 1st sess., House Report 1135; Winfrey and Day, *Indian Papers of Texas and the Southwest*, 4: 155; *Report of the United States Commission to Texas,* U.S. Congress, 43rd Cong., 1st sess., Ex. Doc. 257, 3. Dickson's claim comes from Kenner, "Great New Mexico Cattle Raid," 246.

22. Hatch to Granger, 31 March 1872, in Wallace, *Mackenzie's Official Correspondence*, 45, 46; Gregg to Acting Assistant Adjutant General, 4 June 1872, LS, DNM, RG 393, NA, in Arrott Collection, 27: 138.

23. Kenner, *New Mexican–Plains Indians Relations,* 192; Hämäläinen, *Comanche Empire,* 315.

24. Gregg to Sartle, 9 May 1872, LS, DNM, RG 393, NA, in Arrott Collection, 27: 123; Alexander's quote is from Miller, *Soldiers and Settlers*, 269.

25. McLaughlin to Post Adjutant, Fort Concho, 15 May 1872, in Wallace, *Mackenzie's Official Correspondence*, 65.

26. Hatch, Fort Concho, 21 May 1872, in Wallace, *Mackenzie's Official Correspondence*, 69.

27. Mackenzie to Assistant Adjutant General, Dept. of Texas, 24 April 1872, in Wallace, *Mackenzie's Official Correspondence*, 54–55, 57.

28. Mackenzie to Assistant Adjutant General, Dept. of Tex., "Camp on the Fresh Fork of Brazos, Texas, July 5, 1872," in Wallace, *Mackenzie's Official Correspondence*, 100; "Augur's Special Orders for the Campaign of 1872," Special Orders No. 102, in Wallace, *Mackenzie's Official Correspondence*, 71, 72.

29. Mackenzie to Assistant Adjutant General, Dept. of Texas, "Camp on Las Canaditas, New Mexico, August 7, 1872"; and Mackenzie to Granger, DNM, 15 August 1872, both in Wallace, *Mackenzie's Official Correspondence*, 127, 128, 131; Kenner, *New Mexican–Plains Indians Relations,* 192. Col. C. C. Augur's quote

comes from *Annual Report of the Secretary of War,* 1872, found in Kenner, *New Mexican–Plains Indian Relations,* 56. As noted in chapter 1, both Frederick Rathjen and Ernest Wallace hailed Mackenzie's expedition as the first U.S. military expedition in the Llano Estacado: see Wallace, *Ranald Mackenzie on the Texas Frontier,* 56; Rathjen, *Texas Panhandle Frontier,* 202.

30. Jewett to Kobbe, 15 March 1870, LS, DNM, RG 393, NA; Jewett to Kobbe, 26 August 1870, LS, DNM, RG 393, NA; Curtis to Pope, 1 November 1872, in U.S. Office of Indian Affairs, *Annual Report of the Commissioner of Indian Affairs,* 689. Granger's order is found in Sartle to Commanding Officer [Gregg], Fort Bascom, 1 August 1872, LS, DNM, RG 393, NA, in Arrott Collection, 27: 192. Hämäläinen details the extraction of cattle from Texas by the Comanches, who in turn traded them to the Comancheros for goods during this period, which led to Hittson taking action on his own: see Hämäläinen, *Comanche Empire,* 315; Kenner, "Great New Mexico Cattle Raid," 250.

31. Despite Kenner's mischaracterizations of Fort Bascom's soldiers, no one has detailed the significance of the Comancheros as well as this historian. Emerging scholarship on the region does note this resistance, but not its full implications: see Hämäläinen, *Comanche Empire,* 317; Delay, *War of a Thousand Deserts,* 110, 111; Brooks, *Captives and Cousins,* 291; and Ely, "Gone to Texas and Trading with the Enemy," 445.

32. Matthews, Letters, "Camp at Fort Bascom," 25 June 1872; and "Camp at Fort Bascom," 3 August 1872. While on this expedition, Matthews kept a journal that he later mailed to his parents; all items from this journal are cited hereafter as Journal, followed by the date. Matthews, Journal, 6–7 August 1872. Colonel Gregg did not leave Fort Bascom until after the column left. Company M accompanied him. Matthews estimated 350 soldiers were a part of this caravan. Combining Gregg's official report (214 troopers) with the number of teamsters needed for the wagons gives a more realistic total of 300 soldiers and citizens. Gregg's count is found in Kenner, *New Mexican–Plains Indian Relations,* 198. The count on the wagons is found in Matthews, Journal, 24 August 1872. Matthews later kept the accounting books for the regiment, so his numbers cannot be dismissed.

33. Matthews, Journal, 8–11, 14 August 1872; Morris, *El Llano Estacado,* 191.

34. Matthews, Journal, 16 August 1872; Kenner, *New Mexican–Plains Indian Relations,* 198; Peters, *Indian Battles and Skirmishes,* 33; the second quote is from Matthews, Journal, 12 August 1872.

35. Matthews, Journal, 17–18, 23 August 1872; Kenner, *New Mexican–Plains Indian Relations,* 198, 199; Flores, *Caprock Canyonlands,* 10. The Quitaque Peaks were so named because of a series of geographic landmarks that appear from a distance to be giant boulders stacked on top of one another. According to Larry Banks, a research associate for the National Museum of Natural History's department of anthropology, Quitaque was the Comanche name for "horse-hit": phone conversation with Larry Banks on 23 August 2014.

36. Matthews, Journal, 24 August 1872.

37. Ibid., 25 August 1872.

38. Ibid.

39. Ibid., 6, 14 September 1872.

40. Matthews, Letters, "Fort Bascom, N.M.," 26 March 1873.

41. Matthews, Letters, "Fort Bascom, N.M.," 26 March 1873; Kenner, *New Mexican–Plains Indian Relations,* 201, 202; quote from Matthews, Letters, "Fort Bascom, N.M.," 3 April 1872.

42. Matthews, "Fort Bascom, N.M.," 17 July 1874.

43. Kenner, *New Mexican–Plains Indian Relations* 192.

44. Ibid., 203.

45. On the origin of the trading post, see Kavanagh, *Comanches,* 287.

46. Kavanagh, *Comanches,* 445, 446; Rathjen, *Texas Panhandle Frontier,* 161; Hämäläinen, *Comanche Empire,* 338.

47. Returns, Fort Bascom, 1874; "Programme of Campaign in New Mexico," *Chicago Tribune,* 4 May 1874.

48. Hämäläinen, *Comanche Empire,* 338, 339; Rathjen, *Texas Panhandle Frontier,* 163, 206, 207.

49. The Red River War has been thoroughly covered by others: see Leckie, *Military Conquest of the Southern Plains,* 185–235; Rathjen, *Texas Panhandle Frontier,* 206–20; Utley, *Frontier Regulars,* 219–33.

50. Price to Mahnken, 20 August 1874; and Lafferty to Mahnken, both in Telegrams Sent and Received, DNM, RG 393, NA, in Arrott Collection, 29: 141, 142; Matthews, Letters, "Fort Union, N.M.," 17 August 1874.

51. Price to Mahnken, 20 August 1874, Telegrams Sent and Received, DNM, RG 393, NA, in Arrott Collection, 29: 141; Utley, *Frontier Regulars,* 219–33; Rathjen, *Texas Panhandle Frontier,* 207, 217. The notation regarding scouts and wagons is from Cruse, *Battles of the Red River War,* 95.

52. Price, "Excitement on the Sweetwater," 245, 246.

53. Cruse notes that this battle occurred just north of Mobettie (*Battles of the Red River War,* 95, 96); Price, "Excitement on the Sweetwater," 246. In addition to including edited portions of Major Price's report of the battle, Nye also used two Kiowas' recollections. It was Botalye (also known as Eadle-tau-hain) who described their escape in Price, "Excitement on the Sweetwater," 244.

54. Price, "Excitement on the Sweetwater," 247; Rathjen, *Texas Panhandle Frontier,* 213. Gageby Creek was named after Capt. James H. Gageby, Company I, Thirty-Seventh U.S. Infantry, who was killed during the battle at Soldier Spring in 1868.

55. Price, "Excitement on the Sweetwater," 248, 249; Rathjen, *Texas Panhandle Frontier,* 216. On Miles commandeering Price's supplies, see Mahnken to Chief Quartermaster, Headquarters, 15 February 1875, LR, DNM, RG 393, NA, in Arrott Collection, 29: 233–34.

56. Mackenzie was aided by information regarding Quanah's whereabouts that he extracted from Pecos River Valley Comanchero José Piedad Tafoya: Hämäläinen, *Comanche Empire,* 339; Carter, *On the Border with Mackenzie,* 487–95;

Rathjen, *Texas Panhandle Frontier,* 218, 219. Quanah did not use his Anglo family name, Parker, until he finally moved to the reservation. Frankel details Quanah's transition to reservation life and also covers the facts and legends surrounding this Comanche chief's unusual life story in *The Searchers,* 129. While the destruction of the horses was certainly the most significant loss in this battle, Comanche foodstuffs and winter robes were also destroyed, which contributed to their demise: see Rathjen, *Texas Panhandle Frontier,* 218, 219.

57. Carter, *On the Border with Mackenzie,* 487–95.

58. Peters, *Indian Battles and Skirmishes,* 43; Rathjen, *Texas Panhandle Frontier,* 216–17.

59. Alexander to Acting Assistant Adjutant General, Headquarters, 1 May 1875, LS, DNM, RG 393, NA, in Arrott Collection, 29: 282.

60. An Eighth Cavalry trooper simply known as "Bugler" occasionally sent dispatches to the *Freeport* [Ill.] *Journal* about his exploits on the Canadian River; he used the phrase "horse marine" in these dispatches: see *Freeport Journal,* 16 October 1872. Fort Richardson is designated as such in Texas Parks and Wildlife, "Fort Richardson"; see also Matthews, Journal, 24 August 1872.

CHAPTER 8

1. DeLay, *War of a Thousand Deserts,* 109, 110; Hämäläinen, *Comanche Empire,* 330, 353; Morris, *El Llano Estacado,* 192. John Hittson declared that one hundred thousand head of cattle were redistributed from 1852 to 1872: see Kenner, "Great New Mexico Cattle Raid," 257. Other accounts of the first years after the Civil War state that Texas's northwestern counties were hit the hardest. Carl Rister noted thirty thousand cattle and thirty-six hundred horses were stolen in this period: see Rister, "Fort Griffin," 419.

2. Goetzmann, *Exploration and Empire,* ix.

3. U.S. Congress, *Report on Texas Frontier Troubles*; Utley, *Lone Star Justice,* 164, 165.

4. Remley, *Bell Ranch,* 41, 48; Bickers, "Three Cultures, Four Hooves, and One River," 107, 137; Ellis, *Bell Ranch Sketches,* 74. The old Bell Ranch is now part of the Silver Spur Ranch, headquartered in Wyoming. Three hundred thousand acres of the original ranch remain: see Rutherford, "New Mexico's Iconic Bell Ranch Changes Hands."

5. Sherman to Belknap, 17 November 1870, AGO, RF, RG 94, NA; for the reference to "horse marines" see chapter 7, note 60.

6. Socorro, New Mexico, continued to develop after Fort Craig was closed. As its name indicates, the town of Fort Sumner also survived after its post was closed.

7. Morris to Gregg, Projects Coordinator, NMARBC, 4 February 1976; and Krahling, Director, NMARBC, 19 April 1976, New Mexico American Revolution Bicentennial Commission Records, New Mexico State Archives, Santa Fe, Collection 1977-030, folder 524, box 14.

Bibliography

PRIMARY SOURCES

Unpublished

Arrott, James W. Collection. Donnelly Library, New Mexico Highlands University, Las Vegas.

Letters Sent and Received. Records of the United States Continental Commands, Department of New Mexico, 1854–65, Record Group 393. National Archives, Washington, D.C.

Letters Sent and Received. Records of the United States Army Continental Commands, District of New Mexico, Record Group 393. National Archives, Washington, D.C.

Matthews, Eddie. "Letters from Home and Journal of His Military Years," transcribed by Ora Matthews Bublitz. Archives, Fort Union National Monument, N.Mex.

Letters

"Fort Union, N.M.," 3 March 1871

"Fort Bascom, N.M.," 3 April 1872

"Camp at Fort Bascom," 25 June 1872

"Camp Near Fort Bascom," 1 July 1872

"Camp Near Fort Bascom," 25 July 1872

"Camp at Fort Bascom," 3 August 1872

"Camp at Fort Bascom," 26 August 1872

"Fort Bascom, N.M.," 26 March 1873

"Fort Bascom, N.M.," 30 March 1873

"Summer Camp on the Canadian River," 20 August 1873

"Summer Camp on the Canadian River," 23 September 1873

"Summer Camp on the Canadian River," 5 September 1873

"Fort Union, N.M.," 16 December 1873

"Fort Union, N.M.," 17 April 1874
"Fort Bascom, N.M.," 17 July 1874
"Fort Union, N.M.," 17 August 1874
Journal: 6 August 1872–14 September 1872

Miscellaneous Fort File, Fort Bascom, New Mexico. Record Group 77. National Archives, College Park, Md.

New Mexico Volunteer Muster Rolls. New Mexico State Records Center and Archives, Santa Fe.

Slesick, Leonard. Personal Files. Panhandle Plains Historical Museum Research Center, Canyon, Tex.

Spanish Archives of New Mexico. Series I, Land Grant Documents, Reel 14. Special Collections, Donnelly Library, New Mexico Highlands University, Las Vegas. (José L. Perea Grant)

Spanish Archives of New Mexico. Series I, Surveyor General Records, Reel 12. Special Collections, Donnelly Library, New Mexico Highlands University, Las Vegas. (Preston Beck Grant)

U.S. Bureau of the Census
Ninth Census, 1870. New Mexico, San Miguel County, Division: Fort Bascom Military Reserve, Record Group 29. National Archives, Washington, D.C. http://ftp.us-census.org/pub/usgenweb/census/nm/sanmiguel /1870. Accessed 12 August 2014.

Tenth Census, 1880. New Mexico, Colfax County, Springer, Precinct 12, Record Group 29. National Archives, Washington, D.C. www.ancestry.com.

U.S. Congress, House of Representatives
30th Cong., 1st sess., Ex. Doc. 8 [Serial Set 515].
34th Cong., 1st sess., Ex. Doc. 369, pt. 2 [Serial Set 3436].
40th Cong., 2nd sess., Ex. Doc. 248 [Serial Set 1341].
43rd Cong., 1st sess., Ex. Doc. 181 [Serial Set 1610].
43rd Cong., 1st sess., Ex. Doc. 257 [Serial Set 1615].
44th Cong., 2nd sess., Ex. Doc. 1, pt. 2 [Serial Set 1745].
48th Cong., 1st sess., House Report 1135 [Serial Set 2256].
50th Cong., 2nd sess., Ex. Doc. 103 [Serial Set 2651].

U.S. Department of War
Compiled Service Records of Union Soldiers Who Served in Organizations from the State of California. Record Group 94. National Archives, Washington, D.C. www.fold3.com.

Compiled Service Records of Union Soldiers Who Served in Organizations from the State of Kentucky. Record Group 94. National Archives, Washington, D.C. www.archive.org/details/compiledrecordss0217unit. Accessed 21 August 2011.

Compiled Service Records of Union Soldiers Who Served in Organizations from the Territory of New Mexico. Record Group 94. National Archives, Washington, D.C. www.fold3.com. Accessed 15 August 2012.

Records of the Adjutant General's Office. Record Group 94. National Archives, Washington, D.C. www.fold3.com.

Returns from Military Posts. Fort Bascom. Record Group 94. National Archives, Washington, D.C. www.ancestry.com.

Returns from Military Posts. Fort Sumner. Record Group 94. National Archives, Washington, D.C. www.ancestry.com.

Returns from Regular Army Infantry Regiments, 1821–1916. Record Group 94. National Archives, Washington, D.C. http://search.ancestry.com/search/db.aspx?dbid=2229. Accessed 21 June 2012.

PUBLISHED SOURCES

Primary Sources

Alexander, Eveline M. *Cavalry Wife: The Diary of Eveline M. Alexander, 1866–1867.* Edited by Sandra L. Myers. College Station: Texas A&M Press, 1977.

"Condition of the Indian Tribes." *Report to the Special Committee appointed under Joint Resolution of March 3, 1865. An Appendix.* 39th Cong., 2nd sess., Report No. 156. Washington, D.C.: Government Printing Office, 1867.

Courtright, George. *An Expedition against the Indians in 1864, Reminiscences by George S. Courtright, M.D.* Lithopolis, Ohio: Canal Winchester Times Press, 1911.

Cullum, George W. *Biographical Register of the Graduates of the Military Academy.* http://penelope.uchicago.edu/Thayer/E/Gazetteer/Places/America/United_States/Army/USMA/Cullums_Register/home.html.

Darnton, N. H. *"Red Beds" and Associated Formations in New Mexico: With an Outline of the Geology of the State.* Washington, D.C.: Government Printing Office, 1928.

Du Bois, John Van Deusen. *Campaigns in the West 1856–1861: The Journal and Letters of Colonel John Van Deusen Du Bois.* Tucson: Arizona Historical Society, 1949. Reprint, Tucson: Arizona Historical Society, 2003.

Evans, A. W. "Colonel A. W. Evans Christmas Day Indian Fight (1868)." Edited by Carl Coke Rister. *Chronicle of Oklahoma* 3 (September 1938): 275–301.

———. "Headquarters, Canadian River Expedition, Monument Creek Depot, January 23, 1869." Edited by Carl Coke Rister. *Chronicle of Oklahoma* 16 (September 1938), 287.

Gassett, Henry, collator. "List of Elevations: Principally in That Portion of the United States West of the Mississippi River." *U.S. Geological Survey, Miscellaneous Publications,* No. 1. Washington, D.C.: Government Printing Office, 1877.

Gregg, Josiah. *Diary and Letters of Josiah Gregg.* Edited by Maurice Garland Fulton. Norman: University of Oklahoma Press, 1941.

———. *Commerce of the Prairies.* Edited by Max L. Moorhead. Norman: University of Oklahoma Press, 1954.

Hammond, George Peter, and Agapito Rey, eds. *Don Juan de Oñate, Colonizer of New Mexico, 1595–1628*. Vol. 1. Albuquerque: University of New Mexico Press, 1953.

Hilley, Terry E. et al. *Soil Survey of San Miguel County Area, New Mexico*. Washington, D.C.: U. S. Department of Agriculture, 1981.

Kappler, C. J., ed. *Indian Affairs, Laws and Treaties*. Vol. 2. Washington, D.C.: Government Printing Office, 1903.

Marcy, Randolph B. *Adventure on the Red River: Report on the Exploration of the Headwaters of the Red River*. Edited by Grant Foreman. Norman: University of Oklahoma Press, 1937.

Montaignes, François des. *The Plains*. Edited by Nancy Alpert Mower and Don Russell. Norman: University of Oklahoma Press, 1972.

Moore, Frank, and Edward Everett, eds. *From the Rebellion Record: A Diary of American Events*. New York: G. P. Putnam, 1864.

Pettis, George H. *Kit Carson's Fight with the Comanche and Kiowa Indians, at the Adobe Walls on the Canadian River, November 25th, 1864*. Providence: S.S. Rider, 1878.

———. "The California Column, Its Campaigns and Services in New Mexico, Arizona, and Texas during the Civil War." *Historical Society of New Mexico Publications*, No. 11. Santa Fe: New Mexico Printing Co., 1908.

Price, William Redwood. "Excitement on the Sweetwater." Edited by Wilbur S. Nye. *Chronicles of Oklahoma* 16 (June 1938): 241–49.

Ruxton, George Frederick. *Life in the Far West*. 6th ed. Edited by Leroy F. Hafen. Norman: University of Oklahoma Press, 1981.

Scott, Robert N. et al. *The War of the Rebellion: A Compilation of the Official Records of the Union and Confederate Armies*. 128 parts in 70 vols. Washington, D.C.: Government Printing Office, 1888–1901.

Simon, John Y., ed. *The Papers of Ulysses S. Grant*. Vol. 18: Oct. 1, 1867–June 30, 1868. Carbondale: Southern Illinois University Press, 1991.

U.S. Congress. *Report to the Secretary of War*. 42nd Cong., 2nd sess., Ex. Doc. 1, pt. 2 Washington, D.C.: Government Printing Office, 1871.

———. *Report on Texas Frontier Troubles*. 44th Cong., 1st sess., House Report 343. Washington, D.C.: Government Printing Office, [1876?].

———. *Testimony Taken by the Committee on Expenditures in the Department of Justice*. Washington, D.C.: Government Printing Office, 1884.

U.S. Office of Indian Affairs. *Annual Report of the Commissioner of Indian Affairs to the Secretary of the Interior for the Year 1872*. Washington, D.C.: Government Printing Office [1873?].

Whipple, A. W. *A Pathfinder in the Southwest: The Itinerary of Lieutenant A. W. Whipple during His Explorations for a Railway Route from Fort Smith to Los Angeles in the Years 1853 & 1854*. Edited by Grant Foreman. Norman: University of Oklahoma Press, 1941.

Wilhelm, Thomas. *History of the 8th United States Infantry*. Vol. 2. New York Harbor: Eighth Infantry Headquarters, 1873.

Winfrey, Dorman H., and James M. Day, eds. *The Indian Papers of Texas and the Southwest, 1825–1916.* 5 vols. Austin, Tex.: Pemberton Press, 1966–95.

Newspapers

Chicago Tribune
(Santa Fe) *Daily New Mexican*
(Albuquerque) *Evening Citizen*
Freeport (Ill.) *Journal*

SECONDARY SOURCES

Articles in Periodicals

Archambeau, Ernest R. "The Ft. Smith–Santa Fe Trail along the Canadian River in Texas." *Panhandle Plains Historical Review* 27 (1954): 1–26.
Ball, Durwood. "Fort Craig, New Mexico, and the Southwestern Indian Wars, 1854–1884." *New Mexico Historical Review* 73 (April 1998): 153–73.
Brooks, James F. "Served Well by Plunder: La Gran Ladronería and Producers of History astride the Rio Grande." *American Quarterly* 52 (March 2000): 23–58.
———. "Violence, Exchange, and Renewal in the American Southwest." *Ethnohistory* 49 (Winter 2002): 205–18.
Carroll, H. Bailey. "Some New Mexico–West Texas Relationships, 1541–1841." *West Texas Historical Association Year Book* 14 (1938): 92–102.
Carter, Harvey Lewis, and Marcia Carpenter Spencer. "Stereotypes of the Mountain Man." *Western Historical Review* 6 (January 1975): 17–32.
Ely, Glen Sample. "Gone from Texas and Trading with the Enemy: New Perspectives on Civil War West Texas." *Southwestern Historical Quarterly* 110 (April 2007): 438–63.
———. "What To Do about Texas." *New Mexico Historical Review* 85 (Fall 2010): 375–408.
Flores, Dan. "Bison Ecology and Bison Diplomacy: The Southern Plains from 1800 to 1850." *Journal of American History* 78 (September 1991): 465–85.
———. "Argument for Bioregional Review." *Environmental History Review* 18 (Winter 1994): 1–18.
Frazer, Robert W. "Fort Butler: The Fort That Almost Was." *New Mexico Historical Review* 4 (October 1968): 253–70.
Garfield, Marvin. "Defense of the Kansas Frontier, 1868–1869." *Kansas Historical Quarterly* 1 (November 1932): 465–85.
Haley, J. Evetts. "The Comanchero Trade." *Southwestern Historical Quarterly* 38 (January 1935): 157–76.
Hoagland, Alison. "Village Constructions: U.S. Army Forts on the Plains, 1848–1890." *Winterthur Portfolio* 34 (Winter 1999): 225–37.
Kenner, Charles L. "The Great New Mexico Cattle Raid, 1872." *New Mexico Historical Review* 37 (October 1962): 243–59.

Krieger, Alex D. "The Eastward Extension of Puebloan Datings towards the Cultures of the Mississippi Valley." *American Antiquity* 12 (January 1947): 141–48.

Lucas, Spencer P., and Adrian P. Hunt. "Stratigraphy of the Anton Chico and Santa Rosa Formations, Triassic of East-Central New Mexico." *Journal of Arizona-Nevada Academy of Science* 22 (1987): 21–33.

Malin, James. "Ecology and History." *Scientific Monthly* 70 (May 1950): 295–98.

Mares, Curtis. "Signifying Spain, Becoming Comanche, Making Mexicans: Indian Captivity and the History of Chicana/o Popular Performance." *American Quarterly* 153 (June 2001): 267–307.

McGowen, Stanley S. *Horse Sweat and Powder Smoke: The First Texas Cavalry in the Civil War.* College Station: Texas A&M University Press, 1999.

Merlan, Thomas, and Frances Levine. "Comanchero: José Piedad Tafoya, 1834–1913." *New Mexico Historical Review* 81 (Winter 2006): 31–67.

Myers, Lee. "Military Establishments in Southwestern New Mexico: Stepping Stones to Settlement." *New Mexico Historical Review* 43 (January 1968): 5–48.

Porter, Kenneth W. "Negroes and Indians on the Texas Frontier, 1831–1876." *Journal of Negro History* 4 (July 1956): 85–214.

Rister, Carl Coke. "Fort Griffin." *West Texas Historical Association Year Book* 1 (1925): 15–24.

————, ed. "Early Accounting of Indian Depredations." *West Texas Historical Association Year Book* 2 (1926): 18–44.

Romero, José Ynocencio. "Spanish Sheepherders on the Canadian at Old Tascosa, As told to Ernest R. Archambeau." *Panhandle-Plains History Review* 19 (1946): 405–17.

Simmons, Marc. "Comancheros Had a Colorful History in New Mexico." *New Mexican* (Santa Fe), December 30, 2000, b1–b2. http://libproxy.library .unt.edu:2986/us/new-mexico/santa-fe/santa-fe-new-mexican/2000/ 12-30/page-9. Accessed 18 August 2014.

Swagerty, William R. "Marriage and Settlement Patterns of Rocky Mountain Trappers and Traders." *Western Historical Quarterly* 11 (April 1980): 159–80.

Walker, Henry P., and James Teal. "Soldier in the California Column: The Diary of John W. Teal." *Arizona and the West* 13 (Spring 1971): 33–82.

Wallace, Ernest. "The Historic Indians of the Llano Estacado." *West Texas Historical Association Year Book* 58 (1982): 3–18.

Weber, David J. "Spanish Fur Trade from New Mexico, 1540–1821." *The Americas* 24 (October 1967): 122–36.

White, Linda Harper, and Fred R. Gowans. "Andrew Henry and the Rocky Mountain Fur Trade." *Montana: The Magazine of Western History* 43 (Winter 1993): 58–65.

Works, Martha A. "Creating Trading Places on the New Mexico Frontier." *Geographical Review* 82 (July 1992): 268–81.

Worster, Donald. "New West, True West." *Western Historical Quarterly* 18 (April 1987): 141–56.

Books

Alberts, Don. *The Battle of Glorieta: Union Victory in the West.* College Station: Texas A&M University Press, 1998.

Anderson, Gary Clayton. *The Indian Southwest, 1580–1830: Ethnogenesis and Reinvention.* Norman: University of Oklahoma Press, 1999.

Armistead, Gene C. *Horses and Mules in the Civil War: A Complete History with a Roster of More Than 700 War Horses.* Jefferson, N.C.: McFarland, 2013.

Averill, Charles. *The Prince of the Gold Hunters.* Boston: G. H. Williams, 1849.

Bailey, Lynn R. *Bosque Redondo: An American Concentration Camp.* Pasadena, Calif.: Socio-Technical Books, 1970.

———. *Indian Slave Trade in the Southwest: A Study of Slave-Taking and the Traffic in Indian Captives.* Los Angeles: Westernlore Press, 1973.

Ball, Durwood. *Army Regulars in the Western Frontier, 1848–1861.* Norman: University of Oklahoma Press, 2001.

———. "Ranald Mackenzie: War on the Plains Indians." In *Chiefs and Generals: Nine Men Who Shaped the American West,* edited by Richard W. Etulain and Glenda Riley. Golden, Colo.: Fulcrum Publishing, 2004.

Barr, Juliana. *Peace Came in the Form of a Woman: Indians and Spaniards in the Texas Borderlands.* Chapel Hill: University of North Carolina Press, 2007.

Baxter, John O. *Las Carneradas: Sheep Trade in New Mexico 1700–1860.* Albuquerque: University of New Mexico Press, 1987.

Billington, Monroe Lee. *New Mexico's Buffalo Soldiers, 1866–1900.* Niwot: University of Colorado Press, 1991.

Brooks, James F. *Captives and Cousins: Slavery, Kinship, and Community in the Southwest Borderlands.* Chapel Hill: University of North Carolina Press for the Omohundro Institute of Early American History and Culture, 2002.

Caffey, David L. *Chasing the Santa Fe Ring: Power and Privilege in Territorial New Mexico.* Albuquerque: University of New Mexico Press, 2014.

Caldwell, Clifford R. *John Simpson Chisum: Cattle King of the Pecos Revisited.* Santa Fe: Sunstone Press, 2010.

Carlson, Paul H. *The Buffalo Soldier Tragedy of 1877.* College Station: Texas A&M University Press, 2003.

Carricker, Robert C. *Fort Supply, Indian Territory: Frontier Outpost on the Plains.* Norman: University of Oklahoma Press, 1970.

Carter, Robert G. *On the Border with Mackenzie, or Winning West Texas from the Comanche.* New York: Antiquarian, 1961.

Clark, Mary Grooms. *A History of New Mexico: A Mark of Time.* Canyon, Tex.: Staked Plains Press, 1983.

Clary, David A. *These Relics of Barbarism: A History of Furniture in Barracks and Guardhouses of the U.S. Army, 1800–1880.* Harpers Ferry, W.Va.: U. S. Department of the Interior, National Park Service, 1981.

Cruse, J. Brett. *Battles of the Red River War: Archeological Perspectives on the Indian Campaign of 1874.* College Station: Texas A&M University Press, 2008.

Crutchfield, James A. *Tragedy at Taos: The Revolt of 1847*. Plano: Republic of Texas Press, 1995.

Dary, David. *The Santa Fe Trail: Its History, Legends, and Lore*. New York: Penguin Books, 2000.

DeBuys, William. *Enchantment and Exploitation: The Life and Hard Times of a New Mexico Mountain Range*. Albuquerque: University of New Mexico Press, 1985.

Delay, Brian. *War of a Thousand Deserts: Indian Raids and the U.S.-Mexican War*. New Haven, Conn.: Yale University Press, 2008.

Dobak, William A. *Freedom by the Sword: The U.S. Colored Troops, 1862–1867*. Washington, D.C.: U.S. Army Center for Military History, 2011.

Dunham, Harold H. "Ceran St. Vrain." In *The Mountain Men and Fur Trade of the Far West: Eighteen Biographical Sketches*, edited by LeRoy R. Hafen. Lincoln: University of Nebraska Press, 1982.

Dunlay, Thomas W. *Wolves for Blue Soldiers: Indian Scouts and Auxiliaries with the U.S. Army, 1860–1890*. Lincoln: University of Nebraska Press, 1982.

———. *Kit Carson and the Indians*. Lincoln: University of Nebraska Press, 2000.

Ely, Glen Sample. *Where the West Begins: Debating Texas Identity*. Lubbock: Texas Tech University Press, 2011.

Emmet, Chris. *Fort Union and the Winning of the Southwest*. Norman: University of Oklahoma Press, 1965.

Emmons, David M. *Beyond the American Pale: The Irish in the West, 1845–1910*. Norman: University of Oklahoma Press, 2010.

Flores, Dan. *Caprock Canyonlands: Journeys into the Heart of the Southern Plains*. Austin: University of Texas Press, 1990.

———. *Horizontal Yellow: Nature and History in the Near Southwest*. Albuquerque: University of New Mexico Press, 1999.

Frankel, Glenn. *The Searchers: The Making of an American Legend*. New York: Bloomsbury, 2013.

Frazer, Robert W. *Forts of the West*. Norman: University of Oklahoma Press, 1965.

———. *Forts and Supplies: The Role of the Army in the Economy of the Southwest, 1846–1861*. Albuquerque: University of New Mexico Press, 1983.

Frazier, Donald S. *Blood and Treasure: Confederate Empire in the Southwest*. College Station: Texas A&M University Press, 1995.

Goetzmann, William H. *Exploration and Empire: The Explorer and the Scientific Winning of the American West*. Austin: Texas State Historical Association, 1993.

Hafen, LeRoy R., ed. *The Mountain Men and the Fur Trade of the Far West*. Vol. 2. Glendale, Calif.: Arthur H. Clark, 1965–72.

———, and Carl Coke Rister. *Western America: The Exploration, Settlement, and Development of the Region beyond the Mississippi*. New York: Prentice-Hall, 1950.

Haley, J. Evetts. *Charles Goodnight: Cowman and Plainsman*. Norman: University of Oklahoma Press, 1987.

Hall, Martin Hardwick. *Sibley's New Mexico Campaign*. Albuquerque: University of New Mexico Press, 2000.

Hämäläinen, Pekka. *The Comanche Empire*. New Haven, Conn.: Yale University Press, 2008.

———. "The Emergence of New Texas Indian History." In *Beyond Texas through Time: Breaking Away from Past Interpretations*, edited by Walter Buenger and Arnoldo de León. College Station: Texas A &M University Press, 2011.

Hammack, Lauren C. *Archaeology of the Ute Dam and Reservoir of Northeastern New Mexico*. Papers in Anthropology, No. 14. Santa Fe: Museum of New Mexico Press, 1965.

Holmes, Alan J. *Fort Selden, 1865–1891: The Birth, Life, and Death of a Frontier Fort in New Mexico*. Santa Fe: Sunstone Press, 2010.

Hughes, Jack T., and Patrick S. Wiley, eds. *Archeology at Mackenzie Reservoir*. Austin: Texas Historical Commission, 1978.

Hunt, Aurora. *The Army of the Pacific: Its Operations in California, Texas, Arizona, and New Mexico*. Mechanicsville, Pa.: Stackpole Books, 2004.

Hutton, Paul. *Phil Sheridan and His Army*. Lincoln: University of Nebraska Press, 1985.

Hyslop, Stephen G. *Bound for Santa Fe: The Road to New Mexico and the American Conquest*. Norman: University of Oklahoma Press, 2012.

Inman, Henry. *The Old Santa Fe Trail: The Story of the Great Highway*. Topeka, Kans.: Crane & Co., 1916.

Johnson, David. *The Horrell Wars: Feuding in Texas and New Mexico*. Denton: University of North Texas Press, 2014.

Julyan, Robert. *The Place Names of New Mexico*. Albuquerque: University of New Mexico Press, 1998.

Kavanaugh, Thomas W. *Comanche Political History: An Ethnohistorical Perspective, 1706–1875*. Lincoln: University of Nebraska Press, 1996.

———. *The Comanches: A History, 1706–1875*. Lincoln: University of Nebraska Press, 1999.

Kelly, Lawrence. *Navajo Roundup: Selected Correspondences of Kit Carson's Expedition against the Navajo, 1863–65*. Boulder, Colo.: Pruett Publishing Company.

Kenner, Charles L. *A History of New Mexican–Plains Indian Relations*. Norman: University of Oklahoma Press, 1969. Reprinted as *The Comanchero Frontier: A History of New Mexican–Plains Indian Relations*. Norman: University of Oklahoma Press, 1994.

Kessell, John L. *Kiva, Cross, and Crown: The Pecos Indians and New Mexico, 1540–1840*. Washington, D.C.: National Park Service, 1979.

———. *Spain in the Southwest: A Narrative History of Colonial New Mexico, Arizona, Texas, and California*. Norman: University of Oklahoma Press, 2002.

Klein, Alan M. "Political Economy of the Buffalo Hide Trade: Race and Class on the Plains." In *The Political Economy of North American Indians*, edited by John H. Moore. Norman: University of Oklahoma Press, 1993.

Lamar, Howard. *Texas Crossings: The Lone Star State and the American Far West, 1836–1986.* Austin: University of Texas Press, 1991.

Leckie, William H. *The Military Conquest of the Southern Plains.* Norman: University of Oklahoma Press, 1963.

Levine, Frances. "Economic Perspectives on the Comanchero Trade." In *Farmers, Hunters, and Colonials,* edited by Katherine A. Spielmann. Tucson: University of Arizona Press, 1991.

Limerick, Patricia. *Legacy of Conquest: The Unbroken Past of the American West.* New York: W. W. Norton, 1987.

Lintz, Christopher. "Texas Panhandle–Pueblo Interactions from the Thirteenth through the Sixteenth Century." In *Farmers, Hunters, and Colonials,* edited by Katherine A. Spielmann. Tucson: University of Arizona Press, 1991.

Lynn, Alvin R. *Kit Carson and the First Battle of Adobe Walls.* Lubbock: Texas Tech University Press, 2014.

MacCameron, Robert. "Environmental Change in Colonial New Mexico." In *A Sense of the American West: An Anthology of American History,* edited by James E. Sherow. Albuquerque: University of New Mexico Press, 1998.

Malone, Michael. *Historians and the American West.* Lincoln: University of Nebraska Press, 1983.

Masich, Andrew E. *The Civil War in Arizona: The Story of the California Volunteers, 1861–1865.* Norman: University of Oklahoma Press, 2006.

McChristian, Douglas C. *Frontier Cavalry Trooper: The Letters of Private Eddie Matthews 1869–1874.* Albuquerque: University of New Mexico Press, 2013.

McLemore, Laura Lyons. *Inventing Texas: Early Historians of the Lone Star State.* College Station: Texas A&M University Press, 2004.

McNitt, Frank. *Navajo Wars: Military Campaigns, Slave Raids, and Reprisals.* Albuquerque: University of New Mexico Press, 1972.

Meketa, Charles, and Jacquelina Meketa. *One Blanket and Ten Days Rations: First New Mexico Volunteers in Arizona, 1864–1866.* Globe, Ariz.: Southwest Parks and Monuments Association, 1980.

Meketa, Jacqueline Dorgan. *Legacy of Honor: The Life of Rafael Chacón, a Nineteenth-Century New Mexican.* Albuquerque: University of New Mexico Press, 1986.

Merrill, William L. "Cultural Creativity and Raiding Bands in Eighteenth-Century Northern New Spain." In *Violence, Resistance, and Survival in the Americas: Native Americans and the Legacy of Conquest,* edited by William B. Taylor and Franklin Pease. Washington, D.C.: Smithsonian Institution Press, 1994.

Michno, Gregory, and Susan Michno. *A Fate Worse Than Death: Indian Captives in the West.* Caldwell, Idaho: Caxton Press, 2007.

Miller, Darlis A. *The California Column in New Mexico.* Albuquerque: University of New Mexico Press, 1982.

———. *Soldiers and Settlers: Military Supply in the Southwest, 1861–1885.* Albuquerque: University of New Mexico Press, 1989.

Millett, Allan R., and Peter Maslowski. *A Military History of the United States of America.* New York: Free Press, 1994.

Monroy, Douglas. *Thrown among Strangers: The Making of Mexican Culture in Frontier California.* Berkeley: University of California Press, 1990.

Morris, John Miller. *El Llano Estacado: Explorations and Imagination on the High Plains of Texas and New Mexico, 1536–1860.* Austin: Texas State Historical Association, 1997.

Nathans, Benjamin. *Beyond the Pale: The Jewish Encounter with Late Imperial Russia.* Berkeley: University of California Press, 2002.

Nolan, Frederick. *The Lincoln County War: A Documentary History.* Norman: University of Oklahoma Press, 1992.

———. *The West of Billy the Kid.* Norman: University of Oklahoma Press, 1998.

Nye, Wilbur S. *Carbine and Lance.* Norman: University of Oklahoma Press, 1969.

Oliva, Leo E. *Soldiers on the Santa Fe Trail.* Norman: University of Oklahoma Press, 1967.

———. *Fort Union and the Frontier Army in the Southwest: A Historic Resource Study.* Santa Fe: National Park Service, 1993.

Parish, William. *The Charles Ilfeld Company—A Study in the Rise and Decline of Mercantile Capitalism in New Mexico.* Cambridge, Mass.: Harvard University Press, 1961.

Peters, Joseph P. *Indian Battles and Skirmishes on the American Frontier, 1790–1898.* Ann Arbor, N.Y.: Argonaut Press, 1966.

Rathjen, Frederick W. *The Texas Panhandle Frontier.* Austin: University of Texas Press, 1973.

Remley, David. *Bell Ranch: Cattle Ranching in the Southwest, 1824–1947.* Albuquerque: University of New Mexico Press, 1993.

Reséndez, Andrés. *Changing National Identities at the Frontier: Texas and New Mexico, 1800–1850.* New York: Cambridge University Press, 2005.

Rickey, David, Jr. *Forty Miles on Beans and Hay: The Enlisted Soldiers Fighting the Indian Wars.* Norman: University of Oklahoma Press, 1963.

Rosenbaum, Robert J. *Mexicano Resistance in the Southwest: The Sacred Right to Self Preservation.* Austin: University of Texas Press, 1981. Reprint, Dallas: Southern Methodist University Press, 1998.

Rothman, Hal. *On Rims and Ridges: The Los Alamos Area Since 1882.* Lincoln: University of Nebraska Press, 1992.

Russell, Marion Sloan. *Land of Enchantment: Memoirs of Marion Russell along the Santa Fe Trail,* as dictated to Mrs. Hal Russell. Albuquerque: University of New Mexico Press, 1981.

Sargent, Charles Sprague. *The Silva of North American.* Vol. 8. New York: Houghton Mifflin, 1902.

Sherow, James E. "Workings of the Geodialectic." In *A Sense of the American West: An Environmental History Anthology,* edited by James E. Sherow. Albuquerque: University of New Mexico Press, 1998.

Sides, Hampton. *Blood and Thunder: An Epic of the American West.* New York: Doubleday, 2006.

Simmons, Marc. *The Little Lion of the Southwest: The Life of Manuel Antonio Chaves.* Chicago: Swallow Press, 1973.

———. *Following the Santa Fe Trail: A Guide For Modern Travelers.* Santa Fe: Ancient City Press, 1986.

———. *The Last Conquistador: Juan de Oñate and the Settling of the Far Southwest.* Norman: University of Oklahoma Press, 1991.

Smith, David Paul. *Frontier Defense in the Civil War: Texas Rangers and Rebels.* College Station: Texas A&M University Press, 1992.

Smith, F. Todd. *The Wichita Indians: Traders of Texas and the Southern Plains, 1540–1845.* College Station: Texas A&M University Press, 2000.

———. *From Dominance to Disappearance: The Indians of Texas and the Near Southwest, 1786–1859.* Lincoln: University of Nebraska Press, 2005.

Smith, Sherry L. *The View from Officers' Row: Army Perceptions of Western Indians.* Tucson: University of Arizona Press, 1990.

Smith, Thomas T. *Fort Inge: Sharps, Spurs, and Sabers on the Texas Frontier, 1849– 1869.* Austin, Tex.: Eakin Press, 1993.

———. *The Old Army in Texas: A Research Guide to the U.S. Army in Nineteenth-Century Texas.* Austin: Texas State Historical Association, 2000.

Stanley, F. *Fort Bascom: Comanche-Kiowa Barrier.* Pampa, Tex.: Pampa Print Shop, 1961.

Stegmaier, Mark. *Texas, New Mexico, and the Compromise of 1850: Boundary Dispute and Sectional Crisis.* Kent, Ohio: Kent State University Press, 1996.

Taylor, John McLellan. *Bloody Valverde: A Civil War Battle on the Rio Grande.* Albuquerque: University of New Mexico Press, 1995.

Taylor, Quintard. *In Search of the Racial Frontier: African Americans in the American West, 1528–1990.* New York: W. W. Norton, 1998.

Thompson, Jerry D. *Henry Hopkins Sibley: Confederate General in the West.* Natchitoches, La.: Northwestern State University Press, 1987.

———, ed. *New Mexico Territory during the Civil War: Wallen and Evans Inspection Reports, 1862–1863.* Albuquerque: University of New Mexico Press, 2008.

Thrapp, Dan. *The Conquest of Apacheria.* Norman: University of Oklahoma Press, 1967.

Tiller, Veronica A. *The Jicarilla Apache Tribe: A History.* Revised edition. Albuquerque: Bow Arrow Publishing, 2000.

Utley, Robert M. *Frontier Regulars: The United States Army and the Indians, 1866–1891.* New York: MacMillan, 1973.

———. *Frontiersmen in Blue: The United States Army and the Indian, 1848–1865.* Lincoln: University of Nebraska Press, 1981.

———. *High Noon in Lincoln: Violence on the Western Frontier.* Albuquerque: University of New Mexico Press, 1987.

———. *Frontier Justice: The First Century of the Texas Rangers.* New York: Berkeley Books, 2002.

———, and Wilcomb E. Washburn. *Indian Wars.* Boston: Houghton Mifflin, 1977.

Wallace, Ernest. *Ranald Mackenzie on the Texas Frontier.* Lubbock: West Texas Museum Association, 1964.

———, ed. *Ranald S. Mackenzie's Official Correspondence Relating to Texas.* 2 vols. Lubbock: West Texas Museum Association, 1967–68.

Ward, Albert E., John D. Schelberg, and Jerold G. Widdison, eds. *Archaeological Investigations at Los Esteros Reservoir, Northeastern New Mexico.* Albuquerque: Center for Anthropological Studies, 1987.

Webb, Walter Prescott. *The Great Plains.* Waltham, Mass.: Ginn and Company, 1931.

Weber, David J. *The Taos Trappers: The Fur Trade in the Far Southwest, 1540–1846.* Norman: University of Oklahoma Press, 1971.

———. *The Mexican Frontier, 1821–1846: The American Southwest under Mexico.* Albuquerque: University of New Mexico Press, 1982.

———. "'Scarce More Than Apes': Historical Roots of Anglo-American Stereotypes of Mexicans." In *New Spain's Far Northern Frontier: Essays on Spain in the American West, 1540–1821,* edited by David J. Weber. Dallas: Southern Methodist University Press, 1988.

Williams, Jerry, and Paul E. McAllister, eds. *New Mexico in Maps.* Second edition. Albuquerque: University of New Mexico Press, 1986.

Wilson, James H. *The Life and Services of Brevet Brigadier-General Andrew Jonathan Alexander, United States Army.* New York, 1887.

Wilson, John P. *When the Texans Came: Missing Records from the Civil War in the Southwest, 1861–1862.* Albuquerque: University of New Mexico Press, 2001.

Wooster, Robert. *Frontier Crossroads.* College Station: Texas A&M Press, 2006.

Wozniak, Frank E. *Across the Caprock: A Cultural Resource Survey on the Llano Estacado and in the Canadian River Valley of East Central New Mexico.* Albuquerque: University of New Mexico Press, 1985.

Dissertations, Presentations, and Special Publications

Bickers, Margaret A. "Three Cultures, Four Hooves, and One River: The Canadian River in Texas and New Mexico, 1848–1939." PhD diss., Kansas State University, 2010.

Blackshear, James B. "Between Comancheros and Comanchería: A History of Fort Bascom, New Mexico." PhD diss., University of North Texas, 2013.

Foster, James Monroe. "History of Fort Bascom, New Mexico." MA thesis, Eastern New Mexico University, 1955.

Lester, Paul Arnold. "Michael Steck and New Mexico Indian Affairs, 1852–1865." PhD diss., University of Oklahoma, 1986.

Levine, Frances. "The Unified Anthropological Approach to Historical Archaeology: A Study from Los Esteros Lake, Guadalupe County, New Mexico." PhD diss., Southern Methodist University, 1980.

Prucha, Francis Paul. "Commentary." In *The American Military on the Frontier: Proceedings of the Seventh Military History Symposium.* Washington, D.C.: Office of Air Force History, Headquarters USAF, 1978.

Sánchez, Joseph P. et al. *Fort Union National Monument: Ethnographic Overview and Assessment.* Santa Fe: National Park Service, 2006.

Turner, Frederick Jackson. "The Significance of the Frontier in American History." In *Does the Frontier Experience Make America Exceptional?* Readings selected and introduced by Richard W. Etulain. New York: Bedford St. Martin's, 1999.

Miscellaneous Online Sources

Anderson, H. Allen. "Canadian River Expedition." *Handbook of Texas Online.* www.tshaonline.org/handbook/online/articles/qfc01. Accessed 10 March 2013.

Devita, Christina. "Civil War Burial Records in New Mexico." http://New Mexicoalhn.net/military/tsfortbascom. Accessed June 2011.

"Internal Revenue Assessment Lists for the Territory of New Mexico, 1862–1870, 1872–1874." National Archives Microfilm Publication M782, 1 roll. Records of the Internal Revenue Service, Record Group 58, National Archives, Washington, D.C. http://search.ancestry.com/search/dbextra .aspx?dbid=1264. Accessed 8 August 2014.

National Park Service. "Hornos." www.nps.gov/petr/planyourvisit/hornos.htm. Accessed 21 August 2014.

Office of the New Mexico State Historian. "Fort Wingate." www.newmexico history.org/filedetails_docs.php?fileID=21315. Accessed 15 September-ber 2012.

———. "Santo Domingo Traders—Comancheros 1880." www.newmexicohistory .org/filedetails_docs.php?fileID=216. Accessed 25 October 2010.

Rutherford, Burt. "New Mexico's Iconic Bell Ranch Changes Hands." beef magazine.com/cowcalfweekly/1105-new-mexico-bell-ranch. 5 November-ber 2010. Accessed 4 April 2013.

Texas Parks and Wildlife. "Fort Richardson." www.tpwd.state.tx.us. Accessed 30 June 2011.

U.S. Army Medical Department. "Medal of Honor Awardees: Bernard J. D. Irwin." http://ameddregiment.amedd.army.mil/moh/bios/irwin.html. Accessed 21 August 2011.

U.S. Forest Service, Department of Agriculture. "Pike and San Isabel National Forests: Cimarron and Comanche National Grasslands." www.fs.usda. gov/detail/psicc/about-forest/districts/?cid=fsm9_032536. Accessed 29 December 2014.

Index

23, 36, 65, 202n10; environment
in, 37, 56, 85, 125; geology of,
16–17; Indians in, 57, 95, 116,
146–47, 157, 181; Mackenzie in,
175. *See also* Battle of Adobe
Walls; Red River War; Sheridan's
winter campaign
Canby, Edward R. S., 43–44, 46–48,
51–52, 60
Cañón del Rescate (Ransom Canyon),
Tex., 26, 29, 34, 121, 205n40
Cañón Largo, N.Mex., 65, 96, 97,
117, 152
Caprock Escarpment, 15
Carleton, James H., 51–56, 68, 95,
109, 112–39, 147, 156, 158,
210n32, 219n39; and Battle of
Adobe Walls, 100, 103–14; and
Comancheros, 112–14, 131, 138;
and Comanches, 115, 123; fear
of Confederate invasion, 57;
founding of post, 57–58, 61, 68;
and shoot-to-kill policy, 128, 130
Carr, Eugene A., 148
carretas, 24, 26
Carrick, Robert, 91, 162
Carros Creek, 108
Carson, Christopher (Kit), 32–33,
36, 47, 49, 51–52, 56, 100, 115–16,
133; and Battle of Adobe Walls,
103–15, 121–23, 147–48, 150,
152–53, 156, 174, 179, 184; and
Comancheros, 112–14, 118; leading
Navajo campaign, 95, 97, 147
cart paths, 24
Catron, Thomas B., 74, 213n15
Chaperito, N.Mex., 28, 34, 83, 119,
138, 141
Chaperito Road, 119
Cháves, J. Francisco, 3, 102, 217n14,
218n15
Cháves, Manuel, 138, 141
Cheyennes, 41, 85, 107, 114, 155–57,
162–63, 180, 183, 188

Chiricahua Apaches, 49, 50
Chisholm, John, 172
Chivington, John M., 107, 123
Cimarron River, 41; and Santa Fe
Trail, 98
Cimarron Route, 40, 96, 98–100,
102, 118, 217n6
Clark, J., 93
Clay County, Tex., 170
Clendenin, David R., 163, 168–69,
191; on scouts and patrols, 165;
and stolen cattle, 165
Cochise, 49, 50
Cold Spring, 100, 102
Colorado Volunteers, 52, 53, 107,
117; at Camp Easton, 55, 58,
60, 210n32
Comanche County, Tex., 146
Comanchería, 8–9, 25, 28, 32, 34,
55, 94–95, 101–102, 109, 111–13,
120, 124
Comanchero road, 8, 29, 65, 108,
120–21, 125, 135, 140, 169, 173,
185, 194
Comanchero trade, 10–11, 15,
24–37, 42, 95, 102, 113–14,
124, 126, 132, 134–35, 138,
141–43, 158, 162, 165, 169–72,
176, 180, 190–91. *See also*
black market
Comanches, 8–13, 22–29, 33, 35–36,
39, 41–42, 45, 53–54, 58, 64–65,
67–68, 79–80, 82, 88–89, 96,
98–101, 114–16, 126–27, 129,
131, 144, 146–47, 170–71, 173;
captives of, 35, 114, 119, 120–23;
homeland of, 9, 12, 55, 94–95,
114, 145, 161, 163; trade with,
23–24, 27, 33, 37, 113, 124,
135–38, 142, 144, 158, 172, 181,
190. *See also* Battle of Adobe
Walls; Red River War; Sheridan's
winter campaign
Comanche Springs, N.Mex., 130